ANTI-TERRORISM LAWS

INDIA, THE UNITED STATES, THE UNITED KINGDOM AND ISRAEL

VOLUME I

Edited by

K.R. GUPTA

ATLANTIC

ATLANTIC PUBLISHERS AND DISTRIBUTORS

Published by
ATLANTIC PUBLISHERS AND DISTRIBUTORS
B-2, Vishal Enclave, Opp. Rajouri Garden, New Delhi-27
Phones : 5413460, 5429987

Sales Office
4215/1, Ansari Road, Darya Ganj, New Delhi-02
Phones : 3273880, 3285873, 3280451
Fax : 91-11-3285873
e-mail : info@atlanticbooks.com
web : www.atlanticbooks.com

ISBN 81-269-0137-3 (Vol. I)
ISBN 81-269-0138-1 (Set)

Typeset at
APD Computer Graphics, Delhi

Printed in India at
Mehra Offset Press, Delhi

PREFACE

Terrorism now has become a world-wide phenomenon. During the last two decades the world has been marked by an increasing number of terrorist attacks. Terrorism occurs when a group, whether holding governmental office, or outside government, resolves to pursue a set of ideological objectives by methods which not only subvert or ignore the requirements of domestic and international law, but which rely for their success primarily upon the threat or use of violence. There are now over one lakh *jehadis* all over the Islamic world, in Afghanistan, Kashmir, Albania, Chechnaya (Russia), Xin-jiang (China), Central Asia and elsewhere.

The United Nations has mandated that all states must adopt necessary legal instruments "to prevent terrorism and strengthen international cooperation in combating terrorism." India promulgated Prevention of Terrorism Act (POTO) in October 2001 and re-promulgated it with some changes on 31st December, 2001. Unfortunately the Bill for converting the Ordinance into an Act could not be introduced in the 2001 Winter Session of the Parliament due to resistance of some Opposition Parties and because of the need for unity of all Political Parties to meet with the war-like situation on the Indo-Pak horizon.

The book provides information about anti-terrorism laws of important countries like the United States, the United Kingdom, Israel etc. A study of anti-terrorism laws of these countries would be of great help in formulating a similar law for India and also in softening resistance of Opposition Parties to such a law.

It is hoped that the book would be found useful by the executives of the world and regional organisations, non-government organisations concerned with world peace and security, government executives and parliamentarians in different countries concerned with tackling terrorism, students of Political Science and Law and the common man interested in day-to-day world affairs.

K.R. GUPTA

CONTENTS

Introduction

PREVENTION OF TERRORISM ACT

Need for POTO

Prevention of Terrorism Ordinance (POTO) was approved by the Union Cabinet on October 16, 2001, and replaces the Prevention of Terrorism Bill, which the Atal Bihari Vajpayee government sought to pass last year but failed to bring for discussion in Parliament following sharp criticism from opposition parties and the National Human Rights Commission.

India is largely governed by Indian Panel Code, an omnibus anti-criminal law enacted in 1860 during the British colonial rule. The law has been amended from time to time but officials say it is still not strong enough the deal with terrorism. The security forces had demanded an anti-terrorism legislation with adequate teeth in it.

The existing criminal justice system was not designed to deal with the heinous terrorist crimes being witnessed since the 1980s. We had no law that defined a terrorist act, no provisions relating to financing terrorists, use of weapons of mass destruction, chemical and biological attacks, the possibility of which are so real after September 11, 2001 attack.

No country of the world has suffered even a small fraction of the casualties suffered by India as a result of terrorism. Inspite of this the anti-terrorism laws of the most liberal countries in the West are far more comprehensive and stringent than POTO. Even the United Nations has mandated that all states must adopt necessary legal instruments "to prevent terrorism and to strengthen international cooperation in combating terrorism".

The Terrorism and Disruptive Activities Act (TADA), introduced in 1980s, was allowed to lapse in 1995 after criticism from human rights activists that it was misused against minority Sikh and Muslim separatists in Punjab and Kashmir.

POTO defines a terrorist act as "An act done by using weapons and explosive substances or other methods in a manner as to cause or likely to cause death or injuries to any person or persons or loss or damage to property or disruption of essential supplies and services or by any other means necessary with intent to threaten the unity and integrity of India or to strike terror in any section of the people." The maximum punishment for committing a terrorist act is death, and the minimum punishment is five years' imprisonment.

Home Secretary Kamal Pande says that unlike TADA, the confession of an accused will not be admissible as evidence against a co-accused under POTO. The maximum period of police custody under POTO is 30 days as against 60 days under TADA. And, under section 48(7), a magistrate needs to satisfy himself only about the innocence of the accused before granting bail, not whether he is also unlikely to commit a similar offence after being let out, as required by TADA. Also, appeals against an order of a POTO special court can be made to a high court instead of the Supreme Court as required by TADA. Even Ram Jethmalani, who opposed TADA, admits POTO is more humane.

Under POTO, intimation of the arrest of an accused will have to be provided to a family member immediately after the arrest and this fact has to be recorded by a police officer. The time for the confirmation of the first information report has been reduced. More important, confessions made to an officer below the rank of deputy superintendent of police will not be admissible as evidence. And a legal practitioner shall be allowed to be present during interrogation, but not throughout the interrogation in line with the Supreme Court's judgment in the D.K. Basu case.

India, a country of over one billion people and dozens of diverse ethnic groups, has been plagued for years by bloody separatist rebellions in Kashmir and the Northeast. Radical political groups often resort to violent attacks against government agencies and the public in other parts of the country to highlight their agenda.

Criticism

Critics point out that India already has some two dozen special security laws and, if used effectively, they are adequate to fight terrorism. They feel that all the acts of violence mentioned in POTO are already illegal under the Indian Penal Code; so what is the need for POTO if it is not to "criminalise dissent", they ask. Moreover, the human rights group Amnesty International feels the vague definition of a "terrorist act" might expose non-violent human rights defenders, minority communities and the media to a discriminatory enforcement of POTO. And Communist Party of India, Marxist, leader Sitaram Yechuri feels that the "by any other means necessary" clause is so open-ended that even legitimate political activities such as a *bandh* against the government's economic policies or a trade union meeting can be interpreted as a terrorist act.

The sweeping powers it invests in the police to arrest, detain and interrogate those it considers terrorists, and the tight bail provisions, have heightened fears of their misuse, leading to harassment, extortion and torture of innocent people. Answering this criticism of POTO, K.P.S. Gill says, "It contains strong safeguards against abuse and significant penalties against malicious prosecution by the police. The argument that POTO 'may be misused', moreover, cannot hold water. There is not a single law on the statute book that cannot be 'misused', and potential for misuse cannot be a serious argument for the exclusion or repeal of laws."

Arrests can be made on mere suspicion that a person is a terrorist. A statement which is made for the first time remains valid till the end. Under POTO, a suspect can be detained without trial for 30 days, while in some Western countries with similar laws the limit is three or four days. Premises can be searched without a warrant. All kinds of messages and communications can be intercepted without warrant. The identity of witnesses deposing against an accused can be withheld from the accused. Confessions to the police can be used as evidence. Passport and travel documents of any citizen suspected to be a terrorist or having links with terrorists can be suspended. Charge sheets can be delayed for up to 180 days. Property acquired through terrorist activities can be confiscated. Bail can be applied for and obtained only after a year. There is no time frame for special courts to deal with cases. And the onus of proving innocence is on the accused, not on the investigating authorities.

The safeguards will not work because the responsibility to oversee them has been left to the bureaucracy, which is also responsible for implementing POTO, and not the courts. Any law that takes away the jurisdiction of the courts should not exist in a democratic society. It is pointed out that under a tough law like TADA, seventy per cent of the seventy thousand persons arrested across the country were acquitted, showing how it was misused. Answering this criticism, K.P.S. Gill says, "But what is the conviction rate for all crimes in this country? 6.5 per cent, with processes of litigation that extend over decades. More significantly, what are the conviction rates under normal laws, for terrorist crimes in the regions afflicted by widespread terrorism? These would probably be less than 0.001 per cent. If the inefficiency and incompetence of India's criminal justice system are to be accepted as an argument against the existence of specific laws, we would have to throw the entire book of criminal statutes into the dust bin."

POTO compels journalists to disclose all information regarding any person or persons perceived by the police as terrorists, with provision for imprisonment (from a period of one year to 10 years) for failure to do so. In other words, a journalist can be arrested for not revealing his sources, for refusing to tell the police what he/she knows about a terrorist's plans or hideouts, and/or for meeting sources and receiving information.

Any such new law needs to be carefully tailored to the needs of the people, enforced for a specific period of time and should be subject to judicial review at all times. That is not the case with POTO.

In Defence of POTO

The Government maintains that it has learnt its lessons from TADA and has built safeguards into POTO. It is said under POTO, it is easier for those detained to obtain bail, it is tougher to convict on the basis of confessions made during detention and provisions to punish errant police officers are allowed.

Defending POTO Indian Home Minister, L.K. Advani, remarked : "If POTO becomes an Act, it will display national determination and strengthen national resolve to fight against terrorism. The people of India will not forgive the opposition parties if they oppose the introduction of such legislation." "Those opposing POTO are wittingly or unwittingly appeasing terrorists. Considering the security situation in the country, a national perspective and not a partisan view is required." He said POTO had been put together taking into account several state legislations against organised crime. "If the states are implementing laws like this, why should a new similar law to deal with a bigger menace like terrorism be called draconian?" Advani said such a law was not directed against any religion or group but was only meant to fight terrorism.

Rural Development Minister Venkaiah Naidu says, point-blank, that civil rights are for civil people and human rights are for human beings, not for terrorists.

Federal Law Minister Arun Jaitley strongly defended POTO, saying identical laws against organized crime had been adopted by many states, including Maharashtra where an opposition Congress-led coalition is in power. "If India is going to oppose

POTO (Prevention of Terrorism Ordinance), then our commitment to a legislative and investigative framework to fight terrorism is highly suspect," Jaitley said. "All states have a similar law against organized crime. The language of POTO on what constitutes a terrorist act is verbatim that for state legislation, except that 'organized crime' has been substituted with 'terrorism,'" he said.

POTO, he said, was a step ahead of any law holding intercepts of confessions made to police officers admissible. "Within 60 days the intercepts have to be ratified by a review committee, headed by a high court judge." When it was pointed out that even TADA held confessions to police officers admissible, a provision that could lead to its misuse, the minister said : "But for the special rules of evidence under TADA that holds confessions made to a police officer admissible, no person would have been convicted in the Rajiv Gandhi assassination. Let (Congress president) Sonia Gandhi decide about POTO now."

Asked about a reported provision that required the media to reveal information about terrorism-related activities, Jaitley said : "There is firstly no provision for media in the proposed act. It only says whoever gets any information about terrorists has to inform the authorities." "That is a pre-existing clause even in the Code of Criminal Procedure or the Indian Penal Code. Why should such a law that has existed for so long, affect journalists now?"

Arun Jaitley says the provision doesn't make it an offence to meet a terrorist or report news of a terrorist organisation, unless the purpose was to support the activities of the terrorist or terrorist organisation. But information should be provided if asked for, which he says applies to everybody else as well, not just journalists. Home Secretary Kamal Pande points out that these provisions are merely a reiteration of similar provisions in section 39 of the CrPC and section 187 of the IPC.

The Law Commission says national security comes above freedom of the press. It says it has been repeatedly upheld by the Supreme Court that the rights and privileges of the press are no greater than those of any citizen of India. And that even in the UK and US, no immunity in favour of journalists or the press is recognised.

Police seem to be in its favour. D.R. Karthikeyan, who investigated the Rajiv Gandhi assassination, says the existing laws are antiquated to deal with modern-day terrorists. Others like Bombay Police Commissioner M.N. Singh feel that with terrorist groups ruthlessly using modern technology and operating across international borders, the agencies facing them need strong laws and proper equipment to deal with them.

Prevention of Terrorism Bill

The Government had desired to convert the Prevention of Terrorism Ordinance into an Act during the winter session of the Parliament. But the Bill could not be introduced because of strong resistance from some opposition parties. In an attempt to make Prevention of Terrorism Bill more acceptable to the critics, the Union Cabinet had decided to make three amendments in the Prevention of Terrorism Ordinance (POTO).

The first was to reduce the period the law would remain in force from five to three years. In this context it may be mentioned that the Atal Bihari Bajpai government has only three years left in office.

Second, while property could be attached under POTO by a designated authority, under the amended Bill only judicial authority would have been able to decide on forfeiture.

Third, the provisions relating to non-disclosure of relevant information by any citizen, including a journalist, had been amended in the bill. This had been done to allay the apprehensions of the media.

I.D. Swami, Minister of State for Home Affairs, pointed out that the UK and the US had passed anti-terrorist legislation without much murmur. He said : "In the US it took three days to pass the law. On the first day, the House of Representatives passed it. Second day, the Senate passed the law and the third day President Bush put his seal on it. And here we are still faced with how to pass the law."

Referring to caution of National Human Rights Commission (NHRC) Chairman Justice J.S. Verma that governments have to do a "fine balancing act between maintaining peace and security and human rights," Swami said, "this balancing, this tightrope-walking cannot be done always". He added that "since the right to life had been destroyed by terrorists, there is a need to create such a law to meet this extraordinary situation." He also claimed the government had information that some human rights organisations had links with terrorists and were being funded by them. However, he did not name these organisations.

TADA has been criticised on the ground, that "From 1985 ever since the statute was passed, terrorism has not decreased, terrorism has increased in volume and in the extent of its operations. This shows that there is something wrong with your remedy." The implication of this argument is that, unless the 'root causes' of terrorism are not addressed, no legal remedy is of any use. Answering this criticism, K.P.S. Gill states, "But TADA was in existence for just ten years. There has been a law against murder in every society since the beginning of human history. Yet, murder 'has not decreased'. No one has thought to ask whether the law against murder or rape actually stops or reduces murder and rape; the evidence of a very long history of laws against these crimes suggests that the law certainly fails in this regard. This has not been advanced, in any serious jurisprudential discourse, as sufficient grounds to dispense with these laws. Are we, moreover, to understand that crimes other than terrorism arise without 'root causes'? That murder and rape are committed by happy, prosperous, educated, well-adjusted individuals who have no legitimate grievances against society? Most — if not all — crimes of violence are committed in subjectively justifiable states of rage, of distress, of confusion and alienation. Does this mean that, until a perfect world has been created, where all the 'root causes' have been eliminated, no such crimes are to be punished?"

First Application of POTO in Delhi

Mohammad Afzal, Shaukat Hussain, Syed Abdul Rehman Gilani and Afsan Guru will share the dubious distinction of being the first in Delhi to be tried under the Prevention of Terrorism Ordinance (POTO). Commissioner of Police Ajai Raj Sharma said that although the case lodged against the four militants was under the provisions of the Indian Penal Code, sections of POTO have also been applied.

Speaking to the Hindustan Times, the police chief also said that the fact that the militants were Pak nationals was confirmed through intercepts of telephone conversations that the police got. In POTO, scientific evidence such as this is admissible in a court of law, while in the Indian Evidence Act it is not. Had the anti-terror ordinance not been passed, it is possible that the investigating agencies would have had no clinching evidence to strengthen their case. The vital links in this case have been the mobile phone printouts and the conversation intercepts. Under the Evidence Act, these are not admissible as evidence. Sources reveal that in this case, the link between Mohammad the human bomb and Afzal can only be established through the conversations they had. The case would be further strengthened as under the POTO provisions confessions made before a DCP are admissible in the court of law. Under IPC, they are not.

Under POTO, electronic communication including exchange of e-mails on the Net, transmissions of signs or encryptic messages in whole or part can also be read against the accused. "In the Red Fort shootout case, the alleged terrorists used to communicate through pornographic sites. If such evidence is procured in case of the Parliament House attack, it will be read against them," a lawyer said.

Another fact that will help the prosecuting agency is that under POTO the accused are not entitled for bail till the trial is completed. And only the Supreme Court has powers to hear the bail application of the accused. In IPC, bail can be granted by a trial judge too.

"The investigating agency is not under any duress to complete investigations in 90 days as under IPC," adds a leading criminal lawyer Ashish Bhagat. He says under IPC, if investigations are incomplete, the accused is entitled to bail. "Under POTO he is not, till the trial is completed," he added.

According to legal experts if the police adds the sections of POTO in the FIR itself, it can get an extension of 90 days to file its final report before the trial can start, which means that the police has 180 days in hand to file it. But the extension can be granted only after the police files a report indicating the progress of the investigation and states specific reason for the accused's detention. Under the IPC, there is no provision to extend the period of filing a final report. If the police fails to file it within 90 days, the court has to grant bail immediately. If POTO sections are not added to the FIR, the police is bound to file the final report in 90 days.

Under POTO, anybody who funds a terrorist organisation or supports one can also be tried. POTO is a combination of several laws like the Explosives Act, Arms Act and also brings conspiracy within its ambit. An accused, therefore, if found guilty under POTO, can be convicted and sentenced to a minimum of five years in jail. The maximum sentence is life imprisonment or death penalty.

Under POTO, confessions made before an assistant commissioner of police are also admissible. The IPC, however, is governed by the Evidence Act which does not allow a confessional statement to be read against the accused or a co-accused.

Amended POTO Re-promulgated

The Prevention of Terrorism Ordinance (POTO) was re-promulgated, after Cabinet approval, on December 31 with some key changes relating to the duration of the measures and freedom of press.

The Union Cabinet on December 30 modified the earlier POTO curtailing its duration from five to three years and scrapping the provision under which a journalist was required to divulge to police any information he knows or believes could be of material assistance in preventing the commission of a terrorist act.

Another modification made to POTO was the deletion of the reference to Special Courts, thus doing away with concurrent jurisdiction of the Designated Authority and the Special Courts. The new ordinance provides for appeal against the order made by the Designated Authority to the Special Courts.

The revised POTO includes the list of 25 terrorist outfits, including the Communist Party of India-Marxist-Leninist — Peoples War Group (better known as PWG) and the Maoist Communist Centre (MCC), which were added after the promulgation of the ordinance.

INDIA

The Prevention of Terrorism Ordinance, 2001

NO 9 of 2001

Promulgated by the President in the Fifty-second Year of the Republic of India.

An Ordinance to make provisions for the prevention of, and for dealing with, terrorist activities and for matters connected therewith.

WHEREAS Parliament is not in session and the President is satisfied that circumstances exist which render it necessary for him to take immediate action;

NOW, THEREFORE, in exercise of the powers conferred by clause (1) of article 123 of the Constitution, the President is pleased to promulgate the following Ordinance :

CHAPTER I

PRELIMINARY

1. (1) This Ordinance may be called the Prevention of Terrorism Ordinance, 2001.

(2) It extends to the whole of India.

(3) Every person shall be liable to punishment under this Ordinance for every act or omission contrary to the provisions thereof, of which he is held guilty in India.

(4) Any person who commits an offence beyond India which is punishable under this Ordinance shall be dealt with

according to the provisions of this Ordinance in the same manner as if such act had been committed in India.

(5) The provisions of this Ordinance apply also to —

(a) citizens of India outside India;

(b) persons in the service of the Government, wherever they may be; and

(c) persons on ships and aircrafts, registered in India, wherever they may be.

(6) It shall come into force at once and shall remain in force for a period of five years from the date of its commencement, but its expiry under the operation of this sub-section shall not affect —

(a) the previous operation of, or anything duly done or suffered under this Ordinance, or

(b) any right, privilege, obligation or liability acquired, accrued or incurred under this Ordinance, or

(c) any penalty, forfeiture or punishment incurred in respect of any offence under this Ordinance, or

(d) any investigation, legal proceeding or remedy in respect of any such right, privilege, obligation, liability, penalty, forfeiture or punishment as aforesaid,

and, any such investigation, legal proceeding or remedy any be instituted, continued or enforced and any such penalty, forfeiture or punishment may be imposed as if this Ordinance had not expired.

2. (1) In this Ordinance, unless the context otherwise requires, —

(a) "Code" means the Code of Criminal Procedure, 1973;

(b) "Designated Authority" shall mean such officer of the Central Government not below the rank of Joint Secretary to the Government, or such officer of the State Government not below the rank of Secretary to the Government, as the case may be, as may be specified by the Central Government or as the case may be, the State Government, by a notification published in the Official Gazette;

(c) "proceeds of terrorism" shall mean all kinds of properties which have been derived or obtained from commission of any terrorist act or have been acquired through funds traceable to a terrorist act, and shall include cash, irrespective of person in whose name such proceeds are standing or in whose possession they are found;

(d) "property" means property and assets of every description, whether corporeal or incorporeal, movable or immovable, tangible or intangible and deeds and instruments evidencing title to, or interest in, such property or assets;

(e) "Public Prosecutor" means a Public Prosecutor or an Additional Public Prosecutor or a Special Public Prosecutor appointed under section 28 and includes any person acting under the directions of the Public Prosecutor;

(f) "Special Court" means a Special Court constituted under section 23;

(g) "terrorist act" has the meaning assigned to it in sub-section (1) of section 3, and the expression "terrorist" shall be construed accordingly;

(h) "State Government", in relation to a Union territory, means the Administrator thereof;

(i) words and expressions used but not defined in this Ordinance and defined in the Code shall have the meanings respectively assigned to them in the Code.

(2) Any reference in this Ordinance to any enactment or any provision thereof shall, in relation to an area in which such enactment or such provision is not in force, be construed as a reference to the corresponding law or the relevant provision of the corresponding law, if any, in force in that area.

CHAPTER II
PUNISHMENT FOR, AND MEASURES FOR DEALING WITH, TERRORIST ACTIVITIES

3. (1) Whoever, —

(a) with intent to threaten the unity, integrity, security or sovereignty of India or to strike terror in the people or any section of the people does any act or thing by using bombs, dynamite or other explosive substances or inflammable substances or fire arms or other lethal weapons or poisons or noxious gases or other chemicals or by any other substances (whether biological or otherwise) of a hazardous nature or by any other means whatsoever, in such a manner as to cause, or likely to cause, death of, or injuries to any person or persons or loss of, or damage to, or destruction of, property or disruption of any supplies or services essential to the life of the community or causes damage or destruction of any property or equipment used or intended to be used for the defence of India or in connection with any other purposes of the Government of India, any State Government or any of their agencies, or detains any person and threatens to kill or injure such person in order to compel the Government or any other person to do or abstain from doing any act;

(b) is or continues to be a member of an association declared unlawful under the Unlawful Activities (Prevention) Act, 1967, or voluntarily does an act aiding or promoting in any manner the objects of such association and in either case is in possession of any unlicensed firearms, ammunition, explosive or other instrument or substance capable of causing mass destruction and commits any act resulting in loss of human life or grievous injury to any person or causes significant damage to any property, commits a terrorist act.

Explanation : For the purposes of this sub-section, "a terrorist act" shall include the act of raising funds intended for the purpose of terrorism.

(2) Whoever commits a terrorist act, shall, —

(i) if such act has resulted in the death of any person, be punishable with death or imprisonment for life and shall also be liable to fine;

(ii) in any other case, be punishable with imprisonment for a term which shall not be less than five years but which may extend to imprisonment for life and shall also be liable to fine.

(3) Whoever conspires or attempts to commit, or advocates, abets, advises or incites or knowingly facilitates the commission of, a terrorist act or any act preparatory to a terrorist act, shall be punishable with imprisonment for a term which shall not be less than five years but which may extend to imprisonment for life and shall also be liable to fine.

(4) Whoever voluntarily harbours or conceals, or attempts to harbour or conceal any person knowing that such person is a terrorist shall be punishable with imprisonment for a term which shall not be less than three years but which may extend to imprisonment for life and shall also be liable to fine :

Provided that this sub-section shall not apply to any case in which the harbour or concealment is by the husband or wife of the offender.

(5) Any person who is a member of a terrorist gang or a terrorist organisation, which is involved in terrorist acts, shall be punishable with imprisonment for a term which may extend to imprisonment for life or with fine which may extend to rupees ten lakh or with both.

Explanation : For the purposes of this sub-section, "terrorist organisation" means an organisation which is concerned with or involved in terrorism.

(6) Whoever knowingly holds any property derived or obtained from commission of any terrorist act or has been acquired through the terrorist funds shall be punishable with imprisonment for a term which may extend to imprisonment for life or with fine which may extend to rupees ten lakh or with both.

(7) Whoever threatens any person who is a witness or any other person in whom such witness may be interested, with violence, or wrongfully restrains or confines the witness, or any other person in whom the witness may be interested, or does any other unlawful act with the said intent, shall be punishable with imprisonment which may extend to three years and fine.

(8) A person receiving or in possession of information which he knows or believes to be of material assistance —

(i) in preventing the commission by any other person of a terrorist act; or

(ii) in securing the apprehension, prosecution or conviction of any other person for an offence involving the commission, preparation or instigation of such an act,

and fails, without reasonable cause, to disclose that information as soon as reasonably practicable to the police, shall be punishable with imprisonment for a term which may extend to one year or with fine or with both :

Provided that a legal practitioner of the accused shall not be bound to disclose such information which he might have received while defending the accused.

4. Where any person is in unauthorized possession of any, —

(a) arms or ammunition specified in columns (2) and (3) of Category I or Category III (a) of Schedule I to the Arms Rules, 1962, in a notified area,

(b) bombs, dynamite or hazardous explosive substances or other lethal weapons capable of mass destruction or biological or chemical substances of warfare in any area, whether notified or not,

he shall be guilty of terrorist act notwithstanding anything contained in any other law for the time being in force, and be punishable with imprisonment for a term which may extend to imprisonment for life or with fine which may extend to rupees ten lakh or with both.

Explanation : In this section "notified area" means such area as the State Government may, by notification in the Official Gazette, specify.

5. (1) If any person with intent to aid any terrorist contravenes any provision of, or any rule made under, the Arms Act, 1959, the Explosives Act, 1884, the Explosive Substances Act, 1908 or the Inflammable Substances Act, 1952, he shall, notwithstanding anything contained in any of the aforesaid Acts or the rules made thereunder, be punishable with imprisonment for a term which may extend to imprisonment for life and shall also be liable to fine.

(2) For the purposes of this section, any person who attempts to contravene or abets, or does any act preparatory to the contravention of any provision of any law, rule or order, shall be deemed to have contravened that provision, and the provisions of sub-section (1) shall, in relation to such person, have effect subject to the modification that the reference to "imprisonment for life" shall be construed as a reference to "imprisonment for ten years".

6. (1) No person shall hold or be in possession of any proceeds of terrorism.

(2) Proceeds of terrorism, whether held by a terrorist or by any other person and whether or not such person is prosecuted or convicted under this Ordinance, shall be liable to be forfeited to the Central Government or the State Government, as the case may be, in the manner provided under this Chapter.

7. (1) If an officer (not below the rank of Superintendent of Police) investigating an offence committed under this Ordinance, has reason to believe that any property in relation to which an investigation is being conducted, represents proceeds of terrorism, he shall, with the prior approval in writing of the Director General of the Police of the State in which such property is situated, make an order seizing such property and where it is not practicable to seize such property, make an order of attachment directing that such property shall not be transferred or otherwise dealt with except with the prior permission of the officer making such order, or of the Designated Authority, or the Special Court, as the case may be, before whom the properties seized or attached are produced and a copy of such order shall be served on the person concerned.

(2) The investigating officer shall duly inform the Designated Authority or, as the case may be, the Special Court, within forty-eight hours of the seizure or attachment of such property.

(3) It shall be open to the Designated Authority or the Special Court before whom the seized or attached properties are produced either to confirm or revoke the order of attachment so issued :

Provided that an opportunity of making a representation by the person whose property is being attached shall be given.

(4) In the case of immovable property attached by the investigating officer, it shall be deemed to have been produced before the Designated Authority or the Special Court, as the case may be, when the investigating officer notifies his report and places it at the disposal of the Designated Authority or the Special Court, as the case may be.

(5) The investigating officer may seize and detain any cash to which this Chapter applies if he has reasonable grounds for suspecting that —

(a) it is intended to be used for the purposes of terrorism;

(b) it forms the whole or part of the resources of an organisation declared as terrorist organisation under this Ordinance :

Provided that the cash seized under this sub-section by the investigating officer shall be released not later than the period of forty-eight hours beginning with the time when it is seized unless the matter involving the cash is before the Designated Authority, or as the case may be, the Special Court and such authority or, as the case may be, the Court passes an order allowing its retention beyond forty-eight hours.

Explanation : For the purposes of this sub-section "cash" means —

(a) coins and notes in any currency;

(b) postal orders;

(c) traveller's cheques;

(d) banker's drafts; and

(e) such other monetary instruments as the Central Government, or as the case may be, the State Government may specify by an order made in writing.

8. Where any property is seized or attached in the belief that it constitutes proceeds of terrorism and is produced before the Designated Authority, it shall, on being satisfied that the said property consists of proceeds of terrorism, order forfeiture of such property, whether or not the person from whose possession it is seized or attached, is prosecuted in a Special Court for an offence under this Ordinance.

9. (1) No order forfeiting any proceeds of terrorism shall be made under section 8 unless the person holding or in possession of such proceeds is given a notice in writing informing him of the grounds on which it is proposed to forfeit the proceeds of terrorism and such person is given an opportunity of making a representation in writing within such reasonable time as may be specified in the notice against the grounds of forfeiture and is also given a reasonable opportunity of being heard in the matter.

(2) No order of forfeiture shall be made under sub-section (1), if such person establishes that he is a *bona fide* transferee of such proceeds for value without knowing that they represent proceeds of terrorism.

(3) It shall be competent for the Designated Authority to make an order in respect of property seized or attached, —

(a) directing it to be sold if it is a perishable property and the provisions of section 459 of the Code shall, as nearly as may be practicable, apply to the net proceeds of such sale;

(b) nominating any officer of the Central or State Government, in the case of any other property, to perform the function of the Administrator of such property subject to such conditions as may be specified by the Designated Authority.

10. (1) Any person aggrieved by an order of forfeiture under section 8 may, within one month from the date of the receipt of such order, appeal to the High Court within whose jurisdiction, the Designated Authority, who passed the order appealed against, is situated.

(2) Where an order under section 8 is modified or annulled by the High Court or where in a prosecution instituted for the contravention of the provisions of this Ordinance, the person against whom an order of forfeiture has been made under section 8 is acquitted, such property shall be returned to him and in either case if it is not possible for any reason

to return the forfeited property, such person shall be paid the price therefor as if the property had been sold to the Central Government with reasonable interest calculated from the day of seizure of the property and such price shall be determined in the manner prescribed.

11. The order of forfeiture made under this Ordinance by the Designated Authority, shall not prevent the infliction of any other punishment to which the person affected thereby is liable under this Ordinance.

12. (1) Where any claim is preferred, or any objection is made to the seizure of any property under section 7 on the ground that such property is not liable to seizure, the Designated Authority, or as the case may be, the Special Court, before whom such property is produced, shall proceed to investigate the claim or objection :

Provided that no such investigation shall be made where the Designated Authority or the Special Court considers that the claim or objection was designed to cause unnecessary delay.

(2) In case claimant or objector establishes that the property specified in the notice issued under section 9 is not liable to be attached or forfeited under the Ordinance, the said notice shall be withdrawn or modified accordingly.

13. The Designated Authority, acting under the provisions of this Ordinance, shall have all the powers of a Civil Court required for making a full and fair enquiry into the matter before it.

14. (1) Notwithstanding anything contained in any other law, the officer investigating any offence under this Ordinance, with prior approval in writing of an officer not below the rank of a Superintendent of Police, may require any officer or authority of the Central Government or a State Government or a local authority or a Bank, company, or a firm or any other institution, establishment, organisation or any individual to furnish information in their possession in relation to such offence, on points or matters, where the investigating officer has reason to believe that such information will be useful for, or relevant to, the purposes of this Ordinance.

(2) Failure to furnish the information called for under sub-section (1), or deliberately furnishing false information shall be punishable with imprisonment for a term which may extend to three years or with fine or with both.

(3) Notwithstanding anything contained in the Code, the offence under sub-section (1) shall be tried as a summary case and the procedure prescribed in Chapter XXI of the said Code [except sub-section (2) of section 262] shall be applicable thereto.

15. Where, after the issue of an order under section 7 or issue of a notice under section 9, any property referred to in the said order or notice is transferred by any mode whatsoever, such transfer shall, for the purpose of the proceedings under this Ordinance, be ignored and if such property is subsequently forfeited, the transfer of such property shall be deemed to be null and void.

16. (1) Where any person is accused of any offence under this Ordinance, it shall be open to the Special Court trying him to pass an order that all or any of the properties, movable or immovable or both belonging to him, shall, during the period of such trial, be attached, if not already attached under this Ordinance.

(2) Where a person has been convicted of any offence punishable under this Ordinance, the Special Court may, in addition to awarding any punishment, by order in writing, declare that any property, movable or immovable or both, belonging to the accused and specified in the order, shall stand forfeited to the Central Government or the State Government, as the case may be, free from all encumbrances.

17. Where any shares in a company stand forfeited to the Central Government or the State Government, as the case may be, under this Ordinance, then, the company shall on receipt of the order of the Special Court, notwithstanding anything contained in the Companies Act, 1956, or the articles of association of the company, forthwith register the Central Government or the State Government, as the case may be, as the transferee of such shares.

CHAPTER III

TERRORIST ORGANISATIONS

18. (1) For the purposes of this Ordinance an organisation is a terrorist organisation if, —

(a) it is listed in the Schedule, or

(b) it operates under the same name as an organisation listed in that Schedule.

(2) The Central Government may by order, in the Official Gazette, —

(a) add an organisation to the Schedule;

(b) remove an organisation from that Schedule;

(c) amend that Schedule in some other way.

(3) The Central Government may exercise its power under clause (a) of sub-section (2) in respect of an organisation only if it believes that it is involved in terrorism.

(4) For the purposes of sub-section (3) an organisation shall be deemed to be involved in terrorism if it—

(a) commits or participates in acts of terrorism,

(b) prepares for terrorism,

(c) promotes or encourages terrorism, or

(d) is otherwise involved in terrorism.

19. (1) An application may be made to the Central Government for the exercise of its power under clause (b) of sub-section (2) of section 18 to remove an organisation from the Schedule.

(2) An application may be made by —

(a) the organisation, or

(b) any person affected by inclusion of the organisation in the Schedule as a terrorist organisation.

(3) The Central Government may make rules to prescribe the procedure for admission and disposal of an application made under this section.

(4) Where an application under sub-section (1) has been refused, the applicant may apply for a review to the Review Committee constituted by the Central Government

under sub-section (1) of section 59 within one month from the date of receipt of the order by the applicant.

(5) The Review Committee may allow an application for review against refusal to remove an organisation from the Schedule, if it considers that the decision to refuse was flawed when considered in the light of the principles applicable on an application for judicial review.

(6) Where the Review Committee allows review under sub-section (5) by or in respect of an organisation, it may make an order under this sub-section.

(7) Where an order is made under sub-section (6), the Central Government shall as soon as the certified copy of the order is received by it, make an order removing the organisation from the list in the Schedule.

20. (1) A person commits an offence if he belongs or professes to belong to a terrorist organisation :

Provided that this sub-section shall not apply where the person charged is able to prove —

(a) that the organisation was not declared as a terrorist organisation at the time when he became a member or began to profess to be a member; and

(b) that he has not taken part in the activities of the organisation at any time during its inclusion in the Schedule as a terrorist organisation.

(2) A person guilty of an offence under this section shall be liable, on conviction, to imprisonment for a term not exceeding ten years or with fine or with both.

21. (1) A person commits an offence if —

(a) he invites support for a terrorist organisation, and

(b) the support is not, or is not restricted to, the provision of money or other property within the meaning of section 22.

(2) A person commits an offence if he arranges, manages or assists in arranging or managing a meeting which he knows is —

(a) to support a terrorist organisation,

(b) to further the activities of a terrorist organisation, or

(c) to be addressed by a person who belongs or professes to belong to a terrorist organisation.

(3) A person commits an offence if he addresses a meeting for the purpose of encouraging support for a terrorist organisation or to further its activities .

(4) A person guilty of an offence under this section shall be liable on conviction, to imprisonment for a term not exceeding ten years or with fine or with both.

Explanation : For the purposes for this section, the expression "meeting" means a meeting of three or more persons whether or not the public are admitted.

22. (1) A person commits an offence if he —

(a) invites another to provide money or other property, and

(b) intends that it should be used, or has reasonable cause to suspect that it may be used, for the purposes of terrorism.

(2) A person commits an offence if he —

(a) receives money or other property, and

(b) intends that it should be used , or has reasonable cause to suspect that it may be used, for the purposes of terrorism.

(3) A person commits an offence if he —

(a) provides money or other property, and

(b) knows or has reasonable cause to suspect that it will or may be used for the purposes of terrorism.

(4) In this section, a reference to the provision of money or other property is a reference to its being given, lent or otherwise made available, whether or not for consideration.

(5) A person guilty of an offence under this section shall be liable on conviction, to imprisonment for a term not exceeding fourteen years, or with fine or with both.

CHAPTER IV
SPECIAL COURTS

23. (1) The Central Government or a State Government may, by notification in the Official Gazette, constitute one or more Special Courts for such area or areas, or for such case or class or group of cases, as may be specified in the notification.

(2) Where a notification constituting a Special Court for any area or areas or for any case or class or group of cases is issued by the Central Government under sub-section (1), and a notification constituting a Special Court for the same area or areas or for the same case or class or group of cases has also been issued by the State Government under that sub-section, the Special Court constituted by the Central Government, whether the notification constituting such Court is issued before or after the issue of the notification constituting the Special Court by the State Government, shall have, and the Special Court constituted by the State Government shall not have, jurisdiction to try any offence committed in that area or areas or, as the case may be, the case or class or group of cases and all cases pending before any Special Court constituted by the State Government shall stand transferred to the Special Court constituted by the Central Government.

(3) Where any question arises as to the jurisdiction of any Special Court, it shall be referred to the Central Government whose decision in the matter shall be final.

(4) A Special Court shall be presided over by a judge to be appointed by the Central Government or, as the case may be, the State Government, with the concurrence of the Chief Justice of the High Court.

(5) The Central Government or, as the case may be, the State Government may also appoint, with the concurrence of the Chief Justice of the High Court, additional judges to exercise jurisdiction of a Special Court.

(6) A person shall not be qualified for appointment as a judge or an additional judge of a Special Court unless he is, immediately before such appointment, a sessions judge or an additional sessions judge in any State.

(7) For the removal of doubts, it is hereby provided that the attainment, by a person appointed as a judge or an additional judge of a Special Court, of the age of superannuation under the rules applicable to him in the service to which he belongs, shall not affect his continuance as such judge or additional judge.

(8) Where any additional judge or additional judges is or are appointed in a Special Court, the judge of the Special Court may, from time to time, by general or special order, in writing, provide for the distribution of business of the Special Court among all judges including himself and the additional judge or additional judges and also for the disposal of urgent business in the event of his absence or the absence of any additional judge.

24. A Special Court may, on its own motion, or on an application made by the Public Prosecutor and if it considers it expedient or desirable so to do, sit for any of its proceedings at any place, other than its ordinary place of sitting :

Provided that nothing in this section shall be construed to change the place of sitting of a Special Court constituted by a State Government to any place outside that State.

25. (1) Notwithstanding anything contained in the Code, every offence punishable under any provision of this Ordinance shall be triable only by the Special Court within whose local jurisdiction it was committed or, as the case may be, by the Special Court constituted for trying such offence under section 23.

(2) If, having regard to the exigencies of the situation prevailing in a State, —

(i) it is not possible to have a fair, impartial or speedy trial; or

(ii) it is not feasible to have the trial without occasioning the breach of peace or grave risk to the safety of the accused, the witnesses, the Public Prosecutor and a judge of the Special Court or any of them; or

(iii) it is not otherwise in the interests of justice,

the Supreme Court may transfer any case pending before

a Special Court to any other Special Court within that State or in any other State and the High Court may transfer any case pending before a Special Court situated in that State to any other Special Court within the State.

(3) The Supreme Court or the High Court, as the case may be, may act under this section either on the application of the Central Government or a party interested and any such application shall be made by motion, which shall, except when the applicant is the Attorney-General of India, be supported by an affidavit or affirmation.

26. (1) When trying any offence, a Special Court may also try any other offence with which the accused may, under the Code, be charged at the same trial if the offence is connected with such other offence.

(2) If, in the course of any trial under this Ordinance of any offence, it is found that the accused person has committed any other offence under this Ordinance or under any other law, the Special Court may convict such person of such other offence and pass any sentence or award punishment authorized by this Ordinance or such rule or, as the case may be, under such other law.

27. (1) When a police officer investigating a case requests the Court of a Chief Judicial Magistrate or the Court of a Chief Metropolitan Magistrate in writing for obtaining samples of hand writing, finger prints, foot prints, photographs, blood, saliva, semen, hair, voice of any accused person, reasonably suspected to be involved in the commission of an offence under this Ordinance, it shall be lawful for the Court of a Chief Judicial Magistrate or the Court of a Chief Metropolitan Magistrate to direct that such samples be given by the accused person to the police officer either through a medical practitioner or otherwise, as the case may be.

(2) If any accused person refuses to give samples as provided in sub-section (1), the court shall draw adverse inference against the accused.

28. (1) For every Special Court, the Central Government or, as the case may be, the State Government, shall appoint a person to be the Public Prosecutor and may appoint one or more persons to be the Additional Public Prosecutor or Additional Public Prosecutors :

Provided that the Central Government or, as the case may be, the State Government, may also appoint for any case or class or group of cases, a Special Public Prosecutor.

(2) A person shall not be qualified to be appointed as a Public Prosecutor or an Additional Public Prosecutor or a Special Public Prosecutor under this section unless he has been in practice as an Advocate for not less than seven years or has held any post, for a period of not less than seven years, under the Union or a State, requiring special knowledge of law.

(3) Every person appointed as a Public Prosecutor or an Additional Public Prosecutor or a Special Public Prosecutor under this section shall be deemed to be a Public Prosecutor within the meaning of clause (u) of section 2 of the Code, and the provisions of the Code shall have effect accordingly.

29. (1) Subject to the provisions of section 49, a Special Court may take cognizance of any offence, without the accused being committed to it for trial, upon receiving a complaint of facts that constitute such offence or upon a police report of such facts.

(2) Where an offence triable by a Special Court is punishable with imprisonment for a term not exceeding three years or with fine or with both, the Special Court may, notwithstanding anything contained in sub-section (1) of section 260 or section 262 of the Code, try the offence in a summary way in accordance with the procedure prescribed in the Code and the provisions of sections 263 to 265 of the Code, shall so far as may be, apply to such trial :

Provided that when, in the course of a summary trial under this sub-section, it appears to the Special Court that the nature of the case is such that it is undesirable to try it in a summary way, the Special Court shall recall any witnesses who may have been examined and proceed to re-hear the case in the manner provided by the provisions of the Code for the trial of such offence and the said provisions shall apply to and in relation to a Special Court as they apply to and in relation to a Magistrate :

Provided further that in the case of any conviction in a summary trial under this section, it shall be lawful for a Special Court to pass a sentence of imprisonment for a term not exceeding one year and with fine which may extend to rupees five lakh.

(3) Subject to the other provisions of this Ordinance, a Special Court shall, for the purpose of trial of any offence, have all the powers of a Court of Session and shall try such offence as if it were a Court of Session so far as may be in accordance with the procedure prescribed in the Code for the trial before a Court of Session.

(4) Subject to the other provisions of this Ordinance, every case transferred to a Special Court under section 25 shall be dealt with as if such case had been transferred under section 406 of the Code to such Special Court.

(5) Notwithstanding anything contained in the Code, but subject to the provisions of section 299 of the Code, a Special Court may, if it thinks fit and for reasons to be recorded by it, proceed with the trial in the absence of the accused or his pleader and record the evidence of any witness, subject to the right of the accused to recall the witness for cross-examination.

30. (1) Notwithstanding anything contained in the Code, the proceedings under this Ordinance may, for reasons to be recorded in writing, be held in camera if the Special Court so desires.

(2) A Special Court, if on an application made by a witness in any proceeding before it or by the Public Prosecutor in relation to such witness or on its own motion, is satisfied that the life of such witness is in danger, it may, for reasons to be recorded in writing, take such measures as it deems fit for keeping the identity and address of such witness secret.

(3) In particular, and without prejudice to the generality of the provisions of sub-section (2), the measures which a Special Court may take under that sub-section may include —

(a) the holding of the proceedings at a place to be decided by the Special Court;

(b) the avoiding of the mention of the names and addresses of the witnesses in its orders or judgments or in any records of the case accessible to public;

(c) the issuing of any directions for securing that the identity and address of the witnesses are not disclosed;

(d) a decision that it is in the public interest to order that all or any of the proceedings pending before such a court shall not be published in any manner.

(4) Any person who contravenes any decision or direction issued under sub-section (3) shall be punishable with imprisonment for a term which may extend to one year and with fine which may extend to one thousand rupees.

31. The trial under this Ordinance of any offence by a Special Court shall have precedence over the trial of any other case against the accused in any other court (not being a Special Court) and shall be concluded in preference to the trial of such other case and accordingly the trial of such other case shall remain in abeyance.

32. (1) Notwithstanding anything in the Code or in the Indian Evidence Act, 1872, but subject to the provisions of this section, a confession made by a person before a police officer not lower in rank than a Superintendent of Police and recorded by such police officer either in writing or on any mechanical or electronic device like cassettes, tapes or sound tracks from out of which sound or images can be reproduced, shall be admissible in the trial of such person for an offence under this Ordinance or rules made thereunder.

(2) A police officer shall, before recording any confession made by a person under sub-section (1) explain to such person in writing that he is not bound to make a confession and that if he does so, it may be used against him :

Provided that where such person prefers to remain silent, the police officer shall not compel or induce him to make any confession.

(3) The confession shall be recorded in an atmosphere free from threat or inducement and shall be in the same language in which the person makes it.

(4) The person from whom a confession has been recorded

under sub-section (1), shall be produced before the Court of a Chief Metropolitan Magistrate or the Court of a Chief Judicial Magistrate along with the original statement of confession, written or recorded on mechanical or electronic device within forty-eight hours.

(5) The Chief Metropolitan Magistrate or the Chief Judicial Magistrate, shall, record the statement, if any, made by the person so produced and get his signature or thumb impression and if there is any complaint of torture, such person shall be directed to be produced for medical examination before a Medical Officer not lower in rank than an Assistant Civil Surgeon and thereafter, he shall be sent to judicial custody.

33. Where, after taking cognizance of any offence, a Special Court is of the opinion that the offence is not triable by it, it shall, notwithstanding that it has no jurisdiction to try such offence, transfer the case for the trial of such offence to any court having jurisdiction under the Code and the court to which the case is transferred may proceed with the trial of the offence as if it had taken cognizance of the offence.

34. (1) Notwithstanding anything contained in the Code, an appeal shall lie from any judgment, sentence or order, not being an interlocutory order, of a Special Court to the High Court both on facts and on law.

Explanation : For the purposes of this section, "High Court" means a High Court within whose jurisdiction, a Special Court which passed the judgment, sentence or order, is situated.

(2) Every appeal under sub-section (1) shall be heard by a bench of two Judges of the High Court.

(3) Except as aforesaid, no appeal or revision shall lie to any court from any judgment, sentence or order including an interlocutory order of a Special Court.

(4) Notwithstanding anything contained in sub-section (3) of section 378 of the Code, an appeal shall lie to the High Court against an order of the Special Court granting or refusing bail.

(5) Every appeal under this section shall be preferred within a period of thirty days from the date of the judgment, sentence or order appealed from :

Provided that the High Court may entertain an appeal after the expiry of the said period of thirty days if it is satisfied that the appellant had sufficient cause for not preferring the appeal within the period of thirty days.

CHAPTER V

INTERCEPTION OF COMMUNICATION IN CERTAIN CASES

35. In this Chapter, unless the context otherwise requires, —

(a) "electronic communication" means any transmission of signs, signals, writings, images, sounds, data or intelligence of any nature transmitted in whole or in part by a wire, radio, electromagnetic, photo electronic or photo optical system that affects inland or foreign commerce but does not include, —

(i) the radio portion of a cordless telephone communication that is transmitted between the wireless telephone hand-set and the base unit;

(ii) any wire or oral communication;

(iii) any communication made through a tone only paging device; or

(iv) any communication from a tracking device;

(b) "intercept" means the aural or other acquisition of the contents by wire, electronic or oral communication through the use of any electronic, mechanical or other device;

(c) "oral communication" means any oral communication uttered by a person exhibiting an expectation that such communication is not subject to interception under circumstances justifying such expectation but such term does not include any electronic communication;

(d) "wire communication" means any aural transmission made in whole or part through the use of facilities for the transmission of communications by the aid of wire, cable or other like connection between the point of origin and the point of connection, between the point of origin and the point of reception (including the use of such connection in switching station) and such term includes any electronic storage of such communication.

36. The Central Government or the State Government, as the case may be, may appoint an officer not below the rank of Secretary to the Government in case of State Government and not below the rank of Joint Secretary to the Government in the case of Central Government, to be the Competent Authority for the purposes of this Chapter.

37. (1). A police officer not below the rank of Superintendent of Police supervising the investigation of any terrorist act under this Ordinance may submit an application in writing to the Competent Authority for an order authorizing or approving the interception of wire, electronic or oral communication by the investigating officer when he believes that such interception may provide, or has provided evidence of any offence involving a terrorist act.

(2) Each application shall include the following information :

(a) the identity of the investigating officer making the application, and the head of the department authorizing the application;

(b) a statement of the facts and circumstances relied upon by the applicant to justify his belief that an order should be issued, including —

(i) details as to the offence of terrorist act that has been, is being, or is about to be committed;

(ii) a particular description of the nature and location of the facilities from which or the place where the communication is to be intercepted;

(iii) a particular description of the type of communications sought to be intercepted; and

(iv) the identity of the person, if known, committing the terrorist act whose communications are to be intercepted;

(c) a statement of the period of time for which the

interception is required to be maintained, if the nature of the enquiry is such that the authorization of interception should not automatically terminate after the described type of communication has been first obtained;

(d) a particular description of facts establishing probable cause to believe that additional communications of the same type will occur thereafter; and

(e) where the application is for the extension of an order, a statement setting forth the results thus far obtained from the interception, or a reasonable explanation of the failure to obtain such results.

(3) The Competent Authority may require the applicant to furnish additional oral or documentary evidence in support of the application.

38. (1) Upon such application, the Competent Authority may reject the application, or issue an order, as requested or as modified, authorizing or approving interception of wire, electronic or oral communications, if the Competent Authority determines on the basis of the facts submitted by the applicant that —

(a) there is a probable cause for belief that an individual is committing, has committed, or is about to commit a particular offence described and made punishable under sections 3 and 6 of this Ordinance;

(b) there is a probable cause of belief that particular communications concerning that offence may be obtained through such interception;

(c) there is probable cause of belief that the facilities from which, or the place where, the wire, electronic or oral communications are to be intercepted are being used or are about to be used, in connection with the commission of such offence, leased to, or are listed in the name of or commonly used by such person.

(2) Each order by the Competent Authority authorizing or approving the interception of any wire, electronic or oral communication under this section shall specify —

(a) the identity of the person, if known, whose communications are to be intercepted;

(b) the nature and location of the communication facilities as to which, or the place where, authority to intercept is granted;

(c) a particular description of the type of communication sought to be intercepted, and a statement of the particular offence to which it relates;

(d) the identity of the agency authorized to intercept the communications, and the person authorizing the application; and

(e) the period of time during which such interception is authorized , including a statement as to whether or not the interception shall automatically terminate after the described communication has been first obtained.

39. (1) The Competent Authority shall immediately after passing the order under sub-section (1) of section 38, but in any case not later than seven days from the passing of the order, submit a copy of the same to the Review Committee constituted under section 59 along with all the relevant underlying papers, record and his own findings, in respect of the said order, for consideration and approval of the order by the Review Committee.

(2) An order authorizing the interception of a wire, electronic or oral communication under this section shall, upon request of the applicant, direct that a provider of wire or electronic communication service, landlord, custodian or other person shall furnish to the applicant forthwith all information, facilities, and technical assistance necessary to accomplish the interception unobtrusively and with a minimum of interference with the services that such service provider, landlord, custodian, or person is providing to the person whose communications are to be intercepted.

40. (1) No order issued under this section may authorize or approve the interception of any wire, electronic or oral communication for any period longer than is necessary to achieve the objective of the authorization, nor in any event longer than sixty days and such sixty days period shall begin on the day immediately preceding the day on which the investigation officer first begins to conduct an interception under the order or ten days after order is issued whichever is earlier.

(2) The extension of an order may be granted, but only upon an application for an extension made in accordance with sub-section (1) of section 37 and the Competent Authority making the findings required by sub-section (1) of section 38, and the period of such extension shall be no longer than the Competent Authority deems necessary to achieve the purposes for which it was granted and in no event for longer than sixty days at a time.

(3) Every order and extension thereof shall contain a provision that the authorization to intercept shall be executed as soon as practicable and shall be conducted in such manner as to minimize the interception of communications not otherwise subject to interception under this section and shall terminate upon attainment of the authorized objective, or in any event on the expiry of the period of said order or extension thereof.

41. (1) An interception under this Chapter may be conducted in whole or in part by a public servant, acting under the supervision of the investigating officer authorized to conduct the interception.

(2) Whenever an order authorizing an interception is issued pursuant to this section, the order may require reports to be made to the Competent Authority who issued the order showing that progress has been made towards achievement of the authorized objective and the need for continued interception and such report shall be made at such intervals as the Competent Authority may require.

42. (1) Notwithstanding anything contained in any other provision of this section, an officer not below the rank of Additional Director General of Police or a police officer of equivalent rank who reasonably determines that —

(a) an emergency situation exists that involves —

(i) immediate danger of death or serious physical injury to any person;

(ii) conspiratorial activities threatening the security or interest of the State; or

(iii) conspiratorial activities, characteristic of a terrorist act, that requires a wire, electronic or oral communication to be intercepted before an order from the Competent Authority authorizing such interception can, with due diligence, be obtained, and

(b) there are grounds on which an order should be issued under this section to authorize such interception,

may authorize, in writing, the investigating officer to intercept such wire, electronic or oral communication, if an application for an order approving the interception is made in accordance with the provisions of sub-sections (1) and (2) of section 37 within forty-eight hours after the interception has occurred, or begins to occur.

(2) In the absence of an order approving the interception made under sub-section (1), such interception shall immediately terminate when the communication sought is obtained or when the application for the order is rejected, whichever is earlier; and in the event of an application for permitting interception being rejected under sub-section (1) of section 38 or an application under sub-section (1) of section 42 for approval being rejected, or in any other case where the interception is terminated without an order having been issued, the contents of any wire, electronic or oral communication intercepted shall be treated as having been obtained in violation of this section.

43. (a) The contents of any wire, electronic or oral communication intercepted by any means authorized by this section shall as far as possible, be recorded on tape or wire or other comparable device and shall be done in such manner as to protect the recording from editing or other alterations.

(b) Immediately upon the expiration of the period of order, or extension thereof, such recording shall be made available to the Competent Authority issuing such order and shall be sealed under his directions and kept in the custody of such person or authority as the Competent Authority orders, and such recordings shall not be destroyed except upon an order of the Competent Authority and in any event shall be kept for ten years.

(c) Applications made and orders issued under this section shall be sealed by the Competent Authority and custody of the applications and orders shall be kept in such manner as the Competent Authority directs, and shall not be destroyed except on an order of the Competent Authority, and in any event shall be kept for ten years.

44. Notwithstanding anything in the Code or in any other law for the time being in force, the evidence collected through the interception of wire, electronic or oral communication under this Chapter shall be admissible as evidence against the accused in the Court during the trial of a case :

Provided that, the contents of any wire, electronic or oral communication intercepted pursuant to this Chapter or evidence derived therefrom shall not be received in evidence or otherwise disclosed in any trial, hearing or other proceeding in any court unless each accused has been furnished with a copy of the order of the Competent Authority, and accompanying application, under which the interception was authorized or approved not less than ten days before trial, hearing or proceeding :

Provided further that, the period of ten days may be waived by the judge trying the matter, if he comes to the conclusion that it was not possible to furnish the accused with the above information ten days before the trial, hearing or proceeding and that the accused will not be prejudiced by the delay in receiving such information.

45. (1) The Review Committee constituted by the Central Government or the State Government, as the case may be, shall review every order passed by the Competent Authority under section 38.

(2) Every order passed by the Competent Authority under section 38, or disapproved by the officer under section 42, shall be placed before the Review Committee, which shall be considered by the Review Committee within ten days after its receipt, to decide whether the order, was necessary, reasonable and justified.

(3) The Review Committee, after examining the entire record and holding such enquiry, if any, deemed necessary may, by order in writing, either approve the order passed by the

Competent Authority or may issue order disapproving the same.

(4) On issue of an order of disapproval by the Review Committee, the interception, if any, already commenced shall be forthwith discontinued and the intercepted communication, if any, in the form of tape, wire or other device shall, thereupon, not be admissible as evidence in any case and shall be directed to be destroyed.

46. Except as otherwise specifically provided in section 38, any police officer who —

(a) intentionally intercepts, endeavours to intercept, or procures any other person to intercept or endeavour to intercept any wire, electronic or oral communication;

(b) intentionally uses, endeavours to use, or procures any other person to use or endeavours to use any electronic, mechanical or other device to intercept any oral communication when —

(i) such device is affixed to, or otherwise transmits a signal through a wire, cable, or other like connection used in wire communication; or

(ii) such device transmits communications by radio, or interferes with the transmission of such communication;

(c) intentionally discloses, or endeavours to disclose, to any other person the contents of any wire, electronic or oral communication, knowing or having reason to know that the information was obtained through the interception of a wire, electronic or oral communication in violation of this Chapter;

(d) intentionally uses, or endeavours to use, the contents of any wire, electronic or oral communication, knowing or having reason to know that the information was obtained through the interception of a wire, electronic or oral communication in violation of this Chapter; or

(e) intentionally discloses, or endeavours to disclose, to any other unauthorized person the contents of any wire, electronic or oral communication, intercepted by means authorized by section 38;

(f) intentionally continues the interception of wire, electronic or oral communication after the issue of an order of rejection by the Competent Authority under this Chapter.

(g) intentionally continues the interception of wire, electronic or oral communication after the issue of an order of disapproval by the Review Committee under sub-section (3) of section 45,

shall for such violation be punishable with imprisonment for a term which may extend to one year and with fine upto rupees fifty thousand.

47. (1) The Central Government and the State Government, as the case may be, shall cause an annual report to be prepared giving a full account of, —

(i) the number of applications for authorization of interceptions received by the Competent Authority from the Police Department in which prosecutions have been launched;

(ii) the number of such applications permitted or rejected;

(iii) the number of interceptions carried out in emergency situations and the number of approvals granted or rejected in such matters;

(iv) the number of prosecutions launched based on such interceptions and convictions resulting from such interceptions, along with an explanatory memorandum giving general assessment of the utility and importance of the interceptions authorized.

(2) An annual report shall be laid by the State Government before the State Legislature within three months of the completion of every calendar year :

Provided that, if the State Government is of the opinion that the inclusion of any matter in the annual report would be prejudicial to the security of the State or to the prevention or detection of any terrorist act, the State Government may exclude such matter from being included in such annual report.

(3) An annual report shall be laid by the Central Government before each House of Parliament within three months of the completion of every calendar year :

Provided that, if the Central Government is of the opinion that the inclusion of any matter in the annual report would be prejudicial to the security of the country or to the prevention or detection of any terrorist act, the Central Government may exclude such matter from being included in such annual report.

CHAPTER VI

MISCELLANEOUS

48. (1) Notwithstanding anything contained in the Code or any other law, every offence punishable under this Ordinance shall be deemed to be a cognizable offence within the meaning of clause (c) of section 2 of the Code, and "cognizable case" as defined in that clause shall be construed accordingly.

(2) Section 167 of the Code shall apply in relation to a case involving an offence punishable under this Ordinance subject to the modification that in sub-section (2), —

(a) the references to "fifteen days", "ninety days" and "sixty days", wherever they occur, shall be construed as references to "thirty days", "ninety days" and "ninety days", respectively; and

(b) after the proviso, the following provisos shall be inserted, namely —

"Provided further that if it is not possible to complete the investigation within the said period of ninety days, the Special Court shall extend the said period up to one hundred and eighty days, on the report of the Public Prosecutor indicating the progress of the investigation and the specific reasons for the detention of the accused beyond the said period of ninety days :

Provided also that if the police officer making the investigation under this Ordinance, requests, for the purposes of investigation, for police custody from judicial custody of any person from judicial custody, he shall file an affidavit stating the reasons for doing so and shall also explain the delay, if any, for requesting such police custody.".

(3) Section 268 of the Code shall apply in relation to a case involving an offence punishable under this Ordinance subject to the modification that —

(a) the reference in sub-section (1) thereof —

(i) to "the State Government" shall be construed as a reference to "the Central Government or the State Government",

(ii) to "order of the State Government" shall be construed as a reference to "order of the Central Government or the State Government, as the case may be"; and

(b) the reference in sub-section (2) thereof, to "State Government" shall be construed as a reference to "Central Government or the State Government, as the case may be".

(4) Sections 366, 367 and 371 of the Code shall apply in relation to a case involving an offence triable by a Special Court subject to the modification that the reference to "Court of Session", wherever occurring therein, shall be construed as the reference to "Special Court".

(5) Nothing in section 438 of the Code shall apply in relation to any case involving the arrest of any person accused of having committed an offence punishable under this Ordinance.

(6) Notwithstanding anything contained in the Code, no person accused of an offence punishable under this Ordinance shall, if in custody, be released on bail or on his own bond unless the Court gives the Public Prosecutor an opportunity of being heard.

(7) Where the Public Prosecutor opposes the application of the accused to release on bail, no person accused of an offence punishable under this Ordinance or any rule made thereunder shall be released on bail until the court is satisfied that there are grounds for believing that he is not guilty of committing such offence :

Provided that after the expiry of a period of one year from

the date of detention of the accused for an offence under this Ordinance, the provisions of sub-section (6) of this section shall apply.

(8) The restrictions on granting of bail specified in sub-sections (6) and (7) are in addition to the restrictions under the Code or any other law for the time being in force on granting of bail.

(9) Notwithstanding anything contained in sub-sections (6), (7) and (8), no bail shall be granted to a person accused of an offence punishable under this Ordinance, if he is not an Indian citizen and has entered the country unauthorisedly or illegally except in very exceptional circumstances and for reasons to be recorded in writing.

49. No Court shall take cognizance of any offence under this Ordinance without the previous sanction of the Central Government or as the case may be, the State Government.

50. Notwithstanding anything contained in the Code, no police officer, —

(a) in the case of the Delhi Special Police Establishment, not below the rank of a Deputy Superintendent of Police or a police officer of equivalent rank;

(b) in the metropolitan areas of Mumbai, Kolkata, Chennai and Ahmedabad and any other metropolitan area notified as such under sub-section (1) of section 8 of the Code, not below the rank of an Assistant Commissioner of Police;

(c) in any other case not relatable to clause (a) or clause (b), not below the rank of a Deputy Superintendent of Police or a police officer of an equivalent rank,

shall investigate any offence punishable under this Ordinance.

51. (1) Where a police officer arrests a person, he shall prepare a custody memo of the person arrested.

(2) The person arrested shall be informed of his right to consult a legal practitioner as soon as he is brought to the police station.

(3) Whenever any person is arrested, information of his arrest shall be immediately communicated by the police officer to a family member or in his absence to a relative of such

person by telegram, telephone or by any other means and this fact shall be recorded by the police officer under the signature of the person arrested.

(4) The person arrested shall be permitted to meet the legal practitioner representing him during the course of interrogation of the accused person :

Provided that nothing in this sub-section shall entitle the legal practitioner to remain present throughout the period of interrogation.

52. (1) In a prosecution for an offence under sub-section (1) of section 3, if it is proved —

(a) that the arms or explosives or any other substances specified in section 4 were recovered from the possession of the accused and there is reason to believe that such arms or explosives or other substances of a similar nature, were used in the commission of such offence; or

(b) that the finger-prints of the accused were found at the site of the offence or on anything including arms and vehicles used in connection with the commission of such offence,

the Special Court shall draw adverse inference against the accused.

(2) In a prosecution for an offence under sub-section (3) of section 3, if it is proved that the accused rendered any financial assistance to a person, having knowledge that such person is accused of, or reasonably suspected of, an offence under that section, the Special Court shall draw adverse inference against the accused.

53. No civil court or other authority shall have or, be entitled to, exercise any jurisdiction, powers or authority in relation to the matters referred to in section 19 and section 39 of the Ordinance.

54. (1) Nothing in this Ordinance shall affect the jurisdiction exercisable by, or the procedure applicable to, any court or other authority under any law relating to the naval, military or air forces or other armed forces of the Union.

(2) For the removal of doubts, it is hereby declared that for

the purposes of any such law as is referred to in sub-section (1), a Special Court shall be deemed to be a court of ordinary criminal justice.

55. The provisions of this Ordinance shall have effect notwithstanding anything inconsistent therewith contained in any enactment other than this Ordinance or in any instrument having effect by virtue of any enactment other than this Ordinance.

56. No suit, prosecution or other legal proceeding shall lie against the Central Government or a State Government or any officer or authority of the Central Government or State Government or any other authority on whom powers have been conferred under this Ordinance, for anything which is in good faith done or purported to be done in pursuance of this Ordinance :

Provided further that no suit, prosecution or other legal proceedings shall lie against any serving member or retired member of the armed forces or other para-military forces in respect of any action taken or purported to be taken by him in good faith, in the course of any operation directed towards combating terrorism.

57. (1) Any police officer who exercises powers corruptly or maliciously, knowing that there are no reasonable grounds for proceeding under this Ordinance, shall be punishable with imprisonment which may extend to two years, or with fine, or with both.

(2) If the Special Court is of opinion that any person has been corruptly or maliciously proceeded against under this Ordinance, the court may award such compensation as it deems fit to the person, so proceeded against and it shall be paid by the officer, person, authority or Government, as may be specified in the order.

58. Notwithstanding anything contained in any other law for the time being in force, the passport and the arms licence of a person, who is charge sheeted for having committed any offence under this Ordinance, shall be deemed to have been impounded for such period as the Special Court may deem fit.

59. (1) The Central Government and each State Government shall, whenever necessary, constitute one or more Review Committees for the purposes of this Ordinance.

(2) Every such Committee shall consist of a Chairperson and such other members not exceeding three and possessing such qualifications as may be prescribed.

(3) A Chairperson of the Committee shall be a person who is, or who has been, a Judge of a High Court, who shall be appointed by the Central Government, or as the case may be, the State Government, so however, that the concurrence of the Chief Justice of the High Court shall be obtained in the case of a sitting Judge :

Provided that in the case of a Union territory, the appointment of a person who is a Judge of the High Court of a State shall be made as a Chairperson with the concurrence of the Chief Justice of the concerned High Court.

60. The High Courts may, by notifications in the Official Gazette, make such rules, if any, as they may deem necessary for carrying out the provisions of this Ordinance relating to Special Courts within their territories.

61. (1) Without prejudice to the powers of the High Courts to make rules under section 60, the Central Government may, by notification in the Official Gazette, make rules for carrying out the provisions of this Ordinance.

(2) In particular, and without prejudice to the generality of the foregoing power, such rules may provide for all or any of the following matters, namely —

(a) regulating the conduct of persons in respect of areas the control of which is considered necessary or expedient and the removal of such persons from such areas;

(b) the entry into, and search of, —

(i) any vehicle, vessel or aircraft; or

(ii) any place, whatsoever,

reasonably suspected of being used for committing the offences referred to in section 3 or section 4 or for manufacturing or storing anything for the commission of any such offence;

(c) conferring powers upon, —

(i) the Central Government;

(ii) a State Government;

(iii) an Administrator of a Union territory under article 239 of the Constitution;

(iv) an officer of the Central Government not lower in rank than that of a Joint Secretary; or

(v) an officer of a State Government not lower in rank than that of a District Magistrate,

to make general or special orders to prevent or deal with terrorist acts;

(d) the arrest and trial of persons contravening any of the rules or any order made thereunder;

(e) the punishment of any person who contravenes or attempts to contravene or abets or attempts to abet the contravention of any rule or order made thereunder with imprisonment for a term which may extend to one year or fine or both.

(f) providing for the seizure and detention of any property in respect of which such contravention, attempt or abetment as is referred to in clause (e) has been committed and for the adjudication of such seizure and detention, whether by any court or by any other authority.

(g) determination of the price of the forfeited property under sub-section (2) of section 10;

(h) the procedure of making application under sub-section (3) of section 19;

(i) the qualifications of the members of the Review Committee under sub-section (2) of section 59.

SCHEDULE

(see section 18)

TERRORIST ORGANISATIONS

1. BABBAR KHALSA INTERNATIONAL.
2. KHALISTAN COMMANDO FORCE.
3. KHALISTAN ZINDABAD FORCE.

4. INTERNATIONAL SIKH YOUTH FEDERATION.
5. LASHKAR-E-TAIBA/PASBAN-E-AHLE HADIS.
6. JAISH-E-MOHAMMED/TAHRIK-E-FURQAN.
7. HARKAT-UL-MUJAHIDEEN/HARKAR-UL-ANSAR/KARKAT UL-JEHAD-E-ISLAMI.
8. HIZB-UL-MUJAHIDEEN/HIZB-ULMUJAHIDEEN PIR PANJAL REGIMENT.
9. AL-UMAR-MUJAHIDEEN.
10. JAMMU AND KASHMIR ISLAMIC FRONT.
11. UNITED LEBERATION FRONT OF ASSAM (ULFA).
12. NATIONAL DEMOCRATIC FRONT OF BODOLAND (NDFB).
13. PEOPLE'S LIBERATION ARMY (PLA).
14. UNITED NATIONAL LIBERATION FRONT (UNLF).
15. PEOPLE'S REVOLUTIONARY PARTY OF KANGLEIPALK (PREPAK).
16. KANLEIPAK COMMUNIST PARTY (KCP).
17. KANGLEI YAOL KANBA LUP (KYKL)
18. MANIPUR PEOPLE'S LIBRATION FRONT (MPLF).
19. ALL TRIPURA TIGER FORCE.
20. NATIONAL LIBERATION FRONT OF TRIPURA.
21. LIBERATION TIGERS OF TAMIL EELAM (LTTE).
22. STUDENTS ISLAMIC MOVEMENT OF INDIA.
23. DEENDAR ANJUMAN

President.

THE UNITED STATES

Uniting and Strengthening America by Providing Appropriate Tools Required to Intercept and Obstruct Terrorism (USA PATRIOT ACT) Act of 2001

ONE HUNDRED SEVENTH CONGRESS OF THE UNITED STATES OF AMERICA

AT THE FIRST SESSION

Begun and held at the City of Washington on Wednesday, the third day of January, two thousand and one

AN ACT

To deter and punish terrorist acts in the United States and around the world, to enhance law enforcement investigatory tools, and for other purposes.

Be it enacted by the Senate and House of Representatives of the United States of America in Congress assembled,

SECTION 1. SHORT TITLE AND TABLE OF CONTENTS.

(a) SHORT TITLE. — This Act may be cited as the "Uniting and Strengthening America by Providing Appropriate Tools Required to Intercept and Obstruct Terrorism (USA PATRIOT ACT) Act of 2001".

(b) TABLE OF CONTENTS. — The table of contents for this Act is as follows :

TITLE IV — PROTECTING THE BORDER

Subtitle A — Protecting the Northern Border

Subtitle B — Enhanced Immigration Provisions

Subtitle C — Preservation of Immigration Benefits for Victims of Terrorism

TITLE V — REMOVING OBSTACLES TO INVESTIGATING TERRORISM

SEC. 2. CONSTRUCTION; SEVERABILITY.

Any provision of this Act held to be invalid or unenforceable by its terms, or as applied to any person or circumstance, shall be construed so as to give it the maximum effect permitted by law, unless such holding shall be one of utter invalidity or unenforceability, in which event such provision shall be deemed severable from this Act and shall not affect the remainder thereof or the application of such provision to other persons not similarly situated or to other, dissimilar circumstances.

TITLE I — ENHANCING DOMESTIC SECURITY AGAINST TERRORISM

SEC. 101. COUNTERTERRORISM FUND.

(a) ESTABLISHMENT; AVAILABILITY. — There is hereby established in the Treasury of the United States a separate fund to be known as the "Counterterrorism Fund", amounts in which shall remain available without fiscal year limitation —

(1) to reimburse any Department of Justice component for any costs incurred in connection with —

(A) reestablishing the operational capability of an office or facility that has been damaged or destroyed as the result of any domestic or international terrorism incident;

(B) providing support to counter, investigate, or prosecute domestic or international terrorism, including, without limitation, paying rewards in connection with these activities; and

(C) conducting terrorism threat assessments of Federal agencies and their facilities; and

(2) to reimburse any department or agency of the Federal Government for any costs incurred in connection with detaining in foreign countries individuals accused of acts of terrorism that violate the laws of the United States.

(b) NO EFFECT ON PRIOR APPROPRIATIONS. — Subsection (a) shall not be construed to affect the amount or availability of any appropriation to the Counterterrorism Fund made before the date of the enactment of this Act.

SEC. 102. SENSE OF CONGRESS CONDEMNING DISCRIMINATION AGAINST ARAB AND MUSLIM AMERICANS.

(a) FINDINGS. — Congress makes the following findings :

(1) Arab Americans, Muslim Americans, and Americans from South Asia play a vital role in our Nation and are entitled to nothing less than the full rights of every American.

(2) The acts of violence that have been taken against Arab and Muslim Americans since the September 11, 2001, attacks against the United States should be and are condemned by all Americans who value freedom.

(3) The concept of individual responsibility for wrongdoing is sacrosanct in American society, and applies equally to all religious, racial, and ethnic groups.

(4) When American citizens commit acts of violence against those who are, or are perceived to be, of Arab or

Muslim descent, they should be punished to the full extent of the law.

(5) Muslim Americans have become so fearful of harassment that many Muslim women are changing the way they dress to avoid becoming targets.

(6) Many Arab Americans and Muslim Americans have acted heroically during the attacks on the United States, including Mohammed Salman Hamdani, a 23-year-old New Yorker of Pakistani descent, who is believed to have gone to the World Trade Center to offer rescue assistance and is now missing.

(b) SENSE OF CONGRESS. — It is the sense of Congress that —

(1) the civil rights and civil liberties of all Americans, including Arab Americans, Muslim Americans, and Americans from South Asia, must be protected, and that every effort must be taken to preserve their safety;

(2) any acts of violence or discrimination against any Americans be condemned; and

(3) the Nation is called upon to recognize the patriotism of fellow citizens from all ethnic, racial, and religious back-grounds.

SEC. 103. INCREASED FUNDING FOR THE TECHNICAL SUPPORT CENTER AT THE FEDERAL BUREAU OF INVESTIGATION.

There are authorized to be appropriated for the Technical Support Center established in section 811 of the Antiterrorism and Effective Death Penalty Act of 1996 (Public Law 104–132) to help meet the demands for activities to combat terrorism and support and enhance the technical support and tactical operations of the FBI, $200,000,000 for each of the fiscal years 2002, 2003, and 2004.

SEC. 104. REQUESTS FOR MILITARY ASSISTANCE TO ENFORCE PROHIBITION IN CERTAIN EMERGENCIES.

Section 2332e of title 18, United States Code, is amended —

(1) by striking "2332c" and inserting "2332a"; and

(2) by striking "chemical".

SEC. 105. EXPANSION OF NATIONAL ELECTRONIC CRIME TASK FORCE INITIATIVE.

The Director of the United States Secret Service shall take appropriate actions to develop a national network of electronic crime task forces, based on the New York Electronic Crimes Task Force model, throughout the United States, for the purpose of preventing, detecting, and investigating various forms of electronic crimes, including potential terrorist attacks against critical infrastructure and financial payment systems.

SEC. 106. PRESIDENTIAL AUTHORITY.

Section 203 of the International Emergency Powers Act (50 U.S.C. 1702) is amended —

(1) in subsection (a)(1) —

(A) at the end of subparagraph (A) (flush to that subparagraph), by striking "and" and inserting a comma and the following :

"by any person, or with respect to any property, subject to the jurisdiction of the United States";

(B) in subparagraph (B) —

(i) by inserting "block during the pendency of an investigation" after "investigate"; and

(ii) by striking "interest;" and inserting "interest by any person, or with respect to any property, subject to the jurisdiction of the United States; and";

(C) by striking "by any person, or with respect to any property, subject to the jurisdiction of the United States"; and

(D) by inserting at the end the following :

"(C) when the United States is engaged in armed hostilities or has been attacked by a foreign country or foreign nationals, confiscate any property, subject to the jurisdiction of the United States, of any foreign person, foreign organization, or foreign country that he determines has planned, authorized, aided, or engaged in such hostilities or attacks against the United States; and all right, title, and interest in any property so confiscated shall vest, when, as, and upon the terms directed by the President, in such agency or person as the President may designate from time to time, and upon such terms and conditions as the President may prescribe, such interest or property shall be held, used, administered, liquidated, sold, or otherwise dealt with in the interest of and for the benefit of the United States, and such designated agency or person may perform any and all acts incident to the accomplishment or furtherance of these purposes."; and

(2) by inserting at the end the following :

"(c) CLASSIFIED INFORMATION. — In any judicial review of a determination made under this section, if the determination was based on classified information (as defined in section 1(a) of the Classified Information Procedures Act) such information may be submitted to the reviewing court ex parte and in camera. This subsection does not confer or imply any right to judicial review.".

TITLE II — ENHANCED SURVEILLANCE PROCEDURES

SEC. 201. AUTHORITY TO INTERCEPT WIRE, ORAL, AND ELECTRONIC COMMUNICATIONS RELATING TO TERRORISM.

Section 2516(1) of title 18, United States Code, is amended —

(1) by redesignating paragraph (p), as so redesignated by section 434(2) of the Antiterrorism and Effective Death Penalty Act of 1996 (Public Law 104–132; 110 Stat. 1274), as paragraph (r); and

(2) by inserting after paragraph (p), as so redesignated by section 201(3) of the Illegal Immigration Reform and Immigrant Responsibility Act of 1996 (division C of Public Law 104–208; 110 Stat. 3009–565), the following new paragraph :

"(q) any criminal violation of section 229 (relating to chemical weapons); or sections 2332, 2332a, 2332b, 2332d, 2339A, or 2339B of this title (relating to terrorism); or".

SEC. 202. AUTHORITY TO INTERCEPT WIRE, ORAL, AND ELECTRONIC COMMUNICATIONS RELATING TO COMPUTER FRAUD AND ABUSE OFFENSES.

Section 2516(1)(c) of title 18, United States Code, is amended by striking "and section 1341 (relating to mail fraud)," and inserting "section 1341 (relating to mail fraud), a felony violation of section 1030 (relating to computer fraud and abuse),".

SEC. 203. AUTHORITY TO SHARE CRIMINAL INVESTIGATIVE INFORMATION.

(a) AUTHORITY TO SHARE GRAND JURY INFORMATION. —

(1) IN GENERAL. — Rule 6(e)(3)(C) of the Federal Rules of Criminal Procedure is amended to read as follows :

"(C)(i) Disclosure otherwise prohibited by this rule of matters occurring before the grand jury may also be made —

"(I) when so directed by a court preliminarily to or in connection with a judicial proceeding;

"(II) when permitted by a court at the request of the defendant, upon a showing that grounds may exist for a motion to dismiss the indictment because of matters occurring before the grand jury;

"(III) when the disclosure is made by an attorney for the government to another Federal grand jury;

"(IV) when permitted by a court at the request of an attorney for the government, upon a showing that such matters may disclose a violation of State criminal law, to an appropriate official of a State or subdivision of a State for the purpose of enforcing such law; or

"(V) when the matters involve foreign intelligence or counterintelligence (as defined in section 3 of the National Security Act of 1947 (50 U.S.C. 401a)), or foreign intelligence information (as defined in clause (iv) of this subparagraph), to any Federal law enforcement, intelligence, protective, immigration, national defense, or national security official in order to assist the official receiving that information in the performance of his official duties.

"(ii) If the court orders disclosure of matters occurring before the grand jury, the disclosure shall be made in such manner, at such time, and under such conditions as the court may direct.

"(iii) Any Federal official to whom information is disclosed pursuant to clause (i)(V) of this subparagraph may use that information only as necessary in the conduct of that person's official duties subject to any limitations on the unauthorized disclosure of such information. Within a reasonable time after such disclosure, an attorney for the government shall file under seal a notice with the court stating the fact that such information was disclosed and the departments, agencies, or entities to which the disclosure was made.

"(iv) In clause (i)(V) of this subparagraph, the term 'foreign intelligence information' means —

"(I) information, whether or not concerning a United States person, that relates to the ability of the United States to protect against —

"(aa) actual or potential attack or other grave hostile acts of a foreign power or an agent of a foreign power;

"(bb) sabotage or international terrorism by a foreign power or an agent of a foreign power; or

"(cc) clandestine intelligence activities by an intelligence service or network of a foreign power or by an agent of foreign power; or

"(II) information, whether or not concerning a United States person, with respect to a foreign power or foreign territory that relates to —

"(aa) the national defense or the security of the United States; or "(bb) the conduct of the foreign affairs of the United States.".

(2) CONFORMING AMENDMENT. — Rule 6(e)(3)(D) of the Federal Rules of Criminal Procedure is amended by striking "(e)(3)(C)(i)" and inserting "(e)(3)(C)(i)(I)".

(b) AUTHORITY TO SHARE ELECTRONIC, WIRE, AND ORAL INTERCEPTION INFORMATION. —

(1) LAW ENFORCEMENT. — Section 2517 of title 18, United States Code, is amended by inserting at the end the following :

"(6) Any investigative or law enforcement officer, or attorney for the Government, who by any means authorized by this chapter, has obtained knowledge of the contents of any wire, oral, or electronic communication, or evidence derived therefrom, may disclose such contents to any other Federal law enforcement, intelligence, protective, immigration, national defense, or national security official to the extent that such contents include foreign intelligence or counterintelligence (as defined in section 3 of the National Security Act of 1947 (50 U.S.C. 401a)), or foreign intelligence information (as defined in subsection (19) of section 2510 of this title), to assist the official who is to receive that information in the performance of his official duties. Any Federal official who receives information pursuant to this provision may use that information only as necessary in the conduct of that person's official duties subject to any limitations on the unauthorized disclosure of such information.".

(2) DEFINITION. — Section 2510 of title 18, United States Code, is amended by —

(A) in paragraph (17), by striking "and" after the semicolon;

(B) in paragraph (18), by striking the period and inserting "; and"; and

(C) by inserting at the end the following :

"(19) 'foreign intelligence information' means —

"(A) information, whether or not concerning a United States person, that relates to the ability of the United States to protect against —

"(i) actual or potential attack or other grave hostile acts of a foreign power or an agent of a foreign power;

"(ii) sabotage or international terrorism by a foreign power or an agent of a foreign power; or

"(iii) clandestine intelligence activities by an intelligence service or network of a foreign power or by an agent of a foreign power; or

"(B) information, whether or not concerning a United States person, with respect to a foreign power or foreign territory that relates to —

"(i) the national defense or the security of the United States; or

"(ii) the conduct of the foreign affairs of the United States.".

(c) PROCEDURES. — The Attorney General shall establish procedures for the disclosure of information pursuant to section 2517(6) and Rule 6(e)(3)(C)(i)(V) of the Federal Rules of Criminal Procedure that identifies a United States person, as defined in section 101 of the Foreign Intelligence Surveillance Act of 1978 (50 U.S.C. 1801)).

(d) FOREIGN INTELLIGENCE INFORMATION. —

(1) IN GENERAL. — Notwithstanding any other provision of law, it shall be lawful for foreign intelligence or counterintel-ligence (as defined in section 3 of the National Security Act of 1947 (50 U.S.C. 401a)) or foreign intelligence information obtained as part of a criminal investigation to be disclosed to any Federal law enforcement, intelligence, protective, immigration, national defense, or national security official in order to assist the official receiving that information in the performance of his official duties. Any Federal official who receives information pursuant to this provision may use that information only as necessary in the conduct of that person's official duties subject to any

limitations on the unauthorized disclosure of such information.

(2) DEFINITION. — In this subsection, the term "foreign intelligence information" means —

(A) information, whether or not concerning a United States person, that relates to the ability of the United States to protect against —

(i) actual or potential attack or other grave hostile acts of a foreign power or an agent of a foreign power;

(ii) sabotage or international terrorism by a foreign power or an agent of a foreign power; or

(iii) clandestine intelligence activities by an intelligence service or network of a foreign power or by an agent of a foreign power; or

(B) information, whether or not concerning a United States person, with respect to a foreign power or foreign territory that relates to —

(i) the national defense or the security of the United States; or

(ii) the conduct of the foreign affairs of the United States.

SEC. 204. CLARIFICATION OF INTELLIGENCE EXCEPTIONS FROM LIMITATIONS ON INTERCEPTION AND DISCLOSURE OF WIRE, ORAL, AND ELECTRONIC COMMUNICATIONS.

Section 2511(2)(f) of title 18, United States Code, is amended —

(1) by striking "this chapter or chapter 121" and inserting "this chapter or chapter 121 or 206 of this title"; and

(2) by striking "wire and oral" and inserting "wire, oral, and electronic".

SEC. 205. EMPLOYMENT OF TRANSLATORS BY THE FEDERAL BUREAU OF INVESTIGATION.

(a) AUTHORITY. — The Director of the Federal Bureau of Investigation is authorized to expedite the employment of personnel as translators to support counterterrorism investigations and operations without regard to applicable Federal personnel requirements and limitations.

(b) SECURITY REQUIREMENTS. — The Director of the Federal Bureau of Investigation shall establish such security requirements as are necessary for the personnel employed as translators under subsection (a).

(c) REPORT. — The Attorney General shall report to the Committees on the Judiciary of the House of Representatives and the Senate on —

(1) the number of translators employed by the FBI and other components of the Department of Justice;

(2) any legal or practical impediments to using translators employed by other Federal, State, or local agencies, on a full, parttime, or shared basis; and

(3) the needs of the FBI for specific translation services in certain languages, and recommendations for meeting those needs.

SEC. 206. ROVING SURVEILLANCE AUTHORITY UNDER THE FOREIGN INTELLIGENCE SURVEILLANCE ACT OF 1978.

Section 105(c)(2)(B) of the Foreign Intelligence Surveillance Act of 1978 (50 U.S.C. 1805(c)(2)(B)) is amended by inserting "or in circumstances where the Court finds that the actions of the target of the application may have the effect of thwarting the identification of a specified person, such other persons," after "specified person".

SEC. 207. DURATION OF FISA SURVEILLANCE OF NON-UNITED STATES PERSONS WHO ARE AGENTS OF A FOREIGN POWER.

(a) DURATION.

(1) SURVEILLANCE. — Section 105(e)(1) of the Foreign Intelligence Surveillance Act of 1978 (50 U.S.C. 1805(e)(1)) is amended by —

(A) inserting "(A)" after "except that"; and

(B) inserting before the period the following : ", and (B) an order under this Act for a surveillance targeted against an agent of a foreign power, as defined in section 101(b)(1)(A) may be for the period specified in the application or for 120 days, whichever is less".

(2) PHYSICAL SEARCH. — Section 304(d)(1) of the Foreign Intelligence Surveillance Act of 1978 (50 U.S.C. 1824(d)(1)) is amended by —

(A) striking "forty-five" and inserting "90";

(B) inserting "(A)" after "except that"; and

(C) inserting before the period the following : ", and (B) an order under this section for a physical search targeted against an agent of a foreign power as defined in section 101(b)(1)(A) may be for the period specified in the application or for 120 days, whichever is less".

(b) EXTENSION. —

(1) IN GENERAL. — Section 105(d)(2) of the Foreign Intelligence Surveillance Act of 1978 (50 U.S.C. 1805(d)(2)) is amended by —

(A) inserting "(A)" after "except that"; and

(B) inserting before the period the following : ", and (B) an extension of an order under this Act for a surveillance targeted against an agent of a foreign power as defined in section 101(b)(1)(A) may be for a period not to exceed 1 year".

(2) DEFINED TERM. — Section 304(d)(2) of the Foreign Intelligence Surveillance Act of 1978 (50 U.S.C. 1824(d)(2) is amended by inserting after "not a United States person," the following : "or against an agent of a foreign power as defined in section 101(b)(1)(A),".

SEC. 208. DESIGNATION OF JUDGES.

Section 103(a) of the Foreign Intelligence Surveillance Act of 1978 (50 U.S.C. 1803(a)) is amended by —

(1) striking "seven district court judges" and inserting "11 district court judges"; and

(2) inserting "of whom no fewer than 3 shall reside within 20 miles of the District of Columbia" after "circuits".

SEC. 209. SEIZURE OF VOICE-MAIL MESSAGES PURSUANT TO WARRANTS.

Title 18, United States Code, is amended —

(1) in section 2510 —

(A) in paragraph (1), by striking beginning with "and such" and all that follows through "communication"; and

(B) in paragraph (14), by inserting "wire or" after "transmission of"; and

(2) in subsections (a) and (b) of section 2703 —

(A) by striking "CONTENTS OF ELECTRONIC" and inserting "CONTENTS OF WIRE OR ELECTRONIC" each place it appears;

(B) by striking "contents of an electronic" and inserting "contents of a wire or electronic" each place it appears; and

(C) by striking "any electronic" and inserting "any wire or electronic" each place it appears.

SEC. 210. SCOPE OF SUBPOENAS FOR RECORDS OF ELECTRONIC COMMUNICATIONS.

Section 2703(c)(2) of title 18, United States Code, as redesignated by section 212, is amended —

(1) by striking "entity the name, address, local and long distance telephone toll billing records, telephone number or other subscriber number or identity, and length of service of a subscriber" and inserting the following : "entity the —

"(A) name;

"(B) address;

"(C) local and long distance telephone connection records, or records of session times and durations;

"(D) length of service (including start date) and types of service utilized;

"(E) telephone or instrument number or other subscriber number or identity, including any temporarily assigned network address; and

"(F) means and source of payment for such service (including any credit card or bank account number), of a subscriber"; and

(2) by striking "and the types of services the subscriber or customer utilized,".

SEC. 211. CLARIFICATION OF SCOPE.

Section 631 of the Communications Act of 1934 (47 U.S.C. 551) is amended —

(1) in subsection (c)(2) —

(A) in subparagraph (B), by striking "or";

(B) in subparagraph (C), by striking the period at the end and inserting "; or"; and

(C) by inserting at the end the following :

"(D) to a government entity as authorized under chapters 119, 121, or 206 of title 18, United States Code, except that such disclosure shall not include records revealing cable sub-scriber selection of video programming from a cable operator."; and

(2) in subsection (h), by striking "A governmental entity" and inserting "Except as provided in subsection (c)(2)(D), a governmental entity".

SEC. 212. EMERGENCY DISCLOSURE OF ELECTRONIC COMMUNICATIONS TO PROTECT LIFE AND LIMB.

(a) DISCLOSURE OF CONTENTS. —

(1) IN GENERAL. — Section 2702 of title 18, United States Code, is amended —

(A) by striking the section heading and inserting the following :

"§ 2702. Voluntary disclosure of customer communications or records";

(B) in subsection (a) —

(i) in paragraph (2)(A), by striking "and" at the end;

(ii) in paragraph (2)(B), by striking the period and inserting "; and"; and

(iii) by inserting after paragraph (2) the following :

"(3) a provider of remote computing service or electronic communication service to the public shall not knowingly divulge a record or other information pertaining to a subscriber to or customer of such service (not including the contents of communications covered by paragraph (1) or (2)) to any governmental entity.";

(C) in subsection (b), by striking "EXCEPTIONS. — A person or entity" and inserting "EXCEPTIONS FOR DISCLOSURE OF COMMUNICATIONS. — A provider described in subsection (a)";

(D) in subsection (b)(6) —

(i) in subparagraph (A)(ii), by striking "or";

(ii) in subparagraph (B), by striking the period and inserting "; or"; and

(iii) by adding after subparagraph (B) the following :

"(C) if the provider reasonably believes that an emergency involving immediate danger of death or serious physical injury to any person requires disclosure of the information without delay."; and

(E) by inserting after subsection (b) the following :

"(c) EXCEPTIONS FOR DISCLOSURE OF CUSTOMER RECORDS. — A provider described in subsection (a) may divulge a record or other information pertaining to a subscriber to or customer of such service (not including the contents of communications covered by subsection (a)(1) or (a)(2)) —

"(1) as otherwise authorized in section 2703;

"(2) with the lawful consent of the customer or subscriber;

"(3) as may be necessarily incident to the rendition of the service or to the protection of the rights or property of the provider of that service;

"(4) to a governmental entity, if the provider reasonably believes that an emergency involving immediate danger of death or serious physical injury to any person justifies disclosure of the information; or

"(5) to any person other than a governmental entity.".

(2) TECHNICAL AND CONFORMING AMENDMENT. — The table of sections for chapter 121 of title 18, United States Code, is amended by striking the item relating to section 2702 and inserting the following :

"2702. Voluntary disclosure of customer communications or records.".

(b) REQUIREMENTS FOR GOVERNMENT ACCESS. —

(1) IN GENERAL. — Section 2703 of title 18, United States Code, is amended —

(A) by striking the section heading and inserting the following :

"§ 2703. Required disclosure of customer communications or records";

(B) in subsection (c) by redesignating paragraph (2) as paragraph (3);

(C) in subsection (c)(1) —

(i) by striking "(A) Except as provided in subparagraph (B), a provider of electronic communication service or remote computing service may" and inserting "A governmental entity may require a provider of electronic communication service or remote computing service to";

(ii) by striking "covered by subsection (a) or (b) of this section) to any person other than a governmental entity.

"(B) A provider of electronic communication service or remote computing service shall disclose a record or other information pertaining to a subscriber to or customer of such service (not including the contents of communications covered by subsection (a) or (b) of this section) to a governmental entity" and inserting ")";

(iii) by redesignating subparagraph (C) as paragraph (2);

(iv) by redesignating clauses (i), (ii), (iii), and (iv) as subparagraphs (A), (B), (C), and (D), respectively;

(v) in subparagraph (D) (as redesignated) by striking the period and inserting "; or"; and

(vi) by inserting after subparagraph (D) (as redesignated) the following :

"(E) seeks information under paragraph (2)."; and (D) in paragraph (2) (as redesignated) by striking "subparagraph (B)" and insert "paragraph (1)".

(2) TECHNICAL AND CONFORMING AMENDMENT. — The table of sections for chapter 121 of title 18, United States Code, is amended by striking the item relating to section 2703 and inserting the following :

"2703. Required disclosure of customer communications or records.".

SEC. 213. AUTHORITY FOR DELAYING NOTICE OF THE EXECUTION OF A WARRANT.

Section 3103a of title 18, United States Code, is amended —

(1) by inserting "(a) IN GENERAL. — " before "In addition"; and

(2) by adding at the end the following :

"(b) DELAY. — With respect to the issuance of any warrant or court order under this section, or any other rule of law, to search for and seize any property or material that constitutes evidence of a criminal offense in violation of the laws of the United States, any notice required, or that may be required, to be given may be delayed if —

"(1) the court finds reasonable cause to believe that providing immediate notification of the execution of the warrant may have an adverse result (as defined in section 2705);

"(2) the warrant prohibits the seizure of any tangible property, any wire or electronic communication (as defined in section 2510), or, except as expressly provided in chapter 121, any stored wire or electronic information, except where the court finds reasonable necessity for the seizure; and

"(3) the warrant provides for the giving of such notice within a reasonable period of its execution, which period may thereafter be extended by the court for good cause shown.".

SEC. 214. PEN REGISTER AND TRAP AND TRACE AUTHORITY UNDER FISA.

(a) APPLICATIONS AND ORDERS. — Section 402 of the Foreign Intelligence Surveillance Act of 1978 (50 U.S.C. 1842) is amended —

(1) in subsection (a)(1), by striking "for any investigation to gather foreign intelligence information or information concerning international terrorism" and inserting "for any investigation to obtain foreign intelligence information not concerning a United States person or to protect against international terrorism or clandestine intelligence activities, provided that such investigation of a United States person is not conducted solely upon the basis of activities protected by the first amendment to the Constitution";

(2) by amending subsection (c)(2) to read as follows :

"(2) a certification by the applicant that the information likely to be obtained is foreign intelligence information not concerning a United States person or is relevant to an ongoing investigation to protect against international terrorism or clandestine intelligence activities, provided that such investigation of a United States person is not conducted solely upon the basis of activities protected by the first amendment to the Constitution.";

(3) by striking subsection (c)(3); and

(4) by amending subsection (d)(2)(A) to read as follows :

"(A) shall specify —

"(i) the identity, if known, of the person who is the subject of the investigation;

"(ii) the identity, if known, of the person to whom is leased or in whose name is listed the telephone line or other facility to which the pen register or trap and trace device is to be attached or applied;

"(iii) the attributes of the communications to which the order applies, such as the number or other identifier, and, if known, the location of the telephone line or other facility to which the pen register or trap and trace device is to be attached or applied and, in the case of a trap and trace device, the geographic limits of the trap and trace order.".

(b) AUTHORIZATION DURING EMERGENCIES. — Section 403 of the Foreign Intelligence Surveillance Act of 1978 (50 U.S.C. 1843) is amended —

(1) in subsection (a), by striking "foreign intelligence information or information concerning international terrorism" and inserting "foreign intelligence information not concerning a United States person or information to protect against international terrorism or clandestine intelligence activities, provided that such investigation of a United States person is not conducted solely upon the basis of activities protected by the first amendment to the Constitution"; and

(2) in subsection (b)(1), by striking "foreign intelligence information or information concerning international terrorism" and inserting "foreign intelligence information not concerning a United States person or information to protect against international terrorism or clandestine intelligence activities, provided that such investigation of a United States person is not conducted solely upon the basis of activities protected by the first amendment to the Constitution".

SEC. 215. ACCESS TO RECORDS AND OTHER ITEMS UNDER THE FOREIGN INTELLIGENCE SURVEILLANCE ACT.

Title V of the Foreign Intelligence Surveillance Act of 1978 (50 U.S.C. 1861 et seq.) is amended by striking sections 501 through 503 and inserting the following :

"SEC. 501. ACCESS TO CERTAIN BUSINESS RECORDS FOR FOREIGN INTELLIGENCE AND INTERNATIONAL TERRORISM INVESTIGATIONS.

"(a)(1) The Director of the Federal Bureau of Investigation or a designee of the Director (whose rank shall be no lower than Assistant Special Agent in Charge) may make an application for an order requiring the production of any tangible things (including books, records, papers, documents, and other items) for an investigation to protect against international terrorism or clandestine intelligence activities, provided that such investigation of a United States person is not conducted solely upon the basis of activities protected by the first amendment to the Constitution.

"(2) An investigation conducted under this section shall —

"(A) be conducted under guidelines approved by the Attorney General under Executive Order 12333 (or a successor order); and

"(B) not be conducted of a United States person solely upon the basis of activities protected by the first amendment to the Constitution of the United States.

"(b) Each application under this section —

"(1) shall be made to —

"(A) a judge of the court established by section 103(a); or

"(B) a United States Magistrate Judge under chapter 43 of title 28, United States Code, who is publicly designated by the Chief Justice of the United States to have the power to hear applications and grant orders for the production of tangible things under this section on behalf of a judge of that court; and

"(2) shall specify that the records concerned are sought for an authorized investigation conducted in accordance with subsection (a)(2) to obtain foreign intelligence information not concerning a United States person or to protect against international terrorism or clandestine intelligence activities.

"(c)(1) Upon an application made pursuant to this section, the judge shall enter an ex parte order as requested, or as modified, approving the release of records if the judge finds that the application meets the requirements of this section.

"(2) An order under this subsection shall not disclose that it is issued for purposes of an investigation described in subsection (a).

"(d) No person shall disclose to any other person (other than those persons necessary to produce the tangible things under this section) that the Federal Bureau of Investigation has sought or obtained tangible things under this section.

"(e) A person who, in good faith, produces tangible things under an order pursuant to this section shall not be liable to any other person for such production. Such production shall not be deemed to constitute a waiver of any privilege in any other proceeding or context.

"SEC. 502. CONGRESSIONAL OVERSIGHT.

"(a) On a semiannual basis, the Attorney General shall fully inform the Permanent Select Committee on Intelligence of the House of Representatives and the Select Committee on Intelligence of the Senate concerning all requests for the production of tangible things under section 402.

"(b) On a semiannual basis, the Attorney General shall provide to the Committees on the Judiciary of the House of Representatives and the Senate a report setting forth with respect to the preceding 6-month period —

"(1) the total number of applications made for orders approving requests for the production of tangible things under section 402; and

"(2) the total number of such orders either granted, modified, or denied.".

SEC. 216. MODIFICATION OF AUTHORITIES RELATING TO USE OF PEN REGISTERS AND TRAP AND TRACE DEVICES.

(a) GENERAL LIMITATIONS. — Section 3121(c) of title 18, United States Code, is amended —

(1) by inserting "or trap and trace device" after "pen register";

(2) by inserting ", routing, addressing," after "dialing"; and

(3) by striking "call processing" and inserting "the processing and transmitting of wire or electronic communications so as not to include the contents of any wire or electronic communications".

(b) ISSUANCE OF ORDERS. —

(1) IN GENERAL. — Section 3123(a) of title 18, United States Code, is amended to read as follows :

"(a) IN GENERAL. —

"(1) ATTORNEY FOR THE GOVERNMENT. — Upon an application made under section 3122(a)(1), the court shall enter an ex parte order authorizing the installation and use of a pen register or trap and trace device anywhere within the United States, if the court finds that the attorney for the Government has certified to the court that the information likely to be obtained by such installation and use is relevant to an ongoing criminal investigation. The order, upon service of that order, shall apply to any person or entity providing wire or electronic communication service in the United States whose assistance may facilitate the execution of the order. Whenever such an order is served on any person or entity not specifically named in the order, upon request of such person or entity, the attorney for the Government or law enforcement or investigative officer that is serving the order shall provide written or electronic certification that the order applies to the person or entity being served.

"(2) STATE INVESTIGATIVE OR LAW ENFORCEMENT OFFICER. — Upon an application made under section 3122(a)(2), the court shall enter an ex parte order authorizing the installation and use of a pen register or trap and trace device within the jurisdiction of the court, if the court finds that the State law enforcement or investigative officer has certified to the court that the information likely to be obtained by such installation and use is relevant to an ongoing criminal investigation.

"(3)(A) Where the law enforcement agency implementing an ex parte order under this subsection seeks to do so by installing and using its own pen register or trap and trace device on a packet-switched data network of a provider of electronic communication service to the public, the agency shall ensure that a record will be maintained which will identify —

"(i) any officer or officers who installed the device and any officer or officers who accessed the device to obtain information from the network;

"(ii) the date and time the device was installed, the date and time the device was uninstalled, and the date, time, and duration of each time the device is accessed to obtain information;

"(iii) the configuration of the device at the time of its installation and any subsequent modification thereof; and

"(iv) any information which has been collected by the device.

To the extent that the pen register or trap and trace device can be set automatically to record this information electronically, the record shall be maintained electronically throughout the installation and use of such device.

"(B) The record maintained under subparagraph (A) shall be provided ex parte and under seal to the court which entered the ex parte order authorizing the installation and use of the device within 30 days after termination of the order (including any extensions thereof).".

(2) CONTENTS OF ORDER. — Section 3123(b)(1) of title 18, United States Code, is amended —

(A) in subparagraph (A) —

(i) by inserting "or other facility" after "telephone line"; and

(ii) by inserting before the semicolon at the end "or applied"; and

(B) by striking subparagraph (C) and inserting the following :

"(C) the attributes of the communications to which the order applies, including the number or other identifier and, if known, the location of the telephone line or other facility to which the pen register or trap and trace device is to be attached or applied, and, in the case of an order authorizing installation and use of a trap and trace device under subsection (a)(2), the geographic limits of the order; and".

(3) NONDISCLOSURE REQUIREMENTS. — Section 3123(d)(2) of title 18, United States Code, is amended —

(A) by inserting "or other facility" after "the line"; and

(B) by striking ", or who has been ordered by the court" and inserting "or applied, or who is obligated by the order".

(c) DEFINITIONS. —

(1) COURT OF COMPETENT JURISDICTION. — Section 3127(2) of title 18, United States Code, is amended by striking subparagraph (A) and inserting the following :

"(A) any district court of the United States (including a magistrate judge of such a court) or any United States court of appeals having jurisdiction over the offense being investigated; or".

(2) PEN REGISTER. — Section 3127(3) of title 18, United States Code, is amended —

(A) by striking "electronic or other impulses" and all that follows through "is attached" and inserting "dialing, routing, addressing, or signaling information transmitted by an instrument or facility from which a wire or electronic communication is transmitted, provided, however, that such information shall not include the contents of any communication"; and

(B) by inserting "or process" after "device" each place it appears.

(3) TRAP AND TRACE DEVICE. — Section 3127(4) of title 18, United States Code, is amended —

(A) by striking "of an instrument" and all that follows through the semicolon and inserting "or other dialing, routing, addressing, and signaling information reasonably likely to identify the source of a wire or electronic communication, provided, however, that such information shall not include the contents of any communication;"; and

(B) by inserting "or process" after "a device".

(4) CONFORMING AMENDMENT. — Section 3127(1) of title 18, United States Code, is amended —

(A) by striking "and"; and

(B) by inserting ", and 'contents' " after "electronic communication service".

(5) TECHNICAL AMENDMENT. — Section 3124(d) of title 18, United States Code, is amended by striking "the terms of".

(6) CONFORMING AMENDMENT. — Section 3124(b) of title 18, United States Code, is amended by inserting "or other facility" after "the appropriate line".

SEC. 217. INTERCEPTION OF COMPUTER TRESPASSER COMMUNICATIONS.

Chapter 119 of title 18, United States Code, is amended —

(1) in section 2510 —

(A) in paragraph (18), by striking "and" at the end;

(B) in paragraph (19), by striking the period and inserting a semicolon; and

(C) by inserting after paragraph (19) the following :

"(20) 'protected computer' has the meaning set forth in section 1030; and

"(21) 'computer trespasser' —

"(A) means a person who accesses a protected computer without authorization and thus has no reasonable expectation of privacy in any communication transmitted to, through, or from the protected computer; and

"(B) does not include a person known by the owner or operator of the protected computer to have an existing contractual relationship with the owner or operator of the protected computer for access to all or part of the protected computer."; and

(2) in section 2511(2), by inserting at the end the following : "(i) It shall not be unlawful under this chapter for a person acting under color of law to intercept the wire or electronic communications of a computer trespasser transmitted to, through, or from the protected computer, if —

"(I) the owner or operator of the protected computer authorizes the interception of the computer trespasser's communications on the protected computer;

"(II) the person acting under color of law is lawfully engaged in an investigation;

"(III) the person acting under color of law has reasonable grounds to believe that the contents of the computer trespasser's communications will be relevant to the investigation; and

"(IV) such interception does not acquire communications other than those transmitted to or from the computer trespasser.".

SEC. 218. FOREIGN INTELLIGENCE INFORMATION.

Sections 104(a)(7)(B) and section 303(a)(7)(B) (50 U.S.C. 1804(a)(7)(B) and 1823(a)(7)(B)) of the Foreign Intelligence Surveillance Act of 1978 are each amended by striking "the purpose" and inserting "a significant purpose".

SEC. 219. SINGLE-JURISDICTION SEARCH WARRANTS FOR TERRORISM.

Rule 41(a) of the Federal Rules of Criminal Procedure is amended by inserting after "executed" the following : "and (3) in an investigation of domestic terrorism or international terrorism (as defined in section 2331 of title 18, United States Code), by a Federal magistrate judge in any district in which activities related to the terrorism may have occurred, for a search of property or for a person within or outside the district".

SEC. 220. NATIONWIDE SERVICE OF SEARCH WARRANTS FOR ELECTRONIC EVIDENCE.

(a) IN GENERAL. — Chapter 121 of title 18, United States Code, is amended —

(1) in section 2703, by striking "under the Federal Rules of Criminal Procedure" every place it appears and inserting "using the procedures described in the Federal Rules of Criminal Procedure by a court with jurisdiction over the offense under investigation"; and

(2) in section 2711 —

(A) in paragraph (1), by striking "and";

(B) in paragraph (2), by striking the period and inserting "; and"; and

(C) by inserting at the end the following :

"(3) the term 'court of competent jurisdiction' has the meaning assigned by section 3127, and includes any Federal court within that definition, without geographic limitation.".

(b) CONFORMING AMENDMENT. — Section 2703(d) of title 18, United States Code, is amended by striking "described in section 3127(2)(A)".

SEC. 221. TRADE SANCTIONS.

(a) IN GENERAL. — The Trade Sanctions Reform and Export Enhancement Act of 2000 (Public Law 106–387; 114 Stat. 1549A–67) is amended —

(1) by amending section 904(2)(C) to read as follows :

"(C) used to facilitate the design, development, or production of chemical or biological weapons, missiles, or weapons of mass destruction.";

(2) in section 906(a)(1) —

(A) by inserting ", the Taliban or the territory of Afghanistan controlled by the Taliban," after "Cuba"; and

(B) by inserting ", or in the territory of Afghanistan controlled by the Taliban," after "within such country"; and

(3) in section 906(a)(2), by inserting ", or to any other entity in Syria or North Korea" after "Korea".

(b) APPLICATION OF THE TRADE SANCTIONS REFORM AND EXPORT ENHANCEMENT ACT. — Nothing in the Trade Sanctions Reform and Export Enhancement Act of 2000 shall limit the application or scope of any law establishing criminal or civil penalties, including any Executive order or regulation promulgated pursuant to such laws (or similar or successor laws), for the unlawful export of any agricultural commodity, medicine, or medical device to —

(1) a foreign organization, group, or person designated pursuant to Executive Order No. 12947 of January 23, 1995, as amended;

(2) a Foreign Terrorist Organization pursuant to the Antiterrorism and Effective Death Penalty Act of 1996 (Public Law 104–132);

(3) a foreign organization, group, or person designated pursuant to Executive Order No. 13224 (September 23, 2001);

(4) any narcotics trafficking entity designated pursuant to Executive Order No. 12978 (October 21, 1995) or the Foreign Narcotics Kingpin Designation Act (Public Law 106–120); or

(5) any foreign organization, group, or persons subject to any restriction for its involvement in weapons of mass destruction or missile proliferation.

SEC. 222. ASSISTANCE TO LAW ENFORCEMENT AGENCIES.

Nothing in this Act shall impose any additional technical obligation or requirement on a provider of a wire or electronic communication service or other person to furnish facilities or technical assistance. A provider of a wire or electronic communication service, landlord, custodian, or other person who furnishes facilities or technical assistance pursuant to section 216 shall be reasonably compensated for such reasonable expenditures incurred in providing such facilities or assistance.

SEC. 223. CIVIL LIABILITY FOR CERTAIN UNAUTHORIZED DISCLOSURES.

(a) Section 2520 of title 18, United States Code, is amended —

(1) in subsection (a), after "entity", by inserting ", other than the United States,";

(2) by adding at the end the following :

"(f) ADMINISTRATIVE DISCIPLINE. — If a court or appropriate department or agency determines that the United States or any of its departments or agencies has violated any provision of this chapter, and the court or appropriate department or agency finds that the circumstances surrounding the violation raise serious questions about whether or not an officer or employee of the United States acted willfully or intentionally with respect to the violation, the department or agency shall, upon receipt of a true and correct copy of the decision and findings of the court or appropriate department or agency promptly initiate a proceeding to determine whether disciplinary action against the officer or employee is warranted. If the head of the department or agency involved determines that disciplinary action is not warranted, he or she shall notify the Inspector General with jurisdiction over the department or agency concerned and shall provide the Inspector General with the reasons for such determination."; and

(3) by adding a new subsection (g), as follows :

"(g) IMPROPER DISCLOSURE IS VIOLATION. — Any willful disclosure or use by an investigative or law enforcement officer or governmental entity of information beyond the extent permitted by section 2517 is a violation of this chapter for purposes of section 2520(a).".

(b) Section 2707 of title 18, United States Code, is amended —

(1) in subsection (a), after "entity", by inserting ", other than the United States,";

(2) by striking subsection (d) and inserting the following :

"(d) ADMINISTRATIVE DISCIPLINE. — If a court or appropriate department or agency determines that the United States or any of its departments or agencies has violated any provision of this chapter, and the court or appropriate department or agency finds that the circumstances surrounding the violation raise serious questions about whether or not an officer or employee of the United States acted willfully or intentionally with respect to the violation, the department or agency shall, upon receipt of a true and correct copy of the decision and findings of the court or appropriate department or agency promptly initiate a proceeding to determine whether disciplinary action against the officer or employee is warranted. If the head of the department or agency involved determines that disciplinary action is not warranted, he or she shall notify the Inspector General with jurisdiction over the department or agency concerned and shall provide the Inspector General with the reasons for such determination."; and

(3) by adding a new subsection (g), as follows :

"(g) IMPROPER DISCLOSURE. — Any willful disclosure of a 'record', as that term is defined in section 552a(a) of title 5, United States Code, obtained by an investigative or law enforcement officer, or a governmental entity, pursuant to section 2703 of this title, or from a device installed pursuant to section 3123 or 3125 of this title, that is not a disclosure made in the proper performance of the official functions of the officer or governmental entity making the disclosure, is a violation of this chapter. This provision shall not apply to information previously lawfully disclosed (prior to the commencement of any civil or administrative proceeding under this chapter) to the public by a Federal, State, or local governmental entity or by the plaintiff in a civil action under this chapter.".

(c) (1) Chapter 121 of title 18, United States Code, is amended by adding at the end the following :

"§ 2712. Civil actions against the United States

"(a) IN GENERAL. — Any person who is aggrieved by any willful violation of this chapter or of chapter 119 of this title or of sections 106(a), 305(a), or 405(a) of the Foreign Intelligence Surveillance Act of 1978 (50 U.S.C. 1801 et seq.) may commence an action in United States District Court against the United States to recover money damages. In any such action, if a person who is aggrieved successfully establishes such a violation of this chapter or of chapter 119 of this title or of the above specific provisions of title 50, the Court may assess as damages —

"(1) actual damages, but not less than $10,000, whichever amount is greater; and

"(2) litigation costs, reasonably incurred.

"(b) PROCEDURES. — (1) Any action against the United States under this section may be commenced only after a claim is presented to the appropriate department or agency under the procedures of the Federal Tort Claims Act, as set forth in title 28, United States Code.

"(2) Any action against the United States under this section shall be forever barred unless it is presented in writing to the appropriate Federal agency within 2 years after such claim accrues or unless action is begun within 6 months after the date of mailing, by certified or registered mail, of notice of final denial of the claim by the agency to which it was presented. The claim shall accrue on the date upon which the claimant first has a reasonable opportunity to discover the violation.

"(3) Any action under this section shall be tried to the court without a jury.

"(4) Notwithstanding any other provision of law, the procedures set forth in section 106(f), 305(g), or 405(f) of the Foreign Intelligence Surveillance Act of 1978 (50 U.S.C. 1801 et seq.) shall be the exclusive means by which materials governed by those sections may be reviewed.

"(5) An amount equal to any award against the United States under this section shall be reimbursed by the department or agency concerned to the fund described in section 1304 of title 31, United States Code, out of any appropriation, fund, or other account (excluding any part of such appropriation, fund, or account that is available for the enforcement of any Federal law) that is available for the operating expenses of the department or agency concerned.

"(c) ADMINISTRATIVE DISCIPLINE. — If a court or appropriate department or agency determines that the United States or any of its departments or agencies has violated any provision of this chapter, and the court or appropriate department or agency finds that the circumstances surrounding the violation raise serious questions about whether or not an officer or employee of the United States acted willfully or intentionally with respect to the violation, the department or agency shall, upon receipt of a true and correct copy of the decision and findings of the court or appropriate department or agency promptly initiate a proceeding to determine whether disciplinary action against the officer or employee is warranted. If the head of the department or agency involved determines that disciplinary action is not warranted, he or she shall notify the Inspector General with jurisdiction over the department or agency concerned and shall provide the Inspector General with the reasons for such determination.

"(d) EXCLUSIVE REMEDY. — Any action against the United States under this subsection shall be the exclusive remedy against the United States for any claims within the purview of this section.

"(e) STAY OF PROCEEDINGS. — (1) Upon the motion of the United States, the court shall stay any action commenced under this section if the court determines that civil discovery will adversely affect the ability of the Government to conduct a related investigation or the prosecution of a related criminal case. Such a stay shall toll the limitations periods of paragraph (2) of subsection (b).

"(2) In this subsection, the terms 'related criminal case' and 'related investigation' mean an actual prosecution or investigation in progress at the time at which the request for the stay or any subsequent motion to lift the stay is made. In determining whether an investigation or a criminal case is related to an action commenced under this section, the court shall consider the degree of similarity between the parties, witnesses, facts, and circumstances involved in the 2 proceedings, without requiring that any one or more factors be identical.

"(3) In requesting a stay under paragraph (1), the Government may, in appropriate cases, submit evidence ex parte in order to avoid disclosing any matter that may adversely affect a related investigation or a related criminal case. If the Government makes such an ex parte submission, the plaintiff shall be given an opportunity to make a submission to the court, not ex parte, and the court may, in its discretion, request further information from either party.".

(2) The table of sections at the beginning of chapter 121 is amended to read as follows :

"2712. Civil action against the United States.".

SEC. 224. SUNSET.

(a) IN GENERAL. — Except as provided in subsection (b), this title and the amendments made by this title (other than sections 203(a), 203(c), 205, 208, 210, 211, 213, 216, 219, 221, and 222, and the amendments made by those sections) shall cease to have effect on December 31, 2005.

(b) EXCEPTION. — With respect to any particular foreign intelligence investigation that began before the date on which the provisions referred to in subsection (a) cease to have effect, or with respect to any particular offense or potential offense that began or occurred before the date on which such provisions cease to have effect, such provisions shall continue in effect.

SEC. 225. IMMUNITY FOR COMPLIANCE WITH FISA WIRETAP.

Section 105 of the Foreign Intelligence Surveillance Act of

1978 (50 U.S.C. 1805) is amended by inserting after subsection (g) the following :

"(h) No cause of action shall lie in any court against any provider of a wire or electronic communication service, landlord, custodian, or other person (including any officer, employee, agent, or other specified person thereof) that furnishes any information, facilities, or technical assistance in accordance with a court order or request for emergency assistance under this Act.".

TITLE III — INTERNATIONAL MONEY LAUNDERING ABATEMENT AND ANTITERRORIST FINANCING ACT OF 2001

SEC. 301. SHORT TITLE.

This title may be cited as the "International Money Laundering Abatement and Financial Anti-Terrorism Act of 2001".

SEC. 302. FINDINGS AND PURPOSES.

(a) FINDINGS. — The Congress finds that —

(1) money laundering, estimated by the International Monetary Fund to amount to between 2 and 5 percent of global gross domestic product, which is at least $600,000,000,000 annually, provides the financial fuel that permits transnational criminal enterprises to conduct and expand their operations to the detriment of the safety and security of American citizens;

(2) money laundering, and the defects in financial transparency on which money launderers rely, are critical to the financing of global terrorism and the provision of funds for terrorist attacks;

(3) money launderers subvert legitimate financial mechanisms and banking relationships by using them as protective covering for the movement of criminal proceeds and the financing of crime and terrorism, and, by so doing, can threaten the safety of United States citizens and undermine the integrity of United

States financial institutions and of the global financial and trading systems upon which prosperity and growth depend;

(4) certain jurisdictions outside of the United States that offer "offshore" banking and related facilities designed to provide anonymity, coupled with weak financial supervisory and enforcement regimes, provide essential tools to disguise ownership and movement of criminal funds, derived from, or used to commit, offenses ranging from narcotics trafficking, terrorism, arms smuggling, and trafficking in human beings, to financial frauds that prey on lawabiding citizens;

(5) transactions involving such offshore jurisdictions make it difficult for law enforcement officials and regulators to follow the trail of money earned by criminals, organized international criminal enterprises, and global terrorist organizations;

(6) correspondent banking facilities are one of the banking mechanisms susceptible in some circumstances to manipulation by foreign banks to permit the laundering of funds by hiding the identity of real parties in interest to financial transactions;

(7) private banking services can be susceptible to manipulation by money launderers, for example corrupt foreign government officials, particularly if those services include the creation of offshore accounts and facilities for large personal funds transfers to channel funds into accounts around the globe;

(8) United States anti-money laundering efforts are impeded by outmoded and inadequate statutory provisions that make investigations, prosecutions, and forfeitures more difficult, particularly in cases in which money laundering involves foreign persons, foreign banks, or foreign countries;

(9) the ability to mount effective counter-measures to international money launderers requires national, as well as bilateral and multilateral action, using tools specially designed for that effort; and

(10) the Basle Committee on Banking Regulation and Supervisory Practices and the Financial Action Task Force on Money Laundering, of both of which the United States is a member, have each adopted international anti-money laundering principles and recommendations.

(b) PURPOSES. — The purposes of this title are —

(1) to increase the strength of United States measures to prevent, detect, and prosecute international money laundering and the financing of terrorism;

(2) to ensure that —

(A) banking transactions and financial relationships and the conduct of such transactions and relationships, do not contravene the purposes of subchapter II of chapter 53 of title 31, United States Code, section 21 of the Federal Deposit Insurance Act, or chapter 2 of title I of Public Law 91–508 (84 Stat. 1116), or facilitate the evasion of any such provision; and

(B) the purposes of such provisions of law continue to be fulfilled, and such provisions of law are effectively and efficiently administered;

(3) to strengthen the provisions put into place by the Money Laundering Control Act of 1986 (18 U.S.C. 981 note), especially with respect to crimes by non-United States nationals and foreign financial institutions;

(4) to provide a clear national mandate for subjecting to special scrutiny those foreign jurisdictions, financial institutions operating outside of the United States, and classes of international transactions or types of accounts that pose particular, identifiable opportunities for criminal abuse;

(5) to provide the Secretary of the Treasury (in this title referred to as the "Secretary") with broad discretion, subject to the safeguards provided by the Administrative Procedure Act under title 5, United States Code, to take measures tailored to the particular money laundering problems presented by specific foreign jurisdictions,

financial institutions operating outside of the United States, and classes of international transactions or types of accounts;

(6) to ensure that the employment of such measures by the Secretary permits appropriate opportunity for comment by affected financial institutions; (7) to provide guidance to domestic financial institutions on particular foreign jurisdictions, financial institutions operating outside of the United States, and classes of international transactions that are of primary money laundering concern to the United States Government;

(8) to ensure that the forfeiture of any assets in connection with the anti-terrorist efforts of the United States permits for adequate challenge consistent with providing due process rights;

(9) to clarify the terms of the safe harbor from civil liability for filing suspicious activity reports;

(10) to strengthen the authority of the Secretary to issue and administer geographic targeting orders, and to clarify that violations of such orders or any other requirement imposed under the authority contained in chapter 2 of title I of Public Law 91–508 and subchapters II and III of chapter 53 of title 31, United States Code, may result in criminal and civil penalties;

(11) to ensure that all appropriate elements of the financial services industry are subject to appropriate requirements to report potential money laundering transactions to proper authorities, and that jurisdictional disputes do not hinder examination of compliance by financial institutions with relevant reporting requirements;

(12) to strengthen the ability of financial institutions to maintain the integrity of their employee population; and

(13) to strengthen measures to prevent the use of the United States financial system for personal gain by corrupt foreign officials and to facilitate the repatriation of any stolen assets to the citizens of countries to whom such assets belong.

SEC. 303. 4-YEAR CONGRESSIONAL REVIEW; EXPEDITED CONSIDERATION.

(a) IN GENERAL. — Effective on and after the first day of fiscal year 2005, the provisions of this title and the amendments made by this title shall terminate if the Congress enacts a joint resolution, the text after the resolving clause of which is as follows : "That provisions of the International Money Laundering Abatement and Anti-Terrorist Financing Act of 2001, and the amendments made thereby, shall no longer have the force of law.".

(b) EXPEDITED CONSIDERATION. — Any joint resolution submitted pursuant to this section should be considered by the Congress expeditiously. In particular, it shall be considered in the Senate in accordance with the provisions of section 601(b) of the International Security Assistance and Arms Control Act of 1976.

Subtitle A — International Counter Money Laundering and Related Measures

SEC. 311. SPECIAL MEASURES FOR JURISDICTIONS, FINANCIAL INSTITUTIONS, OR INTERNATIONAL TRANSACTIONS OF PRIMARY MONEY LAUNDERING CONCERN.

(a) IN GENERAL. — Subchapter II of chapter 53 of title 31, United States Code, is amended by inserting after section 5318 the following new section :

"§ 5318A. Special measures for jurisdictions, financial institutions, or international transactions of primary money laundering concern

"(a) INTERNATIONAL COUNTER-MONEY LAUNDERING REQUIREMENTS. —

"(1) IN GENERAL. — The Secretary of the Treasury may require domestic financial institutions and domestic financial agencies to take 1 or more of the special measures described in subsection (b) if the Secretary finds that reasonable grounds exist for concluding that a jurisdiction outside of the United States, 1 or more financial institutions operating outside of the United States, 1 or more classes of transactions within, or involving, a jurisdiction outside of the United States, or 1 or more types of accounts is of primary money laundering concern, in accordance with subsection (c).

"(2) FORM OF REQUIREMENT. — The special measures described in —

"(A) subsection (b) may be imposed in such sequence or combination as the Secretary shall determine;

"(B) paragraphs (1) through (4) of subsection (b) may be imposed by regulation, order, or otherwise as permitted by law; and

"(C) subsection (b)(5) may be imposed only by regulation.

"(3) DURATION OF ORDERS; RULEMAKING. — Any order by which a special measure described in paragraphs (1) through (4) of subsection (b) is imposed (other than an order described in section 5326) —

"(A) shall be issued together with a notice of proposed rulemaking relating to the imposition of such special measure; and

"(B) may not remain in effect for more than 120 days, except pursuant to a rule promulgated on or before the end of the 120-day period beginning on the date of issuance of such order.

"(4) PROCESS FOR SELECTING SPECIAL MEASURES. — In selecting which special measure or measures to take under this subsection, the Secretary of the Treasury —

"(A) shall consult with the Chairman of the Board of Governors of the Federal Reserve System, any other appropriate Federal banking agency, as defined in section 3 of the Federal Deposit Insurance Act, the Secretary of State, the Securities and Exchange Commission, the Commodity Futures Trading Commission, the National Credit Union Administration Board, and in the sole discretion of the Secretary, such other agencies and interested parties as the Secretary may find to be appropriate; and

"(B) shall consider —

"(i) whether similar action has been or is being taken by other nations or multilateral groups;

"(ii) whether the imposition of any particular special measure would create a significant competitive disadvantage, including any undue cost or burden associated with compliance, for financial institutions organized or licensed in the United States;

"(iii) the extent to which the action or the timing of the action would have a significant adverse systemic impact on the international payment, clearance, and settlement system, or on legitimate business activities involving the particular jurisdiction, institution, or class of transactions; and

"(iv) the effect of the action on United States national security and foreign policy.

"(5) NO LIMITATION ON OTHER AUTHORITY. — This section shall not be construed as superseding or otherwise restricting any other authority granted to the Secretary, or to any other agency, by this subchapter or otherwise.

"(b) SPECIAL MEASURES. — The special measures referred to in subsection (a), with respect to a jurisdiction outside of the United States, financial institution operating outside of the United States, class of transaction within, or involving, a jurisdiction outside of the United States, or 1 or more types of accounts are as follows :

"(1) RECORDKEEPING AND REPORTING OF CERTAIN FINANCIAL TRANSACTIONS. —

"(A) IN GENERAL. — The Secretary of the Treasury may require any domestic financial institution or domestic financial agency to maintain records, file reports, or both, concerning the aggregate amount of transactions, or concerning each transaction, with respect to a jurisdiction outside of the United States, 1 or more financial institutions operating outside of the United States, 1 or more classes of transactions within, or involving, a jurisdiction outside of the United States, or 1 or more types of accounts if the Secretary finds any such jurisdiction, institution, or class of transactions to be of primary money laundering concern.

"(B) FORM OF RECORDS AND REPORTS. — Such records and reports shall be made and retained at such time, in such manner, and for such period of time, as the Secretary shall determine, and shall include such information as the Secretary may determine, including —

"(i) the identity and address of the participants in a transaction or relationship, including the identity of the originator of any funds transfer;

"(ii) the legal capacity in which a participant in any transaction is acting;

"(iii) the identity of the beneficial owner of the funds involved in any transaction, in accordance with such procedures as the Secretary determines to be reasonable and practicable to obtain and retain the information; and

"(iv) a description of any transaction.

"(2) INFORMATION RELATING TO BENEFICIAL OWNERSHIP. — In addition to any other requirement under any other provision of law, the Secretary may require any domestic financial institution or domestic financial agency to take such steps as the Secretary may determine to be reasonable and practicable to obtain and retain information concerning the beneficial ownership of any account opened or maintained in the United States by a foreign person (other than a foreign entity whose shares are subject to public reporting requirements or are listed and traded on a regulated exchange or trading market), or a representative of such a foreign person, that involves a jurisdiction outside of the United States, 1 or more financial institutions operating outside of the United States, 1 or more classes of transactions within, or involving, a jurisdiction outside of the United States, or 1 or more types of accounts if the Secretary finds any such jurisdiction, institution, or transaction or type of account to be of primary money laundering concern.

"(3) INFORMATION RELATING TO CERTAIN PAYABLETHROUGH ACCOUNTS. — If the Secretary finds a jurisdiction outside of the United States, 1 or more financial institutions operating outside of the United States, or 1 or more classes of transactions within, or involving, a jurisdiction outside of the United States to be of primary money laundering concern, the Secretary may require any domestic financial institution or domestic financial agency that opens or maintains a payable-through account in the United States for a foreign financial institution involving any such jurisdiction or any such financial institution operating outside of the United States, or a payable through account through which any such transaction may be conducted, as a condition of opening or maintaining such account —

"(A) to identify each customer (and representative of such customer) of such financial institution who is permitted to use, or whose transactions are routed through, such payable-through account; and

"(B) to obtain, with respect to each such customer (and each such representative), information that is substantially comparable to that which the depository institution obtains in the ordinary course of business with respect to its customers residing in the United States.

"(4) INFORMATION RELATING TO CERTAIN CORRESPONDENT ACCOUNTS. — If the Secretary finds a jurisdiction outside of the United States, 1 or more financial institutions operating outside of the United States, or 1 or more classes of transactions within, or involving, a jurisdiction outside of the United States to be of primary money laundering concern, the Secretary may require any domestic financial institution or domestic financial agency that opens or maintains a correspondent account in the United States for a foreign financial institution involving any such jurisdiction or any such financial institution operating outside of the United States, or a correspondent account through which any such transaction may be conducted, as a condition of opening or maintaining such account —

"(A) to identify each customer (and representative of such customer) of any such financial institution who is permitted to use, or whose transactions are routed through, such correspondent account; and

"(B) to obtain, with respect to each such customer (and each such representative), information that is substantially comparable to that which the depository institution obtains in the ordinary course of business with respect to its customers residing in the United States.

"(5) PROHIBITIONS OR CONDITIONS ON OPENING OR MAINTAINING CERTAIN CORRESPONDENT OR PAYABLE-THROUGH ACCOUNTS. — If the Secretary finds a jurisdiction outside of the United States, 1 or more financial institutions operating outside of the United States, or 1 or more classes of transactions within, or involving, a jurisdiction outside of the United States to be of primary money laundering concern, the Secretary, in consultation with the Secretary of State, the Attorney General, and the Chairman of the Board of Governors of the Federal Reserve System, may prohibit, or impose conditions upon, the opening or maintaining in the United States of a correspondent account or payable-through account by any domestic financial institution or domestic financial agency for or on behalf of a foreign banking institution, if such correspondent account or payable-through account involves any such jurisdiction or institution, or if any such transaction may be conducted through such correspondent account or payable-through account.

"(c) CONSULTATIONS AND INFORMATION TO BE CONSIDERED IN FINDING JURISDICTIONS, INSTITUTIONS, TYPES OF ACCOUNTS, OR TRANSACTIONS TO BE OFPRIMARY MONEY LAUNDERING CONCERN. —

"(1) IN GENERAL. — In making a finding that reasonable grounds exist for concluding that a jurisdiction outside of the United States, 1 or more financial institutions operating outside of the United States, 1 or more classes of transactions within, or involving, a jurisdiction outside of the United States, or 1 or more types of accounts is of primary money laundering concern so as to authorize the Secretary of the Treasury to take 1 or more of the special measures described in subsection (b), the Secretary shall consult with the Secretary of State and the Attorney General.

"(2) ADDITIONAL CONSIDERATIONS. — In making a finding described in paragraph (1), the Secretary shall consider in addition such information as the Secretary determines to be relevant, including the following potentially relevant factors :

"(A) JURISDICTIONAL FACTORS. — In the case of a particular jurisdiction —

"(i) evidence that organized criminal groups, international terrorists, or both, have transacted business in that jurisdiction;

"(ii) the extent to which that jurisdiction or financial institutions operating in that jurisdiction offer bank secrecy or special regulatory advantages to non-residents or nondomiciliaries of that jurisdiction;

"(iii) the substance and quality of administration of the bank supervisory and counter-money laundering laws of that jurisdiction;

"(iv) the relationship between the volume of financial transactions occurring in that jurisdiction and the size of the economy of the jurisdiction;

"(v) the extent to which that jurisdiction is characterized as an offshore banking or secrecy haven by credible international organizations or multilateral expert groups;

"(vi) whether the United States has a mutual legal assistance treaty with that jurisdiction, and the experience of United States law enforcement officials and regulatory officials in obtaining information about transactions originating in or routed through or to such jurisdiction; and

"(vii) the extent to which that jurisdiction is characterized by high levels of official or institutional corruption.

"(B) INSTITUTIONAL FACTORS. — In the case of a decision to apply 1 or more of the special measures described in subsection (b) only to a financial institution or institutions, or to a transaction or class of transactions, or to a type of account, or to all 3, within or involving a particular jurisdiction —

"(i) the extent to which such financial institutions, transactions, or types of accounts are used to facilitate or promote money laundering in or through the jurisdiction;

"(ii) the extent to which such institutions, transactions, or types of accounts are used for legitimate business purposes in the jurisdiction; and

"(iii) the extent to which such action is sufficient to ensure, with respect to transactions involving the jurisdiction and institutions operating in the jurisdiction, that the purposes of this subchapter continue to be fulfilled, and to guard against international money laundering and other financial crimes.

"(d) NOTIFICATION OF SPECIAL MEASURES INVOKED BY THE SECRETARY. — Not later than 10 days after the date of any action taken by the Secretary of the Treasury under subsection (a)(1), the Secretary shall notify, in writing, the Committee on Financial Services of the House of Representatives and the Committee on Banking, Housing, and Urban Affairs of the Senate of any such action.

"(e) DEFINITIONS. — Notwithstanding any other provision of this subchapter, for purposes of this section and subsections (i) and (j) of section 5318, the following definitions shall apply :

"(1) BANK DEFINITIONS. — The following definitions shall apply with respect to a bank :

"(A) ACCOUNT. — The term 'account'

"(i) means a formal banking or business relationship established to provide regular services, dealings, and other financial transactions; and

"(ii) includes a demand deposit, savings deposit, or other transaction or asset account and a credit account or other extension of credit.

"(B) CORRESPONDENT ACCOUNT. — The term 'correspondent account' means an account established to receive deposits from, make payments on behalf of a foreign financial institution, or handle other financial transactions related to such institution.

"(C) PAYABLE-THROUGH ACCOUNT. — The term 'payable-through account' means an account, including a transaction account (as defined in section 19(b)(1)(C) of the Federal Reserve Act), opened at a depository institution by a foreign financial institution by means of which the foreign financial institution permits its customers to engage, either directly or through a subaccount, in banking activities usual in connection with the business of banking in the United States.

"(2) DEFINITIONS APPLICABLE TO INSTITUTIONS OTHER THAN BANKS. — With respect to any financial institution other than a bank, the Secretary shall, after consultation with the appropriate Federal functional regulators (as defined in section 509 of the Gramm-Leach-Bliley Act), define by regulation the term 'account', and shall include within the meaning of that term, to the extent, if any, that the Secretary deems appropriate, arrangements similar to payable-through and correspondent accounts.

"(3) REGULATORY DEFINITION OF BENEFICIAL OWNERSHIP. — The Secretary shall promulgate regulations defining beneficial ownership of an account for purposes of this section and sub-sections (i) and (j) of section 5318. Such regulations shall address issues related to an individual's authority to fund, direct, or manage the account (including, without limitation, the power to direct payments into or out of the account), and an individual's material interest in the income or corpus of the account, and shall ensure that the identification of individuals under this section does not extend to any individual whose beneficial interest in the income or corpus of the account is immaterial.

"(4) OTHER TERMS. -- The Secretary may, by regulation, further define the terms in paragraphs (1), (2), and (3), and define other terms for the purposes of this section, as the Secretary deems appropriate.".

(b) CLERICAL AMENDMENT. — The table of sections for subchapter II of chapter 53 of title 31, United States Code, is amended by inserting after the item relating to section 5318 the following new item :

"5318A. Special measures for jurisdictions, financial institutions, or international transactions of primary money laundering concern.".

SEC. 312. SPECIAL DUE DILIGENCE FOR CORRESPONDENT ACCOUNTS AND PRIVATE BANKING ACCOUNTS.

(a) IN GENERAL. — Section 5318 of title 31, United States Code, is amended by adding at the end the following :

"(i) DUE DILIGENCE FOR UNITED STATES PRIVATE BANKING AND CORRESPONDENT BANK ACCOUNTS INVOLVING FOREIGN PERSONS. —

"(1) IN GENERAL. — Each financial institution that establishes, maintains, administers, or manages a private banking account or a correspondent account in the United States for a non-United States person, including a foreign individual visiting the United States, or a representative of a non-United States person shall establish appropriate, specific, and, where necessary, enhanced, due diligence policies, procedures, and controls that are reasonably designed to detect and report instances of money laundering through those accounts.

"(2) ADDITIONAL STANDARDS FOR CERTAIN CORRESPONDENT ACCOUNTS. —

"(A) IN GENERAL. — Subparagraph (B) shall apply if a correspondent account is requested or maintained by, or on behalf of, a foreign bank operating —

"(i) under an offshore banking license; or

"(ii) under a banking license issued by a foreign country that has been designated —

"(I) as noncooperative with international anti-money laundering principles or procedures by an intergovernmental group or organization of which the United States is a member, with which designation the United States representative to the group or organization concurs; or

"(II) by the Secretary of the Treasury as warranting special measures due to money laundering concerns.

"(B) POLICIES, PROCEDURES, AND CONTROLS. — The enhanced due diligence policies, procedures, and controls required under paragraph (1) shall, at a minimum, ensure that the financial institution in the United States takes reasonable steps —

"(i) to ascertain for any such foreign bank, the shares of which are not publicly traded, the identity of each of the owners of the foreign bank, and the nature and extent of the ownership interest of each such owner;

"(ii) to conduct enhanced scrutiny of such account to guard against money laundering and report any suspicious transactions under subsection (g); and

"(iii) to ascertain whether such foreign bank provides correspondent accounts to other foreign banks and, if so, the identity of those foreign banks and related due diligence information, as appropriate under paragraph (1).

"(3) MINIMUM STANDARDS FOR PRIVATE BANKING ACCOUNTS. — If a private banking account is requested or maintained by, or on behalf of, a non-United States person, then the due diligence policies, procedures, and controls required under paragraph (1) shall, at a minimum, ensure that the financial institution takes reasonable steps —

"(A) to ascertain the identity of the nominal and beneficial owners of, and the source of funds deposited into, such account as needed to guard against money laundering and report any suspicious transactions under subsection (g); and

"(B) to conduct enhanced scrutiny of any such account that is requested or maintained by, or on behalf of, a senior foreign political figure, or any immediate family member or close associate of a senior foreign political figure that is reasonably designed to detect and report transactions that may involve the proceeds of foreign corruption.

"(4) DEFINITION. — For purposes of this subsection, the following definitions shall apply :

"(A) OFFSHORE BANKING LICENSE. — The term 'offshore banking license' means a license to conduct banking activities which, as a condition of the license, prohibits the licensed entity from conducting banking activities with the citizens of, or with the local currency of, the country which issued the license.

"(B) PRIVATE BANKING ACCOUNT. — The term 'private banking account' means an account (or any combination of accounts) that —

"(i) requires a minimum aggregate deposits of funds or other assets of not less than $1,000,000;

"(ii) is established on behalf of 1 or more individuals who have a direct or beneficial ownership interest in the account; and "(iii) is assigned to, or is administered or managed by, in whole or in part, an officer, employee, or agent of a financial institution acting as a liaison between the financial institution and the direct or beneficial owner of the account.".

(b) REGULATORY AUTHORITY AND EFFECTIVE DATE.—

(1) REGULATORY AUTHORITY.—Not later than 180 days after the date of enactment of this Act, the Secretary, in consultation with the appropriate Federal functional regulators (as defined in section 509 of the Gramm-Leach-Bliley Act) of the affected financial institutions, shall further delineate, by regulation, the due diligence policies, procedures, and controls required under section 5318(i)(1) of title 31, United States Code, as added by this section.

(2) EFFECTIVE DATE. — Section 5318(i) of title 31, United States Code, as added by this section, shall take effect 270 days after the date of enactment of this Act, whether or not final regulations are issued under paragraph (1), and the failure to issue such regulations shall in no way affect the enforceability of this section or the amendments made by this section. Section 5318(i) of title 31, United States Code, as added by this section, shall apply with respect to accounts covered by that section 5318(i), that are opened before, on, or after the date of enactment of this Act.

SEC. 313. PROHIBITION ON UNITED STATES CORRESPONDENT ACCOUNTS WITH FOREIGN SHELL BANKS.

(a) IN GENERAL. — Section 5318 of title 31, United States Code, as amended by this title, is amended by adding at the end the following :

"(j) PROHIBITION ON UNITED STATES CORRESPONDENT ACCOUNTS WITH FOREIGN SHELL BANKS. —

"(1) IN GENERAL. — A financial institution described in sub-paragraphs (A) through (G) of section 5312(a)(2) (in this sub-section referred to as a 'covered financial institution') shall not establish, maintain, administer, or manage a correspondent account in the United

States for, or on behalf of, a foreign bank that does not have a physical presence in any country.

"(2) PREVENTION OF INDIRECT SERVICE TO FOREIGN SHELL BANKS. — A covered financial institution shall take reasonable steps to ensure that any correspondent account established, maintained, administered, or managed by that covered financial institution in the United States for a foreign bank is not being used by that foreign bank to indirectly provide banking services to another foreign bank that does not have a physical presence in any country. The Secretary of the Treasury shall, by regulation, delineate the reasonable steps necessary to comply with this paragraph.

"(3) EXCEPTION. — Paragraphs (1) and (2) do not prohibit a covered financial institution from providing a correspondent account to a foreign bank, if the foreign bank —

"(A) is an affiliate of a depository institution, credit union, or foreign bank that maintains a physical presence in the United States or a foreign country, as applicable; and

"(B) is subject to supervision by a banking authority in the country regulating the affiliated depository institution, credit union, or foreign bank described in subparagraph (A), as applicable.

"(4) DEFINITIONS. — For purposes of this subsection —

"(A) the term 'affiliate' means a foreign bank that is controlled by or is under common control with a depository institution, credit union, or foreign bank; and

"(B) the term 'physical presence' means a place of business that —

"(i) is maintained by a foreign bank;

"(ii) is located at a fixed address (other than solely an electronic address) in a country in which the foreign bank is authorized to conduct banking activities, at which location the foreign bank —

"(I) employs 1 or more individuals on a full-time basis; and

"(II) maintains operating records related to its banking activities; and

"(iii) is subject to inspection by the banking authority which licensed the foreign bank to conduct banking activities.".

(b) EFFECTIVE DATE. — The amendment made by subsection (a) shall take effect at the end of the 60-day period beginning on the date of enactment of this Act.

SEC. 314. COOPERATIVE EFFORTS TO DETER MONEY LAUNDERING.

(a) COOPERATION AMONG FINANCIAL INSTITUTIONS, REGULATORY AUTHORITIES, AND LAW ENFORCEMENT AUTHORITIES. —

(1) REGULATIONS. — The Secretary shall, within 120 days after the date of enactment of this Act, adopt regulations to encourage further cooperation among financial institutions, their regulatory authorities, and law enforcement authorities, with the specific purpose of encouraging regulatory authorities and law enforcement authorities to share with financial institutions information regarding individuals, entities, and organizations engaged in or reasonably suspected based on credible evidence of engaging in terrorist acts or money laundering activities.

(2) COOPERATION AND INFORMATION SHARING PROCEDURES. — The regulations adopted under paragraph (1) may include or create procedures for cooperation and information sharing focusing on —

(A) matters specifically related to the finances of terrorist groups, the means by which terrorist groups transfer funds around the world and within the United States, including through the use of charitable organizations, non-profit organizations, and nongovernmental organizations, and the extent to which financial institutions in the United States are unwittingly involved in such finances and the extent to which such institutions are at risk as a result;

(B) the relationship, particularly the financial relationship, between international narcotics traffickers and foreign terrorist organizations, the extent to which their memberships overlap and engage in joint activities, and the extent to which they cooperate with each other in raising and transferring funds for their respective purposes; and

(C) means of facilitating the identification of accounts and transactions involving terrorist groups and facilitating the exchange of information concerning such accounts and transactions between financial institutions and law enforcement organizations.

(3) CONTENTS. — The regulations adopted pursuant to paragraph (1) may —

(A) require that each financial institution designate 1 or more persons to receive information concerning, and to monitor accounts of individuals, entities, and organizations identified, pursuant to paragraph (1); and

(B) further establish procedures for the protection of the shared information, consistent with the capacity, size, and nature of the institution to which the particular procedures apply.

(4) RULE OF CONSTRUCTION. — The receipt of information by a financial institution pursuant to this section shall not relieve or otherwise modify the obligations of the financial institution with respect to any other person or account.

(5) USE OF INFORMATION. — Information received by a financial institution pursuant to this section shall not be used for any purpose other than identifying and reporting on activities that may involve terrorist acts or money laundering activities.

(b) COOPERATION AMONG FINANCIAL INSTITUTIONS. — Upon notice provided to the Secretary, 2 or more financial institutions and any association of financial institutions may share information with one another regarding individuals, entities, organizations, and countries suspected of possible terrorist or money laundering activities. A financial institution or association that transmits, receives, or shares such information for the purposes of identifying and reporting activities that may involve terrorist acts or money laundering activities shall not be liable to any person under any law or regulation of the United States, any constitution, law, or regulation of any State or political subdivision thereof, or under any contract or other legally enforceable agreement (including any arbitration agreement), for such disclosure or for any failure to provide notice of such disclosure to the person who is the subject of such disclosure, or any other person identified in the disclosure, except where such transmission, receipt, or sharing violates this section or regulations promulgated pursuant to this section.

(c) RULE OF CONSTRUCTION. — Compliance with the provisions of this title requiring or allowing financial institutions and any association of financial institutions to disclose or share information regarding individuals, entities, and organizations engaged in or suspected of engaging in terrorist acts or money laundering activities shall not constitute a violation of the provisions of title V of the Gramm-Leach-Bliley Act (Public Law 106–102).

(d) REPORTS TO THE FINANCIAL SERVICES INDUSTRY ON SUSPICIOUS FINANCIAL ACTIVITIES. — At least semiannually, the Secretary shall —

(1) publish a report containing a detailed analysis identifying patterns of suspicious activity and other investigative insights derived from suspicious activity reports and investigations conducted by Federal, State, and local law enforcement agencies to the extent appropriate; and

(2) distribute such report to financial institutions (as defined in section 5312 of title 31, United States Code).

SEC. 315. INCLUSION OF FOREIGN CORRUPTION OFFENSES AS MONEY LAUNDERING CRIMES.

Section 1956(c)(7) of title 18, United States Code, is amended —

(1) in subparagraph (B) —

(A) in clause (ii), by striking "or destruction of property by means of explosive or fire" and inserting "destruction of property by means of explosive or fire, or a crime of violence (as defined in section 16)";

(B) in clause (iii), by striking "1978" and inserting "1978)"; and

(C) by adding at the end the following :

"(iv) bribery of a public official, or the misappropriation, theft, or embezzlement of public funds by or for the benefit of a public official;

"(v) smuggling or export control violations involving —

"(I) an item controlled on the United States Munitions List established under section 38 of the Arms Export Control Act (22 U.S.C. 2778); or

"(II) an item controlled under regulations under the Export Administration Regulations (15 C.F.R. Parts 730–774); or

"(vi) an offense with respect to which the United States would be obligated by a multilateral treaty, either to extradite the alleged offender or to submit the case for prosecution, if the offender were found within the territory of the United States;"; and

(2) in subparagraph (D) —

(A) by inserting "section 541 (relating to goods falsely classified)," before "section 542";

(B) by inserting "section 922(1) (relating to the unlawful importation of firearms), section 924(n) (relating to firearms trafficking)," before "section 956";

(C) by inserting "section 1030 (relating to computer fraud and abuse)," before "1032"; and

(D) by inserting "any felony violation of the Foreign Agents Registration Act of 1938," before "or any felony violation of the Foreign Corrupt Practices Act"

SEC. 316. ANTI-TERRORIST FORFEITURE PROTECTION.

(a) RIGHT TO CONTEST. — An owner of property that is confiscated under any provision of law relating to the confiscation of assets of suspected international terrorists, may contest that confiscation by filing a claim in the manner set forth in the Federal Rules of Civil Procedure (Supplemental Rules for Certain Admiralty and Maritime Claims), and asserting as an affirmative defense that —

(1) the property is not subject to confiscation under such provision of law; or

(2) the innocent owner provisions of section 983(d) of title 18, United States Code, apply to the case.

(b) EVIDENCE. — In considering a claim filed under this section, a court may admit evidence that is otherwise inadmissible under the Federal Rules of Evidence, if the court determines that the evidence is reliable, and that compliance with the Federal Rules of Evidence may jeopardize the national security interests of the United States.

(c) CLARIFICATIONS. —

(1) PROTECTION OF RIGHTS. — The exclusion of certain provisions of Federal law from the definition of the term "civil forfeiture statute" in section 983(i) of title 18, United States Code, shall not be construed to deny an owner of property the right to contest the confiscation of assets of suspected international terrorists under —

(A) subsection (a) of this section;

(B) the Constitution; or

(C) subchapter II of chapter 5 of title 5, United States Code (commonly known as the "Administrative Procedure Act").

(2) SAVINGS CLAUSE. — Nothing in this section shall limit or otherwise affect any other remedies that may be available to an owner of property under section 983 of title 18, United States Code, or any other provision of law.

(d) TECHNICAL CORRECTION. — Section 983(i)(2)(D) of title 18, United States Code, is amended by inserting "or the

International Emergency Economic Powers Act (IEEPA) (50 U.S.C. 1701 et seq.)" before the semicolon.

SEC. 317. LONG-ARM JURISDICTION OVER FOREIGN MONEY LAUNDERERS.

Section 1956(b) of title 18, United States Code, is amended —

(1) by redesignating paragraphs (1) and (2) as subparagraphs (A) and (B), respectively, and moving the margins 2 ems to the right;

(2) by inserting after "(b)" the following : "PENALTIES. — "(1) IN GENERAL. — ";

(3) by inserting ", or section 1957" after "or (a)(3)"; and

(4) by adding at the end the following :

"(2) JURISDICTION OVER FOREIGN PERSONS. — For purposes of adjudicating an action filed or enforcing a penalty ordered under this section, the district courts shall have jurisdiction over any foreign person, including any financial institution authorized under the laws of a foreign country, against whom the action is brought, if service of process upon the foreign person is made under the Federal Rules of Civil Procedure or the laws of the country in which the foreign person is found, and —

"(A) the foreign person commits an offense under sub-section (a) involving a financial transaction that occurs in whole or in part in the United States;

"(B) the foreign person converts, to his or her own use, property in which the United States has an ownership interest by virtue of the entry of an order of forfeiture by a court of the United States; or

"(C) the foreign person is a financial institution that maintains a bank account at a financial institution in the United States.

"(3) COURT AUTHORITY OVER ASSETS. — A court described in paragraph (2) may issue a pretrial restraining order or take any other action necessary to ensure that any bank account or other property held by the defendant in the United States is available to satisfy a judgment under this section.

"(4) FEDERAL RECEIVER. —

"(A) IN GENERAL. — A court described in paragraph (2) may appoint a Federal Receiver, in accordance with subparagraph (B) of this paragraph, to collect, marshal, and take custody, control, and possession of all assets of the defendant, wherever located, to satisfy a civil judgment under this subsection, a forfeiture judgment under section 981 or 982, or a criminal sentence under section 1957 or subsection (a) of this section, including an order of restitution to any victim of a specified unlawful activity.

"(B) APPOINTMENT AND AUTHORITY. — A Federal Receiver described in subparagraph (A) —

"(i) may be appointed upon application of a Federal prosecutor or a Federal or State regulator, by the court having jurisdiction over the defendant in the case;

"(ii) shall be an officer of the court, and the powers of the Federal Receiver shall include the powers set out in section 754 of title 28, United States Code; and

"(iii) shall have standing equivalent to that of a Federal prosecutor for the purpose of submitting requests to obtain information regarding the assets of the defendant —

"(I) from the Financial Crimes Enforcement Network of the Department of the Treasury; or

"(II) from a foreign country pursuant to a mutual legal assistance treaty, multilateral agreement, or other arrangement for international law enforcement assistance, provided that such requests are in accordance with the policies and procedures of the Attorney General.".

SEC. 318. LAUNDERING MONEY THROUGH A FOREIGN BANK.

Section 1956(c) of title 18, United States Code, is amended by striking paragraph (6) and inserting the following :

"(6) the term 'financial institution' includes —

"(A) any financial institution, as defined in section 5312(a)(2) of title 31, United States Code, or the regulations promulgated thereunder; and

"(B) any foreign bank, as defined in section 1 of the International Banking Act of 1978 (12 U.S.C. 3101).".

SEC. 319. FORFEITURE OF FUNDS IN UNITED STATES INTERBANK ACCOUNTS.

(a) FORFEITURE FROM UNITED STATES INTERBANK ACCOUNT. — Section 981 of title 18, United States Code, is amended by adding at the end the following :

"(k) INTERBANK ACCOUNTS. —

"(1) IN GENERAL. —

"(A) IN GENERAL. — For the purpose of a forfeiture under this section or under the Controlled Substances Act (21 U.S.C. 801 et seq.), if funds are deposited into an account at a foreign bank, and that foreign bank has an interbank account in the United States with a covered financial institution (as defined in section 5318(j)(1) of title 31), the funds shall be deemed to have been deposited into the interbank account in the United States, and any restraining order, seizure warrant, or arrest warrant in rem regarding the funds may be served on the covered financial institution, and funds in the interbank account, up to the value of the funds deposited into the account at the foreign bank, may be restrained, seized, or arrested.

"(B) AUTHORITY TO SUSPEND. — The Attorney General, in consultation with the Secretary of the Treasury, may suspend or terminate a forfeiture under this section if the Attorney General determines that a conflict of law exists between the laws of the jurisdiction in which the foreign bank is located and the laws of the United States with respect to liabilities arising from the restraint, seizure, or arrest of such funds, and that such suspension or termination would be in the interest of justice and would not harm the national interests of the United States.

"(2) NO REQUIREMENT FOR GOVERNMENT TO TRACE FUNDS. — If a forfeiture action is brought against funds that are restrained, seized, or arrested under paragraph (1), it shall not be necessary for the Government to establish that the funds are directly traceable to the funds that were deposited into the foreign bank, nor shall it be necessary for the Government to rely on the application of section 984.

"(3) CLAIMS BROUGHT BY OWNER OF THE FUNDS. — If a forfeiture action is instituted against funds restrained, seized, or arrested under paragraph (1), the owner of the funds deposited into the account at the foreign bank may contest the forfeiture by filing a claim under section 983.

"(4) DEFINITIONS. — For purposes of this subsection, the following definitions shall apply :

"(A) INTERBANK ACCOUNT. — The term 'interbank account' has the same meaning as in section 984(c)(2)(B).

"(B) OWNER. —

"(i) IN GENERAL. — Except as provided in clause (ii), the term 'owner' —

"(I) means the person who was the owner, as that term is defined in section 983(d)(6), of the funds that were deposited into the foreign bank at the time such funds were deposited; and

"(II) does not include either the foreign bank or any financial institution acting as an intermediary in the transfer of the funds into the interbank account.

"(ii) EXCEPTION. — The foreign bank may be considered the 'owner' of the funds (and no other person shall qualify as the owner of such funds) only if —

"(I) the basis for the forfeiture action is wrongdoing committed by the foreign bank; or

"(II) the foreign bank establishes, by a preponderance of the evidence, that prior to the restraint, seizure, or arrest of the funds, the foreign bank had discharged all or part of its obligation to the prior owner of the funds, in which case the foreign bank shall be deemed the owner of the funds to the extent of such discharged obligation.".

(b) BANK RECORDS. — Section 5318 of title 31, United States Code, as amended by this title, is amended by adding at the end the following :

"(k) BANK RECORDS RELATED TO ANTI-MONEY LAUNDERING PROGRAMS. —

"(1) DEFINITIONS. — For purposes of this subsection, the following definitions shall apply :

"(A) APPROPRIATE FEDERAL BANKING AGENCY. — The term 'appropriate Federal banking agency' has the same meaning as in section 3 of the Federal Deposit Insurance Act (12 U.S.C. 1813).

"(B) INCORPORATED TERM. — The term 'correspondent account' has the same meaning as in section 5318A(f)(1)(B).

"(2) 120-HOUR RULE. — Not later than 120 hours after receiving a request by an appropriate Federal banking agency for information related to anti-money laundering compliance by a covered financial institution or a customer of such institution, a covered financial institution shall provide to the appropriate Federal banking agency, or make available at a location specified by the representative of the appropriate Federal banking agency, information and account documentation for any account opened, maintained, administered or managed in the United States by the covered financial institution.

"(3) FOREIGN BANK RECORDS. —

"(A) SUMMONS OR SUBPOENA OF RECORDS. —

"(i) IN GENERAL. — The Secretary of the Treasury or the Attorney General may issue a summons or subpoena to any foreign bank that maintains a correspondent account in the United States and request records related to such correspondent account, including records maintained outside of the United States relating to the deposit of funds into the foreign bank.

"(ii) SERVICE OF SUMMONS OR SUBPOENA. — A summons or subpoena referred to in clause (i) may be served on the foreign bank in the United States if the foreign bank has a representative in the United States, or in a foreign country pursuant to any mutual legal assistance treaty, multilateral agreement, or other request for international law enforcement assistance.

"(B) ACCEPTANCE OF SERVICE. —

"(i) MAINTAINING RECORDS IN THE UNITED STATES. — Any covered financial institution which maintains a correspondent account in the United States for a foreign bank shall maintain records in the United States identifying the owners of such foreign bank and the name and address of a person who resides in the United States and is authorized to accept service of legal process for records regarding the correspondent account.

"(ii) LAW ENFORCEMENT REQUEST. — Upon receipt of a written request from a Federal law enforcement officer for information required to be maintained under this paragraph, the covered financial institution shall provide the information to the requesting officer not later than 7 days after receipt of the request.

"(C) TERMINATION OF CORRESPONDENT RELATIONSHIP. —

"(i) TERMINATION UPON RECEIPT OF NOTICE. — A covered financial institution shall terminate any correspondent relationship with a foreign bank not later than 10 business days after receipt of written notice from the Secretary or the Attorney General (in each case, after consultation with the other) that the foreign bank has failed —

"(I) to comply with a summons or subpoena issued under subparagraph (A); or

"(II) to initiate proceedings in a United States court contesting such summons or subpoena.

"(ii) LIMITATION ON LIABILITY. — A covered financial institution shall not be liable to any person in any court or arbitration proceeding for terminating a correspondent relationship in accordance with this sub-section.

"(iii) FAILURE TO TERMINATE RELATIONSHIP. — Failure to terminate a correspondent relationship in accordance with this subsection shall render the covered financial institution liable for a civil penalty of up to $10,000 per day until the correspondent relationship is so terminated.".

(c) GRACE PERIOD. — Financial institutions shall have 60 days from the date of enactment of this Act to comply with the provisions of section 5318(k) of title 31, United States Code, as added by this section.

(d) AUTHORITY TO ORDER CONVICTED CRIMINAL TO RETURN PROPERTY LOCATED ABROAD. —

(1) FORFEITURE OF SUBSTITUTE PROPERTY. — Section 413(p) of the Controlled Substances Act (21 U.S.C. 853) is amended to read as follows :

"(p) FORFEITURE OF SUBSTITUTE PROPERTY. —

"(1) IN GENERAL. — Paragraph (2) of this subsection shall apply, if any property described in subsection (a), as a result of any act or omission of the defendant —

"(A) cannot be located upon the exercise of due diligence;

"(B) has been transferred or sold to, or deposited with, a third party;

"(C) has been placed beyond the jurisdiction of the court;

"(D) has been substantially diminished in value; or

"(E) has been commingled with other property which cannot be divided without difficulty.

"(2) SUBSTITUTE PROPERTY. — In any case described in any of subparagraphs (A) through (E) of paragraph (1), the court shall order the forfeiture of any other property of the defendant, up to the value of any property described in subparagraphs (A) through (E) of paragraph (1), as applicable.

"(3) RETURN OF PROPERTY TO JURISDICTION. — In the case of property described in paragraph (1)(C), the court may, in addition to any other action authorized by this subsection, order the defendant to return the property to the jurisdiction of the court so that the property may be seized and forfeited.".

(2) PROTECTIVE ORDERS. — Section 413(e) of the Controlled Substances Act (21 U.S.C. 853(e)) is amended by adding at the end the following :

"(4) ORDER TO REPATRIATE AND DEPOSIT. —

"(A) IN GENERAL. — Pursuant to its authority to enter a pretrial restraining order under this section, the court may order a defendant to repatriate any property that may be seized and forfeited, and to deposit that property pending trial in the registry of the court, or with the United States Marshals Service or the Secretary of the Treasury, in an interest-bearing account, if appropriate.

"(B) FAILURE TO COMPLY. — Failure to comply with an order under this subsection, or an order to repatriate property under subsection (p), shall be punishable as a civil or criminal contempt of court, and may also result in an enhancement of the sentence of the defendant under the obstruction of justice provision of the Federal Sentencing Guidelines.".

SEC. 320. PROCEEDS OF FOREIGN CRIMES.

Section 981(a)(1)(B) of title 18, United States Code, is amended to read as follows :

"(B) Any property, real or personal, within the jurisdiction of the United States, constituting, derived from, or traceable to, any proceeds obtained directly or indirectly from an offense against a foreign nation, or any property used to facilitate such an offense, if the offense —

"(i) involves the manufacture, importation, sale, or distribution of a controlled substance (as that term is defined for purposes of the Controlled Substances Act), or any other conduct described in section 1956(c)(7)(B);

"(ii) would be punishable within the jurisdiction of the foreign nation by death or imprisonment for a term exceeding 1 year; and

"(iii) would be punishable under the laws of the United States by imprisonment for a term exceeding 1 year, if the act or activity constituting the offense had occurred within the jurisdiction of the United States.".

SEC. 321. FINANCIAL INSTITUTIONS SPECIFIED IN SUBCHAPTER II OF CHAPTER 53 OF TITLE 31, UNITED STATES CODE.

(a) CREDIT UNIONS. — Subparagraph (E) of section 5312(2) of title 31, United States Code, is amended to read as follows :

"(E) any credit union;".

(b) FUTURES COMMISSION MERCHANT; COMMODITY TRADING ADVISOR; COMMODITY POOL OPERATOR. — Section 5312 of title 31, United States Code, is amended by adding at the end the following new subsection :

"(c) ADDITIONAL DEFINITIONS. — For purposes of this subchapter, the following definitions shall apply :

"(1) CERTAIN INSTITUTIONS INCLUDED IN DEFINITION. —

The term 'financial institution' (as defined in subsection (a)) includes the following :

"(A) Any futures commission merchant, commodity trading advisor, or commodity pool operator registered, or required to register, under the Commodity Exchange Act.".

(c) CFTC INCLUDED. — For purposes of this Act and any amendment made by this Act to any other provision of law, the term "Federal functional regulator" includes the Commodity Futures Trading Commission.

SEC. 322. CORPORATION REPRESENTED BY A FUGITIVE.

Section 2466 of title 18, United States Code, is amended by designating the present matter as subsection (a), and adding at the end the following :

"(b) Subsection (a) may be applied to a claim filed by a corporation if any majority shareholder, or individual filing the claim on behalf of the corporation is a person to whom subsection (a) applies.".

SEC. 323. ENFORCEMENT OF FOREIGN JUDGMENTS.

Section 2467 of title 28, United States Code, is amended —

(1) in subsection (d), by adding the following after paragraph (2) :

"(3) PRESERVATION OF PROPERTY. —

"(A) IN GENERAL. — To preserve the availability of propert subject to a foreign forfeiture or confiscation judgment the Government may apply for, and the court ma issue, a restraining order pursuant to section 983(j) o title 18, at any time before or after an application i filed pursuant to subsection (c)(1) of this section.

"(B) EVIDENCE. — The court, in issuing a restraining orde under subparagraph (A) —

"(i) may rely on information set forth in an affidav describing the nature of the proceeding investigation underway in the foreign countr and setting forth a reasonable basis to belie that the property to be restrained will be nam in a judgment of forfeiture at the conclusion of such proceeding; or

"(ii) may register and enforce a restraining order that has been issued by a court of competent jurisdiction in the foreign country and certified by the Attorney General pursuant to subsection (b)(2).

"(C) LIMIT ON GROUNDS FOR OBJECTION. — No person may object to a restraining order under subparagraph (A) on any ground that is the subject of parallel litigation involving the same property that is pending in a foreign court.";

(2) in subsection (b)(1)(C), by striking "establishing that the defendant received notice of the proceedings in sufficient time to enable the defendant" and inserting "establishing that the foreign nation took steps, in accordance with the principles of due process, to give notice of the proceedings to all persons with an interest in the property in sufficient time to enable such persons";

(3) in subsection (d)(1)(D), by striking "the defendant in the proceedings in the foreign court did not receive notice" and inserting "the foreign nation did not take steps, in accordance with the principles of due process, to give notice of the proceedings to a person with an interest in the property"; and

(4) in subsection (a)(2)(A), by inserting ", any violation of foreign law that would constitute a violation or an offense for which property could be forfeited under Federal law if the offense were committed in the United States" after "United Nations Convention".

SEC. 324. REPORT AND RECOMMENDATION.

Not later than 30 months after the date of enactment of this Act, the Secretary, in consultation with the Attorney General, the Federal banking agencies (as defined at section 3 of the Federal Deposit Insurance Act), the National Credit Union Administration Board, the Securities and Exchange Commission, and such other agencies as the Secretary may determine, at the discretion of the Secretary, shall evaluate the operations of the provisions of this subtitle and make recommendations to Congress as to any legislative action with respect to this subtitle as the Secretary may determine to be necessary or advisable.

SEC. 325. CONCENTRATION ACCOUNTS AT FINANCIAL INSTITUTIONS.

Section 5318(h) of title 31, United States Code, as amended by section 202 of this title, is amended by adding at the end the following :

"(3) CONCENTRATION ACCOUNTS. — The Secretary may prescribe regulations under this subsection that govern maintenance of concentration accounts by financial institutions, in order to ensure that such accounts are not used to prevent association of the identity of an individual customer with the movement of funds of which the customer is the direct or beneficial owner, which regulations shall, at a minimum —

"(A) prohibit financial institutions from allowing clients to direct transactions that move their funds into, out of, or through the concentration accounts of the financial institution;

"(B) prohibit financial institutions and their employees from informing customers of the existence of, or the means of identifying, the concentration accounts of the institution; and

"(C) require each financial institution to establish written procedures governing the documentation of all transactions involving a concentration account, which procedures shall ensure that, any time a transaction involving a concentration account commingles funds belonging to 1 or more customers, the identity of, and specific amount belonging to, each customer is documented.".

SEC. 326. VERIFICATION OF IDENTIFICATION.

(a) IN GENERAL. — Section 5318 of title 31, United States Code, as amended by this title, is amended by adding at the end the following :

"(l) IDENTIFICATION AND VERIFICATION OF ACCOUNT-HOLDERS. —

"(1) IN GENERAL. — Subject to the requirements of this sub-section, the Secretary of the Treasury shall prescribe regulations setting forth the minimum standards for financial institutions and their customers regarding the identity of the customer that shall apply in connection with the opening of an account at a financial institution.

"(2) MINIMUM REQUIREMENTS. — The regulations shall, at a minimum, require financial institutions to implement, and customers (after being given adequate notice) to comply with, reasonable procedures for —

"(A) verifying the identity of any person seeking to open an account to the extent reasonable and practicable;

"(B) maintaining records of the information used to verify a person's identity, including name, address, and other identifying information; and

"(C) consulting lists of known or suspected terrorists or terrorist organizations provided to the financial institution by any government agency to determine whether a person seeking to open an account appears on any such list.

"(3) FACTORS TO BE CONSIDERED. — In prescribing regulations under this subsection, the Secretary shall take into consideration the various types of accounts maintained by various types of financial institutions, the various methods of opening accounts, and the various types of identifying information available.

"(4) CERTAIN FINANCIAL INSTITUTIONS. — In the case of any financial institution the business of which is engaging in financial activities described in section 4(k) of the Bank Holding Company Act of 1956 (including financial activities subject to the jurisdiction of the Commodity Futures Trading Commission), the regulations prescribed by the Secretary under paragraph (1) shall be prescribed jointly with each Federal functional regulator (as defined in section 509 of the Gramm-Leach-Bliley Act, including the Commodity Futures Trading Commission) appropriate for such financial institution.

"(5) EXEMPTIONS. — The Secretary (and, in the case of any financial institution described in paragraph (4), any Federal agency described in such paragraph) may, by regulation or order, exempt any financial institution or type of account from the requirements of any regulation prescribed under this sub-section in accordance with such standards and procedures as the Secretary may prescribe.

"(6) EFFECTIVE DATE. — Final regulations prescribed under this subsection shall take effect before the end of the 1-year period beginning on the date of enactment of the International Money Laundering Abatement and Financial Anti-Terrorism Act of 2001.".

(b) STUDY AND REPORT REQUIRED. — Within 6 months after the date of enactment of this Act, the Secretary, in consultation with the Federal functional regulators (as defined in section 509 of the Gramm-Leach-Bliley Act) and other appropriate Government agencies, shall submit a report to the Congress containing recommendations for —

(1) determining the most timely and effective way to require foreign nationals to provide domestic financial institutions and agencies with appropriate and accurate information, comparable to that which is required of United States nationals, concerning the identity, address, and other related information about such foreign nationals necessary to enable such institutions and agencies to comply with the requirements of this section;

(2) requiring foreign nationals to apply for and obtain, before opening an account with a domestic financial institution, an identification number which would function similarly to a Social Security number or tax identification number; and

(3) establishing a system for domestic financial institutions and agencies to review information maintained by relevant Government agencies for purposes of verifying the identities of foreign nationals seeking to open accounts at those institutions and agencies.

SEC. 327. CONSIDERATION OF ANTI-MONEY LAUNDERING RECORD.

(a) BANK HOLDING COMPANY ACT OF 1956. —

(1) IN GENERAL. — Section 3(c) of the Bank Holding

Company Act of 1956 (12 U.S.C. 1842(c)) is amended by adding at the end the following new paragraph :

"(6) MONEY LAUNDERING. — In every case, the Board shall take into consideration the effectiveness of the company or companies in combatting money laundering activities, including in overseas branches.".

(2) SCOPE OF APPLICATION. — The amendment made by paragraph (1) shall apply with respect to any application submitted to the Board of Governors of the Federal Reserve System under section 3 of the Bank Holding Company Act of 1956 after December 31, 2001, which has not been approved by the Board before the date of enactment of this Act.

(b) MERGERS SUBJECT TO REVIEW UNDER FEDERAL DEPOSIT INSURANCE ACT. —

(1) IN GENERAL. — Section 18(c) of the Federal Deposit Insurance Act (12 U.S.C. 1828(c)) is amended —

(A) by redesignating paragraph (11) as paragraph (12); and

(B) by inserting after paragraph (10), the following new paragraph :

"(11) MONEY LAUNDERING. — In every case, the responsible agency, shall take into consideration the effectiveness of any insured depository institution involved in the proposed merger transaction in combatting money laundering activities, including in overseas branches.".

(2) SCOPE OF APPLICATION. — The amendment made by paragraph (1) shall apply with respect to any application submitted to the responsible agency under section 18(c) of the Federal Deposit Insurance Act after December 31, 2001, which has not been approved by all appropriate responsible agencies before the date of enactment of this Act.

SEC. 328. INTERNATIONAL COOPERATION ON IDENTIFICATION OF ORIGINATORS OF WIRE TRANSFERS.

The Secretary shall —

(1) in consultation with the Attorney General and the Secretary of State, take all reasonable steps to encourage foreign

governments to require the inclusion of the name of the originator in wire transfer instructions sent to the United States and other countries, with the information to remain with the transfer from its origination until the point of disbursement; and

(2) report annually to the Committee on Financial Services of the House of Representatives and the Committee on Banking, Housing, and Urban Affairs of the Senate on —

(A) progress toward the goal enumerated in paragraph (1), as well as impediments to implementation and an estimated compliance rate; and

(B) impediments to instituting a regime in which all appropriate identification, as defined by the Secretary, about wire transfer recipients shall be included with wire transfers from their point of origination until disbursement.

SEC. 329. CRIMINAL PENALTIES.

Any person who is an official or employee of any department, agency, bureau, office, commission, or other entity of the Federal Government, and any other person who is acting for or on behalf of any such entity, who, directly or indirectly, in connection with the administration of this title, corruptly demands, seeks, receives, accepts, or agrees to receive or accept anything of value personally or for any other person or entity in return for —

(1) being influenced in the performance of any official act;

(2) being influenced to commit or aid in the committing, or to collude in, or allow, any fraud, or make opportunity for the commission of any fraud, on the United States; or

(3) being induced to do or omit to do any act in violation of the official duty of such official or person, shall be fined in an amount not more than 3 times the monetary equivalent of the thing of value, or imprisoned for not more than 15 years, or both. A violation of this section shall be subject to chapter 227 of title 18, United States Code, and the provisions of the United States Sentencing Guidelines.

SEC. 330. INTERNATIONAL COOPERATION IN INVESTIGATIONS OF MONEY LAUNDERING, FINANCIAL CRIMES, AND THE FINANCES OF TERRORIST GROUPS.

(a) NEGOTIATIONS. — It is the sense of the Congress that the President should direct the Secretary of State, the Attorney General, or the Secretary of the Treasury, as appropriate, and in consultation with the Board of Governors of the Federal Reserve System, to seek to enter into negotiations with the appropriate financial supervisory agencies and other officials of any foreign country the financial institutions of which do business with United States financial institutions or which may be utilized by any foreign terrorist organization (as designated under section 219 of the Immigration and Nationality Act), any person who is a member or representative of any such organization, or any person engaged in money laundering or financial or other crimes.

(b) PURPOSES OF NEGOTIATIONS. — It is the sense of the Congress that, in carrying out any negotiations described in paragraph (1), the President should direct the Secretary of State, the Attorney General, or the Secretary of the Treasury, as appropriate, to seek to enter into and further cooperative efforts, voluntary information exchanges, the use of letters rogatory, mutual legal assistance treaties, and international agreements to —

(1) ensure that foreign banks and other financial institutions maintain adequate records of transaction and account information relating to any foreign terrorist organization (as designated under section 219 of the Immigration and Nationality Act), any person who is a member or representative of any such organization, or any person engaged in money laundering or financial or other crimes; and

(2) establish a mechanism whereby such records may be made available to United States law enforcement officials and domestic financial institution supervisors, when appropriate.

Subtitle B — Bank Secrecy Act Amendments and Related Improvements

SEC. 351. AMENDMENTS RELATING TO REPORTING OF SUSPICIOUS ACTIVITIES.

(a) AMENDMENT RELATING TO CIVIL LIABILITY IMMUNITY FOR DISCLOSURES. — Section 5318(g)(3) of title 31, United States Code, is amended to read as follows :

"(3) LIABILITY FOR DISCLOSURES. —

"(A) IN GENERAL. — Any financial institution that makes a voluntary disclosure of any possible violation of law or regulation to a government agency or makes a disclosure pursuant to this subsection or any other authority, and any director, officer, employee, or agent of such institution who makes, or requires another to make any such disclosure, shall not be liable to any person under any law or regulation of the United States, any constitution, law, or regulation of any State or political subdivision of any State, or under any contract or other legally enforceable agreement (including any arbitration agreement), for such disclosure or for any failure to provide notice of such disclosure to the person who is the subject of such disclosure or any other person identified in the disclosure.

"(B) RULE OF CONSTRUCTION. — Subparagraph (A) shall not be construed as creating —

"(i) any inference that the term 'person', as used in such subparagraph, may be construed more broadly than its ordinary usage so as to include any government or agency of government; or

"(ii) any immunity against, or otherwise affecting, any civil or criminal action brought by any government or agency of government to enforce any constitution, law, or regulation of such government or agency.".

(b) PROHIBITION ON NOTIFICATION OF DISCLOSURES. — Section

5318(g)(2) of title 31, United States Code, is amended to read as follows :

"(2) NOTIFICATION PROHIBITED. —

"(A) IN GENERAL. — If a financial institution or any director, officer, employee, or agent of any financial institution, voluntarily or pursuant to this section or any other authority, reports a suspicious transaction to a government agency —

"(i) the financial institution, director, officer, employee, or agent may not notify any person involved in the transaction that the transaction has been reported; and

"(ii) no officer or employee of the Federal Government or of any State, local, tribal, or territorial government within the United States, who has any knowledge that such report was made may disclose to any person involved in the transaction that the transaction has been reported, other than as necessary to fulfill the official duties of such officer or employee.

"(B) DISCLOSURES IN CERTAIN EMPLOYMENT REFERENCES. —

"(i) RULE OF CONSTRUCTION. — Notwithstanding the application of subparagraph (A) in any other context, subparagraph (A) shall not be construed as prohibiting any financial institution, or any director, officer, employee, or agent of such institution, from including information that was included in a report to which subparagraph (A) applies —

"(I) in a written employment reference that is provided in accordance with section 18(w) of the Federal Deposit Insurance Act in response to a request from another financial institution; or

"(II) in a written termination notice or employment reference that is provided in accordance with the rules of a self-regulatory organization registered with the Securities and Exchange Commission or the Commodity Futures Trading Commission,

except that such written reference or notice may not disclose that such information was also included in any such report, or that such report was made.

"(ii) INFORMATION NOT REQUIRED. — Clause (i) shall not be construed, by itself, to create any affirmative duty to include any information described in clause (i) in any employment reference or termination notice referred to in clause (i).".

SEC. 352. ANTI-MONEY LAUNDERING PROGRAMS.

(a) IN GENERAL. — Section 5318(h) of title 31, United States Code, is amended to read as follows :

"(h) ANTI-MONEY LAUNDERING PROGRAMS. —

"(1) IN GENERAL. — In order to guard against money laundering through financial institutions, each financial institution shall establish anti-money laundering programs, including, at a minimum —

"(A) the development of internal policies, procedures, and controls;

"(B) the designation of a compliance officer;

"(C) an ongoing employee training program; and

"(D) an independent audit function to test programs.

"(2) REGULATIONS. — The Secretary of the Treasury, after consultation with the appropriate Federal functional regulator (as defined in section 509 of the Gramm-Leach-Bliley Act), may prescribe minimum standards for programs established under paragraph (1), and may exempt from the application of those standards any financial institution that is not subject to the provisions of the rules contained in part 103 of title 31, of the Code of Federal Regulations, or any successor rule thereto, for so long as such financial institution is not subject to the provisions of such rules.".

(b) EFFECTIVE DATE. — The amendment made by subsection (a) shall take effect at the end of the 180-day period beginning on the date of enactment of this Act.

(c) DATE OF APPLICATION OF REGULATIONS; FACTORS TO BE TAKEN INTO ACCOUNT. — Before the end of the 180-day period beginning on the date of enactment of this Act, the Secretary shall prescribe regulations that consider the extent to which the requirements imposed under this section are commensurate with the size, location, and activities of the financial institutions to which such regulations apply.

SEC. 353. PENALTIES FOR VIOLATIONS OF GEOGRAPHIC TARGETING ORDERS AND CERTAIN RECORDKEEPING REQUIREMENTS, AND LENGTHENING EFFECTIVE PERIOD OF GEOGRAPHIC TARGETING ORDERS.

(a) CIVIL PENALTY FOR VIOLATION OF TARGETING ORDER. — Section 5321(a)(1) of title 31, United States Code, is amended —

(1) by inserting "or order issued" after "subchapter or a regulation prescribed"; and

(2) by inserting ", or willfully violating a regulation prescribed under section 21 of the Federal Deposit Insurance Act or section 123 of Public Law 91–508," after "sections 5314 and 5315)".

(b) CRIMINAL PENALTIES FOR VIOLATION OF TARGETING ORDER. — Section 5322 of title 31, United States Code, is amended —

(1) in subsection (a) —

(A) by inserting "or order issued" after "willfully violating this subchapter or a regulation prescribed"; and

(B) by inserting ", or willfully violating a regulation prescribed under section 21 of the Federal Deposit Insurance Act or section 123 of Public Law 91–508," after "under section 5315 or 5324)"; and

(2) in subsection (b) —

(A) by inserting "or order issued" after "willfully violating this subchapter or a regulation prescribed"; and

(B) by inserting "or willfully violating a regulation prescribed under section 21 of the Federal Deposit Insurance Act or section 123 of Public Law 91–508," after "under section 5315 or 5324),".

(c) STRUCTURING TRANSACTIONS TO EVADE TARGETING ORDER OR CERTAIN RECORDKEEPING REQUIREMENTS. — Section 5324(a) of title 31, United States Code, is amended —

(1) by inserting a comma after "shall";

(2) by striking "section — " and inserting "section, the reporting or recordkeeping requirements imposed by any order issued under section 5326, or the recordkeeping requirements imposed by any regulation prescribed under section 21 of the Federal Deposit Insurance Act or section 123 of Public Law 91–508 — ";

(3) in paragraph (1), by inserting ", to file a report or to maintain a record required by an order issued under section 5326, or to maintain a record required pursuant to any regulation prescribed under section 21 of the Federal Deposit Insurance Act or section 123 of Public Law 91–508" after "regulation prescribed under any such section"; and

(4) in paragraph (2), by inserting ", to file a report or to maintain a record required by any order issued under section 5326, or to maintain a record required pursuant to any regulation prescribed under section 5326, or to maintain a record required pursuant to any regulation prescribed under section 21 of the Federal Deposit Insurance Act or section 123 of Public Law 91–508," after "regulation prescribed under any such section".

(d) LENGTHENING EFFECTIVE PERIOD OF GEOGRAPHIC TARGETING ORDERS. — Section 5326(d) of title 31, United States Code, is amended by striking "more than 60" and inserting "more than 180".

SEC. 354. ANTI-MONEY LAUNDERING STRATEGY.

Section 5341(b) of title 31, United States Code, is amended by adding at the end the following :

"(12) DATA REGARDING FUNDING OF TERRORISM. — Data concerning money laundering efforts related to the funding of acts of international terrorism, and efforts directed at the prevention, detection, and prosecution of such funding.".

SEC. 355. AUTHORIZATION TO INCLUDE SUSPICIONS OF ILLEGAL ACTIVITY IN WRITTEN EMPLOYMENT REFERENCES.

Section 18 of the Federal Deposit Insurance Act (12 U.S.C. 1828) is amended by adding at the end the following :

"(w) WRITTEN EMPLOYMENT REFERENCES MAY CONTAIN SUSPICIONS OF INVOLVEMENT IN ILLEGAL ACTIVITY. —

"(1) AUTHORITY TO DISCLOSE INFORMATION. — Notwithstanding any other provision of law, any insured depository institution, and any director, officer, employee, or agent of such institution, may disclose in any written employment reference relating to a current or former institution-affiliated party of such institution which is provided to another insured depository institution in response to a request from such other institution, information concerning the possible involvement of such institution-affiliated party in potentially unlawful activity.

"(2) INFORMATION NOT REQUIRED. — Nothing in paragraph (1) shall be construed, by itself, to create any affirmative duty to include any information described in paragraph (1) in any employment reference referred to in paragraph (1).

"(3) MALICIOUS INTENT. — Notwithstanding any other provision of this subsection, voluntary disclosure made by an insured depository institution, and any director, officer, employee, or agent of such institution under this subsection concerning potentially unlawful activity that is made with malicious intent, shall not be shielded from liability from the person identified in the disclosure.

"(4) DEFINITION. — For purposes of this subsection, the term 'insured depository institution' includes any uninsured branch or agency of a foreign bank.".

SEC. 356. REPORTING OF SUSPICIOUS ACTIVITIES BY SECURITIES BROKERS AND DEALERS; INVESTMENT COMPANY STUDY.

(a) DEADLINE FOR SUSPICIOUS ACTIVITY REPORTING

REQUIREMENTS FOR REGISTERED BROKERS AND DEALERS. — The Secretary, after consultation with the Securities and Exchange Commission and the Board of Governors of the Federal Reserve System, shall publish proposed regulations in the Federal Register before January 1, 2002, requiring brokers and dealers registered with the Securities and Exchange Commission under the Securities Exchange Act of 1934 to submit suspicious activity reports under section 5318(g) of title 31, United States Code. Such regulations shall be published in final form not later than July 1, 2002.

(b) SUSPICIOUS ACTIVITY REPORTING REQUIREMENTS FOR FUTURES COMMISSION MERCHANTS, COMMODITY TRADING ADVISORS, AND COMMODITY POOL OPERATORS. — The Secretary, in consultation with the Commodity Futures Trading Commission, may prescribe regulations requiring futures commission merchants, commodity trading advisors, and commodity pool operators registered under the Commodity Exchange Act to submit suspicious activity reports under section 5318(g) of title 31, United States Code.

(c) REPORT ON INVESTMENT COMPANIES. —

(1) IN GENERAL. — Not later than 1 year after the date of enactment of this Act, the Secretary, the Board of Governors of the Federal Reserve System, and the Securities and Exchange Commission shall jointly submit a report to the Congress on recommendations for effective regulations to apply the requirements of subchapter II of chapter 53 of title 31, United States Code, to investment companies pursuant to section 5312(a)(2)(I) of title 31, United States Code.

(2) DEFINITION. — For purposes of this subsection, the term "investment company" —

(A) has the same meaning as in section 3 of the Investment Company Act of 1940 (15 U.S.C. 80a–3); and

(B) includes any person that, but for the exceptions provided for in paragraph (1) or (7) of section 3(c) of the Investment Company Act of 1940 (15 U.S.C. 80a–3(c)), would be an investment company.

(3) ADDITIONAL RECOMMENDATIONS. — The report required by paragraph (1) may make different recommendations for different types of entities covered by this subsection.

(4) BENEFICIAL OWNERSHIP OF PERSONAL HOLDING COMPANIES. — The report described in paragraph (1) shall also include recommendations as to whether the Secretary should promulgate regulations to treat any corporation or business or other grantor trust whose assets are predominantly securities, bank certificates of deposit, or other securities or investment instruments (other than such as relate to operating subsidiaries of such corporation or trust) and that has 5 or fewer common shareholders or holders of beneficial or other equity interest, as a financial institution within the meaning of that phrase in section 5312(a)(2)(I) and whether to require such corporations or trusts to disclose their beneficial owners when opening accounts or initiating funds transfers at any domestic financial institution.

SEC. 357. SPECIAL REPORT ON ADMINISTRATION OF BANK SECRECY PROVISIONS.

(a) REPORT REQUIRED. — Not later than 6 months after the date of enactment of this Act, the Secretary shall submit a report to the Congress relating to the role of the Internal Revenue Service in the administration of subchapter II of chapter 53 of title 31, United States Code (commonly known as the "Bank Secrecy Act").

(b) CONTENTS. — The report required by subsection (a) —

(1) shall specifically address, and contain recommendations concerning —

(A) whether it is advisable to shift the processing of information reporting to the Department of the Treasury under the Bank Secrecy Act provisions to facilities other than those managed by the Internal Revenue Service; and

(B) whether it remains reasonable and efficient, in light of the objective of both anti-money-laundering programs and Federal tax administration, for the Internal Revenue Service to retain authority and responsibility for audit and examination of the compliance of money services businesses and gaming institutions with those Bank Secrecy Act provisions; and

(2) shall, if the Secretary determines that the information processing responsibility or the audit and examination responsibility of the Internal Revenue Service, or both, with respect to those Bank Secrecy Act provisions should be transferred to other agencies, include the specific recommendations of the Secretary regarding the agency or agencies to which any such function should be transferred, complete with a budgetary and resources plan for expeditiously accomplishing the transfer.

SEC. 358. BANK SECRECY PROVISIONS AND ACTIVITIES OF UNITED STATES INTELLIGENCE AGENCIES TO FIGHT INTERNATIONAL TERRORISM.

(a) AMENDMENT RELATING TO THE PURPOSES OF CHAPTER 53 OF TITLE 31, UNITED STATES CODE. — Section 5311 of title 31, United States Code, is amended by inserting before the period at the end the following : ", or in the conduct of intelligence or counterintelligence activities, including analysis, to protect against international terrorism".

(b) AMENDMENT RELATING TO REPORTING OF SUSPICIOUS ACTIVITIES. — Section 5318(g)(4)(B) of title 31, United States Code, is amended by striking "or supervisory agency" and inserting ", supervisory agency, or United States intelligence agency for use in the conduct of intelligence or counterintelligence activities, including analysis, to protect against international terrorism".

(c) AMENDMENT RELATING TO AVAILABILITY OF REPORTS. — Section 5319 of title 31, United States Code, is amended to read as follows :

"§ 5319. Availability of reports

"The Secretary of the Treasury shall make information in a report filed under this subchapter available to an agency, including any State financial institutions supervisory agency, United States intelligence agency or self-regulatory organization registered with the Securities and Exchange Commission or the Commodity Futures Trading Commission, upon request of the head of the agency or organization. The report shall be available for a purpose that is consistent with this subchapter. The Secretary may only require reports on the use of such information by any State financial institutions supervisory agency for other than supervisory purposes or by United States intelligence agencies. However, a report and records of reports are exempt from disclosure under section 552 of title 5.".

(d) AMENDMENT RELATING TO THE PURPOSES OF THE BANK SECRECY ACT PROVISIONS. — Section 21(a) of the Federal Deposit Insurance Act (12 U.S.C. 1829b(a)) is amended to read as follows :

"(a) CONGRESSIONAL FINDINGS AND DECLARATION OF PURPOSE. —

"(1) FINDINGS. — Congress finds that —

"(A) adequate records maintained by insured depository institutions have a high degree of usefulness in criminal, tax, and regulatory investigations or proceedings, and that, given the threat posed to the security of the Nation on and after the terrorist attacks against the United States on September 11, 2001, such records may also have a high degree of usefulness in the conduct of intelligence or counterintelligence activities, including analysis, to protect against domestic and international terrorism; and

"(B) microfilm or other reproductions and other records made by insured depository institutions of checks, as well as records kept by such institutions, of the identity of persons maintaining or authorized to act with respect to accounts therein, have been of particular value in proceedings described in subparagraph (A).

"(2) PURPOSE. — It is the purpose of this section to require the maintenance of appropriate types of records by insured depository institutions in the United States where such records have a high degree of usefulness in criminal, tax, or regulatory investigations or proceedings, recognizes that, given the threat posed to the security of the Nation on and after the terrorist attacks against the United States on September 11, 2001, such records may also have a high degree of usefulness in the conduct of intelligence or counterintelligence activities, including analysis, to protect against international terrorism.".

(e) AMENDMENT RELATING TO THE PURPOSES OF THE BANK SECRECY ACT. — Section 123(a) of Public Law 91–508 (12 U.S.C. 1953(a)) is amended to read as follows :

"(a) REGULATIONS. — If the Secretary determines that the maintenance of appropriate records and procedures by any uninsured bank or uninsured institution, or any person engaging in the business of carrying on in the United States any of the functions referred to in subsection (b), has a high degree of usefulness in criminal, tax, or regulatory investigations or proceedings, and that, given the threat posed to the security of the Nation on and after the terrorist attacks against the United States on September 11, 2001, such records may also have a high degree of usefulness in the conduct of intelligence or counterintelligence activities, including analysis, to protect against international terrorism, he may by regulation require such bank, institution, or person.".

(f) AMENDMENTS TO THE RIGHT TO FINANCIAL PRIVACY ACT. — The Right to Financial Privacy Act of 1978 is amended —

(1) in section 1112(a) (12 U.S.C. 3412(a)), by inserting ", or intelligence or counterintelligence activity, investigation or analysis related to international terrorism" after "legitimate law enforcement inquiry";

(2) in section 1114(a)(1) (12 U.S.C. 3414(a)(1)) —

(A) in subparagraph (A), by striking "or" at the end;

(B) in subparagraph (B), by striking the period at the end and inserting "; or"; and

(C) by adding at the end the following :

"(C) a Government authority authorized to conduct investigations of, or intelligence or counterintelligence analyses related to, international terrorism for the purpose of conducting such investigations or analyses."; and

(3) in section 1120(a)(2) (12 U.S.C. 3420(a)(2)), by inserting ", or for a purpose authorized by section 1112(a)" before the semicolon at the end.

(g) AMENDMENT TO THE FAIR CREDIT REPORTING ACT. —

(1) IN GENERAL. — The Fair Credit Reporting Act (15 U.S.C. 1681 et seq.) is amended —

(A) by redesignating the second of the 2 sections designated as section 624 (15 U.S.C. 1681u) (relating to disclosure to FBI for counterintelligence purposes) as section 625; and

(B) by adding at the end the following new section :

"§ 626. Disclosures to governmental agencies for counterterrorism purposes

"(a) DISCLOSURE. — Notwithstanding section 604 or any other provision of this title, a consumer reporting agency shall furnish a consumer report of a consumer and all other information in a consumer's file to a government agency authorized to conduct investigations of, or intelligence or counterintelligence activities or analysis related to, international terrorism when presented with a written certification by such government agency that such information is necessary for the agency's conduct or such investigation, activity or analysis.

"(b) FORM OF CERTIFICATION. — The certification described in subsection (a) shall be signed by a supervisory official designated by the head of a Federal agency or an officer of a Federal agency whose appointment to office is required to be made by the President, by and with the advice and consent of the Senate.

"(c) CONFIDENTIALITY. — No consumer reporting agency, or officer, employee, or agent of such consumer reporting agency, shall disclose to any person, or specify in any consumer report, that a government agency has sought or obtained access to information under subsection (a).

"(d) RULE OF CONSTRUCTION. — Nothing in section 625 shall

be construed to limit the authority of the Director of the Federal Bureau of Investigation under this section.

"(e) SAFE HARBOR. — Notwithstanding any other provision of this title, any consumer reporting agency or agent or employee thereof making disclosure of consumer reports or other information pursuant to this section in good-faith reliance upon a certification of a governmental agency pursuant to the provisions of this section shall not be liable to any person for such disclosure under this subchapter, the constitution of any State, or any law or regulation of any State or any political subdivision of any State.".

(2) CLERICAL AMENDMENTS. — The table of sections for the Fair Credit Reporting Act (15 U.S.C. 1681 et seq.) is amended —

(A) by redesignating the second of the 2 items designated as section 624 as section 625; and

(B) by inserting after the item relating to section 625 (as so redesignated) the following new item :

"626. Disclosures to governmental agencies for counterterrorism purposes.".

(h) APPLICATION OF AMENDMENTS. — The amendments made by this section shall apply with respect to reports filed or records maintained on, before, or after the date of enactment of this Act.

SEC. 359. REPORTING OF SUSPICIOUS ACTIVITIES BY UNDERGROUND BANKING SYSTEMS.

(a) DEFINITION FOR SUBCHAPTER. — Section 5312(a)(2)(R) of title 31, United States Code, is amended to read as follows :

"(R) a licensed sender of money or any other person who engages as a business in the transmission of funds, including any person who engages as a business in an informal money transfer system or any network of people who engage as a business in facilitating the transfer of money domestically or internationally outside of the conventional financial institutions system;".

(b) MONEY TRANSMITTING BUSINESS. — Section 5330(d)(1)(A) of title 31, United States Code, is amended by inserting before the semicolon the following : "or any other person who engages as a business in the transmission of funds, including any person who engages as a business in an informal money transfer system or any network of people who engage as a business in facilitating the transfer of money domestically or internationally outside of the conventional financial institutions system;".

(c) APPLICABILITY OF RULES. — Section 5318 of title 31, United States Code, as amended by this title, is amended by adding at the end the following :

"(l) APPLICABILITY OF RULES. — Any rules promulgated pursuant to the authority contained in section 21 of the Federal Deposit Insurance Act (12 U.S.C. 1829b) shall apply, in addition to any other financial institution to which such rules apply, to any person that engages as a business in the transmission of funds, including any person who engages as a business in an informal money transfer system or any network of people who engage as a business in facilitating the transfer of money domestically or internationally outside of the conventional financial institutions system.".

(d) REPORT. — Not later than 1 year after the date of enactment of this Act, the Secretary of the Treasury shall report to Congress on the need for any additional legislation relating to persons who engage as a business in an informal money transfer system or any network of people who engage as a business in facilitating the transfer of money domestically or internationally outside of the conventional financial institutions system, counter money laundering and regulatory controls relating to underground money movement and banking systems, including whether the threshold for the filing of suspicious activity reports under section 5318(g) of title 31, United States Code should be lowered in the case of such systems.

SEC. 360. USE OF AUTHORITY OF UNITED STATES EXECUTIVE DIRECTORS.

(a) ACTION BY THE PRESIDENT. — If the President determines that a particular foreign country has taken or has committed to take actions that contribute to efforts of the United States to respond to, deter, or prevent acts of international terrorism, the Secretary may, consistent with other applicable provisions of law, instruct the United States Executive Director of each international financial institution to use the voice and vote of the Executive Director to support any loan or other utilization of the funds of respective institutions for such country, or any public or private entity within such country.

(b) USE OF VOICE AND VOTE. — The Secretary may instruct the United States Executive Director of each international financial institution to aggressively use the voice and vote of the Executive Director to require an auditing of disbursements at such institutions to ensure that no funds are paid to persons who commit, threaten to commit, or support terrorism.

(c) DEFINITION. — For purposes of this section, the term "inter-national financial institution" means an institution described in section 1701(c)(2) of the International Financial Institutions Act (22 U.S.C. 262r(c)(2)).

SEC. 361. FINANCIAL CRIMES ENFORCEMENT NETWORK.

(a) IN GENERAL. — Subchapter I of chapter 3 of title 31, United States Code, is amended —

(1) by redesignating section 310 as section 311; and

(2) by inserting after section 309 the following new section :

"§ 310. Financial Crimes Enforcement Network

"(a) IN GENERAL. — The Financial Crimes Enforcement Network established by order of the Secretary of the Treasury (Treasury Order Numbered 105-08, in this section referred to as 'FinCEN') on April 25, 1990, shall be a bureau in the Department of the Treasury.

"(b) DIRECTOR. —

"(1) APPOINTMENT. — The head of FinCEN shall be the Director, who shall be appointed by the Secretary of the Treasury.

"(2) DUTIES AND POWERS. — The duties and powers of the Director are as follows :

"(A) Advise and make recommendations on matters relating to financial intelligence, financial criminal activities, and other financial activities to the Under Secretary of the Treasury for Enforcement.

"(B) Maintain a government-wide data access service, with access, in accordance with applicable legal requirements, to the following :

"(i) Information collected by the Department of the Treasury, including report information filed under subchapter II of chapter 53 of this title (such as reports on cash transactions, foreign financial agency transactions and relationships, foreign currency transactions, exporting and importing monetary instruments, and suspicious activities), chapter 2 of title I of Public Law 91–508, and section 21 of the Federal Deposit Insurance Act.

"(ii) Information regarding national and international currency flows.

"(iii) Other records and data maintained by other Federal, State, local, and foreign agencies, including financial and other records developed in specific cases.

"(iv) Other privately and publicly available information.

"(C) Analyze and disseminate the available data in accordance with applicable legal requirements and policies and guidelines established by the Secretary of the Treasury and the Under Secretary of the Treasury for Enforcement to —

"(i) identify possible criminal activity to appropriate Federal, State, local, and foreign law enforcement agencies;

"(ii) support ongoing criminal financial investigations and prosecutions and related proceedings, including civil and criminal tax and forfeiture proceedings;

"(iii) identify possible instances of noncompliance with subchapter II of chapter 53 of this title, chapter 2 of title I of Public Law 91–508, and section 21 of the Federal Deposit Insurance Act to Federal agencies with statutory responsibility for enforcing compliance with such provisions and other appropriate Federal regulatory agencies;

"(iv) evaluate and recommend possible uses of special currency reporting requirements under section 5326;

"(v) determine emerging trends and methods in money laundering and other financial crimes;

"(vi) support the conduct of intelligence or counter-intelligence activities, including analysis, to protect against international terrorism; and

"(vii) support government initiatives against money laundering.

"(D) Establish and maintain a financial crimes communications center to furnish law enforcement authorities with intelligence information related to emerging or ongoing investigations and undercover operations.

"(E) Furnish research, analytical, and informational services to financial institutions, appropriate Federal regulatory agencies with regard to financial institutions, and appropriate Federal, State, local, and foreign law enforcement authorities, in accordance with policies and guidelines established by the Secretary of the Treasury or the Under Secretary of the Treasury for Enforcement, in the interest of detection, prevention, and prosecution of terrorism, organized crime, money laundering, and other financial crimes.

"(F) Assist Federal, State, local, and foreign law enforcement and regulatory authorities in combatting the use of informal, nonbank networks and payment and barter system mechanisms that permit the transfer of funds or the equivalent of funds without records and without compliance with criminal and tax laws.

"(G) Provide computer and data support and data analysis to the Secretary of the Treasury for tracking and controlling foreign assets.

"(H) Coordinate with financial intelligence units in other countries on anti-terrorism and anti-money laundering initiatives, and similar efforts.

"(I) Administer the requirements of subchapter II of chapter 53 of this title, chapter 2 of title I of Public Law 91–508, and section 21 of the Federal Deposit Insurance Act, to the extent delegated such authority by the Secretary of the Treasury.

"(J) Such other duties and powers as the Secretary of the Treasury may delegate or prescribe.

"(c) REQUIREMENTS RELATING TO MAINTENANCE AND USE OF DATA BANKS. — The Secretary of the Treasury shall establish and maintain operating procedures with respect to the government-wide data access service and the financial crimes communications center maintained by FinCEN which provide —

"(1) for the coordinated and efficient transmittal of information to, entry of information into, and withdrawal of information from, the data maintenance system maintained by the Network, including —

"(A) the submission of reports through the Internet or other secure network, whenever possible;

"(B) the cataloguing of information in a manner that facilitates rapid retrieval by law enforcement personnel of meaningful data; and

"(C) a procedure that provides for a prompt initial review of suspicious activity reports and other reports, or such other means as the Secretary may provide, to identify information that warrants immediate action; and

"(2) in accordance with section 552a of title 5 and the Right to Financial Privacy Act of 1978, appropriate standards and guidelines for determining —

"(A) who is to be given access to the information maintained by the Network;

"(B) what limits are to be imposed on the use of such information; and

"(C) how information about activities or relationships which involve or are closely associated with the exercise of constitutional rights is to be screened out of the data maintenance system.

"(d) AUTHORIZATION OF APPROPRIATIONS. — There are authorized to be appropriated for FinCEN such sums as may be necessary for fiscal years 2002, 2003, 2004, and 2005.".

(b) COMPLIANCE WITH REPORTING REQUIREMENTS. — The Secretary of the Treasury shall study methods for improving compliance with the reporting requirements established in section 5314 of title 31, United States Code, and shall submit a report on such study to the Congress by the end of the 6-month period beginning on the date of enactment of this Act and each 1-year period thereafter. The initial report shall include historical data on compliance with such reporting requirements.

(c) CLERICAL AMENDMENT. — The table of sections for subchapter I of chapter 3 of title 31, United States Code, is amended —

(1) by redesignating the item relating to section 310 as section 311; and

(2) by inserting after the item relating to section 309 the following new item :

"310. Financial Crimes Enforcement Network.".

SEC. 362. ESTABLISHMENT OF HIGHLY SECURE NETWORK.

(a) IN GENERAL. — The Secretary shall establish a highly secure network in the Financial Crimes Enforcement Network that —

(1) allows financial institutions to file reports required under subchapter II or III of chapter 53 of title 31, United States Code, chapter 2 of Public Law 91–508, or section 21 of the Federal Deposit Insurance Act through the secure network; and

(2) provides financial institutions with alerts and other

information regarding suspicious activities that warrant immediate and enhanced scrutiny.

(b) EXPEDITED DEVELOPMENT. — The Secretary shall take such action as may be necessary to ensure that the secure network required under subsection (a) is fully operational before the end of the 9-month period beginning on the date of enactment of this Act.

SEC. 363. INCREASE IN CIVIL AND CRIMINAL PENALTIES FOR MONEY LAUNDERING.

(a) CIVIL PENALTIES. — Section 5321(a) of title 31, United States Code, is amended by adding at the end the following :

"(7) PENALTIES FOR INTERNATIONAL COUNTER MONEY LAUNDERING VIOLATIONS. — The Secretary may impose a civil money penalty in an amount equal to not less than 2 times the amount of the transaction, but not more than $1,000,000, on any financial institution or agency that violates any provision of subsection (i) or (j) of section 5318 or any special measures imposed under section 5318A.".

(b) CRIMINAL PENALTIES. — Section 5322 of title 31, United States Code, is amended by adding at the end the following :

"(d) A financial institution or agency that violates any provision of subsection (i) or (j) of section 5318, or any special measures imposed under section 5318A, or any regulation prescribed under subsection (i) or (j) of section 5318 or section 5318A, shall be fined in an amount equal to not less than 2 times the amount of the transaction, but not more than $1,000,000.".

SEC. 364. UNIFORM PROTECTION AUTHORITY FOR FEDERAL RESERVE FACILITIES.

Section 11 of the Federal Reserve Act (12 U.S.C. 248) is amended by adding at the end the following :

"(q) UNIFORM PROTECTION AUTHORITY FOR FEDERAL RESERVE FACILITIES. —

"(1) Notwithstanding any other provision of law, to authorize personnel to act as law enforcement officers to protect and safeguard the premises, grounds, property, personnel, including members of the Board, of the Board, or any Federal reserve bank, and operations conducted by or on behalf of the Board or a reserve bank.

"(2) The Board may, subject to the regulations prescribed under paragraph (5), delegate authority to a Federal reserve bank to authorize personnel to act as law enforcement officers to protect and safeguard the bank's premises, grounds, property, personnel, and operations conducted by or on behalf of the bank.

"(3) Law enforcement officers designated or authorized by the Board or a reserve bank under paragraph (1) or (2) are authorized while on duty to carry firearms and make arrests without warrants for any offense against the United States committed in their presence, or for any felony cognizable under the laws of the United States committed or being committed within the buildings and grounds of the Board or a reserve bank if they have reasonable grounds to believe that the person to be arrested has committed or is committing such a felony. Such officers shall have access to law enforcement information that may be necessary for the protection of the property or personnel of the Board or a reserve bank.

"(4) For purposes of this subsection, the term 'law enforcement officers' means personnel who have successfully completed law enforcement training and are authorized to carry firearms and make arrests pursuant to this subsection.

"(5) The law enforcement authorities provided for in this subsection may be exercised only pursuant to regulations prescribed by the Board and approved by the Attorney General.".

SEC. 365. REPORTS RELATING TO COINS AND CURRENCY RECEIVED IN NONFINANCIAL TRADE OR BUSINESS.

(a) REPORTS REQUIRED. — Subchapter II of chapter 53 of title 31, United States Code, is amended by adding at the end the following new section :

"§ 5331. Reports relating to coins and currency received in nonfinancial trade or business

"(a) COIN AND CURRENCY RECEIPTS OF MORE THAN $10,000. — Any person —

"(1) who is engaged in a trade or business; and

"(2) who, in the course of such trade or business, receives more than $10,000 in coins or currency in 1 transaction (or 2 or more related transactions),

shall file a report described in subsection (b) with respect to such transaction (or related transactions) with the Financial Crimes Enforcement Network at such time and in such manner as the Secretary may, by regulation, prescribe.

"(b) FORM AND MANNER OF REPORTS. — A report is described in this subsection if such report —

"(1) is in such form as the Secretary may prescribe;

"(2) contains —

"(A) the name and address, and such other identification information as the Secretary may require, of the person from whom the coins or currency was received;

"(B) the amount of coins or currency received;

"(C) the date and nature of the transaction; and

"(D) such other information, including the identification of the person filing the report, as the Secretary may prescribe.

"(c) EXCEPTIONS. —

"(1) AMOUNTS RECEIVED BY FINANCIAL INSTITUTIONS. — Subsection (a) shall not apply to amounts received in a transaction reported under section 5313 and regulations prescribed under such section.

"(2) TRANSACTIONS OCCURRING OUTSIDE THE UNITED STATES. — Except to the extent provided in regulations prescribed by the Secretary, subsection (a) shall not apply to any transaction if the entire transaction occurs outside the United States.

"(d) CURRENCY INCLUDES FOREIGN CURRENCY AND CERTAIN MONETARY INSTRUMENTS. —

"(1) IN GENERAL. — For purposes of this section, the term 'currency' includes —

"(A) foreign currency; and

"(B) to the extent provided in regulations prescribed by the Secretary, any monetary instrument (whether or not in bearer form) with a face amount of not more than $10,000.

"(2) SCOPE OF APPLICATION. — Paragraph (1)(B) shall not apply to any check drawn on the account of the writer in a financial institution referred to in subparagraph (A), (B), (C), (D), (E), (F), (G), (J), (K), (R), or (S) of section 5312(a)(2).".

(b) PROHIBITION ON STRUCTURING TRANSACTIONS. —

(1) IN GENERAL. — Section 5324 of title 31, United States Code, is amended —

(A) by redesignating subsections (b) and (c) as subsections (c) and (d), respectively; and

(B) by inserting after subsection (a) the following new subsection :

"(b) DOMESTIC COIN AND CURRENCY TRANSACTIONS INVOLVING NONFINANCIAL TRADES OR BUSINESSES. — No person shall, for the purpose of evading the report requirements of section 5333 or any regulation prescribed under such section —

"(1) cause or attempt to cause a nonfinancial trade or business to fail to file a report required under section 5333 or any regulation prescribed under such section;

"(2) cause or attempt to cause a nonfinancial trade or business to file a report required under section 5333 or any regulation prescribed under such section that contains a material omission or misstatement of fact; or

"(3) structure or assist in structuring, or attempt to structure or assist in structuring, any transaction with 1 or more nonfinancial trades or businesses.".

(2) TECHNICAL AND CONFORMING AMENDMENTS. —

(A) The heading for subsection (a) of section 5324 of title 31, United States Code, is amended by inserting "INVOLVING FINANCIAL INSTITUTIONS" after "TRANSACTIONS".

(B) Section 5317(c) of title 31, United States Code, is amended by striking "5324(b)" and inserting "5324(c)".

(c) DEFINITION OF NONFINANCIAL TRADE OR BUSINESS. —

(1) IN GENERAL. — Section 5312(a) of title 31, United States Code, is amended —

(A) by redesignating paragraphs (4) and (5) as paragraphs (5) and (6), respectively; and

(B) by inserting after paragraph (3) the following new paragraph :

"(4) NONFINANCIAL TRADE OR BUSINESS. — The term 'nonfinancial trade or business' means any trade or business other than a financial institution that is subject to the reporting requirements of section 5313 and regulations prescribed under such section.".

(2) TECHNICAL AND CONFORMING AMENDMENTS. —

(A) Section 5312(a)(3)(C) of title 31, United States Code, is amended by striking "section 5316," and inserting "sections 5333 and 5316,".

(B) Subsections (a) through (f) of section 5318 of title 31, United States Code, and sections 5321, 5326, and 5328 of such title are each amended —

(i) by inserting "or nonfinancial trade or business" after "financial institution" each place such term appears; and

(ii) by inserting "or nonfinancial trades or businesses" after "financial institutions" each place such term appears.

(c) CLERICAL AMENDMENT. — The table of sections for chapter 53 of title 31, United States Code, is amended by inserting after the item relating to section 5332 (as added by section 112 of this title) the following new item :

"5331. Reports relating to coins and currency received in nonfinancial trade or business.".

(f) REGULATIONS. — Regulations which the Secretary determines are necessary to implement this section shall be published in final form before the end of the 6-month period beginning on the date of enactment of this Act.

SEC. 366. EFFICIENT USE OF CURRENCY TRANSACTION REPORT SYSTEM.

(a) FINDINGS. — The Congress finds the following :

(1) The Congress established the currency transaction reporting requirements in 1970 because the Congress found then that such reports have a high degree of usefulness in criminal, tax, and regulatory investigations and proceedings and the usefulness of such reports has only increased in the years since the requirements were established.

(2) In 1994, in response to reports and testimony that excess amounts of currency transaction reports were interfering with effective law enforcement, the Congress reformed the currency transaction report exemption requirements to provide —

(A) mandatory exemptions for certain reports that had little usefulness for law enforcement, such as cash transfers between depository institutions and cash deposits from government agencies; and

(B) discretionary authority for the Secretary of the Treasury to provide exemptions, subject to criteria and guidelines established by the Secretary, for financial institutions with regard to regular business customers that maintain accounts at an institution into which frequent cash deposits are made.

(3) Today there is evidence that some financial institutions are not utilizing the exemption system, or are filing reports even if there is an exemption in effect, with the result that the volume of currency transaction reports is once again interfering with effective law enforcement.

(b) STUDY AND REPORT. —

(1) STUDY REQUIRED. — The Secretary shall conduct a study of —

(A) the possible expansion of the statutory exemption

system in effect under section 5313 of title 31, United States Code; and

(B) methods for improving financial institution utilization of the statutory exemption provisions as a way of reducing the submission of currency transaction reports that have little or no value for law enforcement purposes, including improvements in the systems in effect at financial institutions for regular review of the exemption procedures used at the institution and the training of personnel in its effective use.

(2) REPORT REQUIRED. — The Secretary of the Treasury shall submit a report to the Congress before the end of the 1-year period beginning on the date of enactment of this Act containing the findings and conclusions of the Secretary with regard to the study required under subsection (a), and such recommendations for legislative or administrative action as the Secretary determines to be appropriate.

Subtitle C — Currency Crimes and Protection

SEC. 371. BULK CASH SMUGGLING INTO OR OUT OF THE UNITED STATES.

(a) FINDINGS. — The Congress finds the following :

(1) Effective enforcement of the currency reporting requirements of subchapter II of chapter 53 of title 31, United States Code, and the regulations prescribed under such subchapter, has forced drug dealers and other criminals engaged in cashbased businesses to avoid using traditional financial institutions.

(2) In their effort to avoid using traditional financial institutions, drug dealers and other criminals are forced to move large quantities of currency in bulk form to and through the airports, border crossings, and other ports of entry where the currency can be smuggled out of the United States and placed in a foreign financial institution or sold on the black market.

(3) The transportation and smuggling of cash in bulk form may now be the most common form of money

laundering, and the movement of large sums of cash is one of the most reliable warning signs of drug trafficking, terrorism, money laundering, racketeering, tax evasion and similar crimes.

(4) The intentional transportation into or out of the United States of large amounts of currency or monetary instruments, in a manner designed to circumvent the mandatory reporting provisions of subchapter II of chapter 53 of title 31, United States Code,, is the equivalent of, and creates the same harm as, the smuggling of goods.

(5) The arrest and prosecution of bulk cash smugglers are important parts of law enforcement's effort to stop the laundering of criminal proceeds, but the couriers who attempt to smuggle the cash out of the United States are typically low-level employees of large criminal organizations, and thus are easily replaced. Accordingly, only the confiscation of the smuggled bulk cash can effectively break the cycle of criminal activity of which the laundering of the bulk cash is a critical part.

(6) The current penalties for violations of the currency reporting requirements are insufficient to provide a deterrent to the laundering of criminal proceeds. In particular, in cases where the only criminal violation under current law is a reporting offense, the law does not adequately provide for the confiscation of smuggled currency. In contrast, if the smuggling of bulk cash were itself an offense, the cash could be confiscated as the corpus delicti of the smuggling offense.

(b) PURPOSES. — The purposes of this section are —

(1) to make the act of smuggling bulk cash itself a criminal offense;

(2) to authorize forfeiture of any cash or instruments of the smuggling offense; and

(3) to emphasize the seriousness of the act of bulk cash smuggling.

(c) ENACTMENT OF BULK CASH SMUGGLING OFFENSE. — Subchapter II of chapter 53 of title 31, United States Code, is amended by adding at the end the following :

"§ 5332. Bulk cash smuggling into or out of the United States

"(a) CRIMINAL OFFENSE. —

"(1) IN GENERAL. — Whoever, with the intent to evade a currency reporting requirement under section 5316, knowingly conceals more than $10,000 in currency or other monetary instruments on the person of such individual or in any conveyance, article of luggage, merchandise, or other container, and transports or transfers or attempts to transport or transfer such currency or monetary instruments from a place within the United States to a place outside of the United States, or from a place outside the United States to a place within the United States, shall be guilty of a currency smuggling offense and subject to punishment pursuant to subsection (b).

"(2) CONCEALMENT ON PERSON. — For purposes of this section, the concealment of currency on the person of any individual includes concealment in any article of clothing worn by the individual or in any luggage, backpack, or other container worn or carried by such individual.

"(b) PENALTY. —

"(1) TERM OF IMPRISONMENT. — A person convicted of a currency smuggling offense under subsection (a), or a conspiracy to commit such offense, shall be imprisoned for not more than 5 years.

"(2) FORFEITURE. — In addition, the court, in imposing sentence under paragraph (1), shall order that the defendant forfeit to the United States, any property, real or personal, involved in the offense, and any property traceable to such property, subject to subsection (d) of this section.

"(3) PROCEDURE. — The seizure, restraint, and forfeiture of property under this section shall be governed by section 413 of the Controlled Substances Act.

"(4) PERSONAL MONEY JUDGMENT. — If the property subject to forfeiture under paragraph (2) is unavailable, and the defendant has insufficient substitute property that may be forfeited pursuant to section 413(p) of the Controlled Substances Act, the court shall enter a personal money judgment against the defendant for the amount that would be subject to forfeiture.

"(c) CIVIL FORFEITURE. —

"(1) IN GENERAL. — Any property involved in a violation of subsection (a), or a conspiracy to commit such violation, and any property traceable to such violation or conspiracy, may be seized and, subject to subsection (d) of this section, forfeited to the United States.

"(2) PROCEDURE. — The seizure and forfeiture shall be governed by the procedures governing civil forfeitures in money laundering cases pursuant to section 981(a)(1)(A) of title 18, United States Code.

"(3) TREATMENT OF CERTAIN PROPERTY AS INVOLVED IN THE OFFENSE. — For purposes of this subsection and subsection (b), any currency or other monetary instrument that is concealed or intended to be concealed in violation of subsection (a) or a conspiracy to commit such violation, any article, container, or conveyance used, or intended to be used, to conceal or transport the currency or other monetary instrument, and any other property used, or intended to be used, to facilitate the offense, shall be considered property involved in the offense.".

(c) CLERICAL AMENDMENT. — The table of sections for subchapter II of chapter 53 of title 31, United States Code, is amended by inserting after the item relating to section 5331, as added by this Act, the following new item :

"5332. Bulk cash smuggling into or out of the United States.".

SEC. 372. FORFEITURE IN CURRENCY REPORTING CASES.

(a) IN GENERAL. — Subsection (c) of section 5317 of title 31, United States Code, is amended to read as follows :

"(c) FORFEITURE. —

"(1) CRIMINAL FORFEITURE. —

"(A) IN GENERAL. — The court in imposing sentence for any violation of section 5313, 5316, or 5324 of this title, or any conspiracy to commit such violation, shall order the defendant to forfeit all property, real or personal, involved in the offense and any property traceable thereto.

"(B) PROCEDURE. — Forfeitures under this paragraph shall be governed by the procedures established in section 413 of the Controlled Substances Act.

"(2) CIVIL FORFEITURE. — Any property involved in a violation of section 5313, 5316, or 5324 of this title, or any conspiracy to commit any such violation, and any property traceable to any such violation or conspiracy, may be seized and forfeited to the United States in accordance with the procedures governing civil forfeitures in money laundering cases pursuant to section 981(a)(1)(A) of title 18, United States Code.".

(b) CONFORMING AMENDMENTS. —

(1) Section 981(a)(1)(A) of title 18, United States Code, is amended —

(A) by striking "of section 5313(a) or 5324(a) of title 31, or"; and

(B) by striking "However" and all that follows through the end of the subparagraph.

(2) Section 982(a)(1) of title 18, United States Code, is amended —

(A) by striking "of section 5313(a), 5316, or 5324 of title 31, or"; and

(B) by striking "However" and all that follows through the end of the paragraph.

SEC. 373. ILLEGAL MONEY TRANSMITTING BUSINESSES.

(a) SCIENTER REQUIREMENT FOR SECTION 1960 VIOLATION. — Section 1960 of title 18, United States Code, is amended to read as follows :

"§ 1960. Prohibition of unlicensed money transmitting businesses

"(a) Whoever knowingly conducts, controls, manages, supervises, directs, or owns all or part of an unlicensed money transmitting business, shall be fined in accordance with this title or imprisoned not more than 5 years, or both.

"(b) As used in this section —

"(1) the term 'unlicensed money transmitting business' means a money transmitting business which affects interstate or foreign commerce in any manner or degree and —

"(A) is operated without an appropriate money transmitting license in a State where such operation is punishable as a misdemeanor or a felony under State law, whether or not the defendant knew that the operation was required to be licensed or that the operation was so punishable;

"(B) fails to comply with the money transmitting business registration requirements under section 5330 of title 31, United States Code, or regulations prescribed under such section; or

"(C) otherwise involves the transportation or transmission of funds that are known to the defendant to have been derived from a criminal offense or are intended to be used to be used to promote or support unlawful activity;

"(2) the term 'money transmitting' includes transferring funds on behalf of the public by any and all means including but not limited to transfers within this country or to locations abroad by wire, check, draft, facsimile, or courier; and

"(3) the term 'State' means any State of the United States, the District of Columbia, the Northern Mariana Islands, and any commonwealth, territory, or possession of the United States.".

(b) SEIZURE OF ILLEGALLY TRANSMITTED FUNDS. — Section 981(a)(1)(A) of title 18, United States Code, is amended by striking "or 1957" and inserting ", 1957 or 1960".

(c) CLERICAL AMENDMENT. — The table of sections for chapter 95 of title 18, United States Code, is amended in the item relating to section 1960 by striking "illegal" and inserting "unlicensed".

SEC. 374. COUNTERFEITING DOMESTIC CURRENCY AND OBLIGATIONS.

(a) COUNTERFEIT ACTS COMMITTED OUTSIDE THE UNITED

STATES. — Section 470 of title 18, United States Code, is amended —

(1) in paragraph (2), by inserting "analog, digital, or electronic image," after "plate, stone,"; and

(2) by striking "shall be fined under this title, imprisoned not more than 20 years, or both" and inserting "shall be punished as is provided for the like offense within the United States".

(b) OBLIGATIONS OR SECURITIES OF THE UNITED STATES. — Section 471 of title 18, United States Code, is amended by striking "fifteen years" and inserting "20 years".

(c) UTTERING COUNTERFEIT OBLIGATIONS OR SECURITIES. — Section 472 of title 18, United States Code, is amended by striking "fifteen years" and inserting "20 years".

(d) DEALING IN COUNTERFEIT OBLIGATIONS OR SECURITIES. — Section 473 of title 18, United States Code, is amended by striking "ten years" and inserting "20 years".

(e) PLATES, STONES, OR ANALOG, DIGITAL, OR ELECTRONIC IMAGES FOR COUNTERFEITING OBLIGATIONS OR SECURITIES. —

(1) IN GENERAL. — Section 474(a) of title 18, United States Code, is amended by inserting after the second paragraph the following new paragraph :

"Whoever, with intent to defraud, makes, executes, acquires, scans, captures, records, receives, transmits, reproduces, sells, or has in such person's control, custody, or possession, an analog, digital, or electronic image of any obligation or other security of the United States; or".

(2) AMENDMENT TO DEFINITION. — Section 474(b) of title 18, United States Code, is amended by striking the first sentence and inserting the following new sentence : "For purposes of this section, the term 'analog, digital, or electronic image' includes any analog, digital, or electronic method used for the making, execution, acquisition, scanning, capturing, recording, retrieval, transmission, or reproduction of any obligation or security, unless such use is authorized by the Secretary of the Treasury.".

(3) TECHNICAL AND CONFORMING AMENDMENT. — The heading for section 474 of title 18, United States Code, is amended by striking "or stones" and inserting ", stones, or analog, digital, or electronic images".

(4) CLERICAL AMENDMENT. — The table of sections for chapter 25 of title 18, United States Code, is amended in the item relating to section 474 by striking "or stones" and inserting ", stones, or analog, digital, or electronic images".

(f) TAKING IMPRESSIONS OF TOOLS USED FOR OBLIGATIONS OR SECURITIES. — Section 476 of title 18, United States Code, is amended —

(1) by inserting "analog, digital, or electronic image," after "impression, stamp,"; and

(2) by striking "ten years" and inserting "25 years".

(g) POSSESSING OR SELLING IMPRESSIONS OF TOOLS USED FOR OBLIGATIONS OR SECURITIES. — Section 477 of title 18, United States Code, is amended —

(1) in the first paragraph, by inserting "analog, digital, or electronic image," after "imprint, stamp,";

(2) in the second paragraph, by inserting "analog, digital, or electronic image," after "imprint, stamp,"; and

(3) in the third paragraph, by striking "ten years" and inserting "25 years".

(h) CONNECTING PARTS OF DIFFERENT NOTES. — Section 484 of title 18, United States Code, is amended by striking "five years" and inserting "10 years".

(i) BONDS AND OBLIGATIONS OF CERTAIN LENDING AGENCIES. — The first and second paragraphs of section 493 of title 18, United States Code, are each amended by striking "five years" and inserting "10 years"

SEC. 375. COUNTERFEITING FOREIGN CURRENCY AND OBLIGATIONS.

(a) FOREIGN OBLIGATIONS OR SECURITIES. — Section 478 of title 18, United States Code, is amended by striking "five years" and inserting "20 years".

(b) UTTERING COUNTERFEIT FOREIGN OBLIGATIONS OR SECURITIES. — Section 479 of title 18, United States

Code, is amended by striking "three years" and inserting "20 years".

(c) POSSESSING COUNTERFEIT FOREIGN OBLIGATIONS OR SECURITIES. — Section 480 of title 18, United States Code, is amended by striking "one year" and inserting "20 years".

(d) PLATES, STONES, OR ANALOG, DIGITAL, OR ELECTRONIC IMAGES FOR COUNTERFEITING FOREIGN OBLIGATIONS OR SECURITIES. —

(1) IN GENERAL. — Section 481 of title 18, United States Code, is amended by inserting after the second paragraph the following new paragraph :

"Whoever, with intent to defraud, makes, executes, acquires, scans, captures, records, receives, transmits, reproduces, sells, or has in such person's control, custody, or possession, an analog, digital, or electronic image of any bond, certificate, obligation, or other security of any foreign government, or of any treasury note, bill, or promise to pay, lawfully issued by such foreign government and intended to circulate as money; or".

(2) INCREASED SENTENCE. — The last paragraph of section 481 of title 18, United States Code, is amended by striking "five years" and inserting "25 years".

(3) TECHNICAL AND CONFORMING AMENDMENT. — The heading for section 481 of title 18, United States Code, is amended by striking "**or stones**" and inserting "**, stones, or analog, digital, or electronic images**".

(4) CLERICAL AMENDMENT. — The table of sections for chapter 25 of title 18, United States Code, is amended in the item relating to section 481 by striking "or stones" and inserting ", stones, or analog, digital, or electronic images".

(e) FOREIGN BANK NOTES. — Section 482 of title 18, United States Code, is amended by striking "two years" and inserting "20 years".

(f) UTTERING COUNTERFEIT FOREIGN BANK NOTES. — Section 483 of title 18, United States Code, is amended by striking "one year" and inserting "20 years".

SEC. 376. LAUNDERING THE PROCEEDS OF TERRORISM.

Section 1956(c)(7)(D) of title 18, United States Code, is amended by inserting "or 2339B" after "2339A".

SEC. 377. EXTRATERRITORIAL JURISDICTION.

Section 1029 of title 18, United States Code, is amended by adding at the end the following :

"(h) Any person who, outside the jurisdiction of the United States, engages in any act that, if committed within the jurisdiction of the United States, would constitute an offense under subsection (a) or (b) of this section, shall be subject to the fines, penalties, imprisonment, and forfeiture provided in this title if —

"(1) the offense involves an access device issued, owned, managed, or controlled by a financial institution, account issuer, credit card system member, or other entity within the jurisdiction of the United States; and

"(2) the person transports, delivers, conveys, transfers to or through, or otherwise stores, secrets, or holds within the jurisdiction of the United States, any article used to assist in the commission of the offense or the proceeds of such offense or property derived therefrom.".

TITLE IV — PROTECTING THE BORDER

Subtitle A — Protecting the Northern Border

SEC. 401. ENSURING ADEQUATE PERSONNEL ON THE NORTHERN BORDER.

The Attorney General is authorized to waive any FTE cap on personnel assigned to the Immigration and Naturalization Service on the Northern border.

SEC. 402. NORTHERN BORDER PERSONNEL.

There are authorized to be appropriated —

(1) such sums as may be necessary to triple the number of Border Patrol personnel (from the number authorized under current law), and the necessary personnel and facilities to

support such personnel, in each State along the Northern Border;

(2) such sums as may be necessary to triple the number of Customs Service personnel (from the number authorized under current law), and the necessary personnel and facilities to support such personnel, at ports of entry in each State along the Northern Border;

(3) such sums as may be necessary to triple the number of INS inspectors (from the number authorized on the date of the enactment of this Act), and the necessary personnel and facilities to support such personnel, at ports of entry in each State along the Northern Border; and

(4) an additional $50,000,000 each to the Immigration and Naturalization Service and the United States Customs Service for purposes of making improvements in technology for monitoring the Northern Border and acquiring additional equipment at the Northern Border.

SEC. 403. ACCESS BY THE DEPARTMENT OF STATE AND THE INS TO CERTAIN IDENTIFYING INFORMATION IN THE CRIMINAL HISTORY RECORDS OF VISA APPLICANTS AND APPLICANTS FOR ADMISSION TO THE UNITED STATES.

(a) AMENDMENT OF THE IMMIGRATION AND NATIONALITY ACT. — Section 105 of the Immigration and Nationality Act (8 U.S.C. 1105) is amended —

(1) in the section heading, by inserting "; DATA EXCHANGE" after "SECURITY OFFICERS";

(2) by inserting "(a)" after "SEC. 105.";

(3) in subsection (a), by inserting "and border" after "internal" the second place it appears; and

(4) by adding at the end the following :

"(b) (1) The Attorney General and the Director of the Federal Bureau of Investigation shall provide the Department of State and the Service access to the criminal history record information contained in the National Crime Information Center's Interstate Identification Index (NCIC-III), Wanted Persons File, and to any other files maintained by the National Crime Information Center that may be mutually agreed upon by the Attorney General and the agency receiving the access, for the purpose of determining whether or not a visa applicant or applicant for admission has a criminal history record indexed in any such file.

"(2) Such access shall be provided by means of extracts of the records for placement in the automated visa lookout or other appropriate database, and shall be provided without any fee or charge.

"(3) The Federal Bureau of Investigation shall provide periodic updates of the extracts at intervals mutually agreed upon with the agency receiving the access. Upon receipt of such updated extracts, the receiving agency shall make corresponding updates to its database and destroy previously provided extracts.

"(4) Access to an extract does not entitle the Department of State to obtain the full content of the corresponding automated criminal history record. To obtain the full content of a criminal history record, the Department of State shall submit the applicant's fingerprints and any appropriate fingerprint processing fee authorized by law to the Criminal Justice Information Services Division of the Federal Bureau of Investigation.

"(c) The provision of the extracts described in subsection (b) may be reconsidered by the Attorney General and the receiving agency upon the development and deployment of a more costeffective and efficient means of sharing the information.

"(d) For purposes of administering this section, the Department of State shall, prior to receiving access to NCIC data but not later than 4 months after the date of enactment of this subsection, promulgate final regulations —

"(1) to implement procedures for the taking of fingerprints; and

"(2) to establish the conditions for the use of the information received from the Federal Bureau of Investigation, in order —

"(A) to limit the redissemination of such information;

"(B) to ensure that such information is used solely to

determine whether or not to issue a visa to an alien or to admit an alien to the United States;

"(C) to ensure the security, confidentiality, and destruction of such information; and

"(D) to protect any privacy rights of individuals who are subjects of such information.".

(b) REPORTING REQUIREMENT. — Not later than 2 years after the date of enactment of this Act, the Attorney General and the Secretary of State jointly shall report to Congress on the implementation of the amendments made by this section.

(c) TECHNOLOGY STANDARD TO CONFIRM IDENTITY. —

(1) IN GENERAL. — The Attorney General and the Secretary of State jointly, through the National Institute of Standards and Technology (NIST), and in consultation with the Secretary of the Treasury and other Federal law enforcement and intelligence agencies the Attorney General or Secretary of State deems appropriate and in consultation with Congress, shall within 2 years after the date of the enactment of this section, develop and certify a technology standard that can be used to verify the identity of persons applying for a United States visa or such persons seeking to enter the United States pursuant to a visa for the purposes of conducting background checks, confirming identity, and ensuring that a person has not received a visa under a different name or such person seeking to enter the United States pursuant to a visa.

(2) INTEGRATED. — The technology standard developed pursuant to paragraph (1), shall be the technological basis for a cross-agency, cross-platform electronic system that is a cost-effective, efficient, fully integrated means to share law enforcement and intelligence information necessary to confirm the identity of such persons applying for a United States visa or such person seeking to enter the United States pursuant to a visa.

(3) ACCESSIBLE. — The electronic system described in paragraph (2), once implemented, shall be readily and easily accessible to —

(A) all consular officers responsible for the issuance of visas;

(B) all Federal inspection agents at all United States border inspection points; and

(C) all law enforcement and intelligence officers as determined by regulation to be responsible for investigation or identification of aliens admitted to the United States pursuant to a visa.

(4) REPORT. — Not later than 18 months after the date of the enactment of this Act, and every 2 years thereafter, the Attorney General and the Secretary of State shall jointly, in consultation with the Secretary of Treasury, report to Congress describing the development, implementation, efficacy, and privacy implications of the technology standard and electronic database system described in this subsection.

(5) FUNDING. — There is authorized to be appropriated to the Secretary of State, the Attorney General, and the Director of the National Institute of Standards and Technology such sums as may be necessary to carry out the provisions of this subsection.

(d) STATUTORY CONSTRUCTION. — Nothing in this section, or in any other law, shall be construed to limit the authority of the Attorney General or the Director of the Federal Bureau of Investigation to provide access to the criminal history record information contained in the National Crime Information Center's (NCIC) Interstate Identification Index (NCIC-III), or to any other information maintained by the NCIC, to any Federal agency or officer authorized to enforce or administer the immigration laws of the United States, for the purpose of such enforcement or administration, upon terms that are consistent with the National Crime Prevention and Privacy Compact Act of 1998 (subtitle A of title II of Public Law 105–251; 42 U.S.C. 14611–16) and section 552a of title 5, United States Code.

SEC. 404. LIMITED AUTHORITY TO PAY OVERTIME.

The matter under the headings "Immigration And Naturalization Service : Salaries and Expenses, Enforcement And Border Affairs" and "Immigration And Naturalization Service : Salaries and Expenses, Citizenship And Benefits, Immigration And Program Direction" in the Department of Justice Appropriations Act, 2001 (as enacted into law by Appendix B (H.R. 5548) of Public Law 106–553 (114 Stat. 2762A–58 to 2762A–59)) is amended by striking the following each place it occurs : "*Provide*d, That none of the funds available to the Immigration and Naturalization Service shall be available to pay any employee overtime pay in an amount in excess of $30,000 during the calendar year beginning January 1, 2001 :".

SEC. 405. REPORT ON THE INTEGRATED AUTOMATED FINGERPRINT IDENTIFICATION SYSTEM FOR PORTS OF ENTRY AND OVERSEAS CONSULAR POSTS.

(a) IN GENERAL. — The Attorney General, in consultation with the appropriate heads of other Federal agencies, including the Secretary of State, Secretary of the Treasury, and the Secretary of Transportation, shall report to Congress on the feasibility of enhancing the Integrated Automated Fingerprint Identification System (IAFIS) of the Federal Bureau of Investigation and other identification systems in order to better identify a person who holds a foreign passport or a visa and may be wanted in connection with a criminal investigation in the United States or abroad, before the issuance of a visa to that person or the entry or exit from the United States by that person.

(b) AUTHORIZATION OF APPROPRIATIONS. — There is authorized to be appropriated not less than $2,000,000 to carry out this section.

Subtitle B — Enhanced Immigration Provisions

SEC. 411. DEFINITIONS RELATING TO TERRORISM.

(a) GROUNDS OF INADMISSIBILITY. — Section 212(a)(3) of the Immigration and Nationality Act (8 U.S.C. 1182(a)(3)) is amended —

(1) in subparagraph (B) —

(A) in clause (i) —

(i) by amending subclause (IV) to read as follows :

"(IV) is a representative (as defined in clause (v)) of —

"(aa) a foreign terrorist organization, as designated by the Secretary of State under section 219, or

"(bb) a political, social or other similar group whose public endorsement of acts of terrorist activity the Secretary of State has determined undermines United States efforts to reduce or eliminate terrorist activities,";

(ii) in subclause (V), by inserting "or" after "section 219,"; and

(iii) by adding at the end the following new subclauses :

"(VI) has used the alien's position of prominence within any country to endorse or espouse terrorist activity, or to persuade others to support terrorist activity or a terrorist organization, in a way that the Secretary of State has determined undermines United States efforts to reduce or eliminate terrorist activities, or

"(VII) is the spouse or child of an alien who is inadmissible under this section, if the activity causing the alien to be found inadmissible occurred within the last 5 years,";

(B) by redesignating clauses (ii), (iii), and (iv) as clauses (iii), (iv), and (v), respectively;

(C) in clause (i)(II), by striking "clause (iii)" and inserting "clause (iv)";

(D) by inserting after clause (i) the following :

"(ii) EXCEPTION. — Subclause (VII) of clause (i) does not apply to a spouse or child —

"(I) who did not know or should not reasonably have known of the activity causing the alien to be found inadmissible under this section; or

"(II) whom the consular officer or Attorney General has reasonable grounds to believe has renounced the activity causing the alien to be found inadmissible under this section.";

(E) in clause (iii) (as redesignated by subparagraph (B)) —

(i) by inserting "it had been" before "committed in the United States"; and

(ii) in subclause (V)(b), by striking "or firearm" and inserting ", firearm, or other weapon or dangerous device";

(F) by amending clause (iv) (as redesignated by subparagraph (B)) to read as follows :

"(iv) ENGAGE IN TERRORIST ACTIVITY DEFINED. — As used in this chapter, the term 'engage in terrorist activity' means, in an individual capacity or as a member of an organization —

"(I) to commit or to incite to commit, under circumstances indicating an intention to cause death or serious bodily injury, a terrorist activity;

"(II) to prepare or plan a terrorist activity;

"(III) to gather information on potential targets for terrorist activity;

"(IV) to solicit funds or other things of value for —

"(aa) a terrorist activity;

"(bb) a terrorist organization described in clause (vi)(I) or (vi)(II); or

"(cc) a terrorist organization described in clause (vi)(III), unless the solicitor can demonstrate that he did not know, and should not reasonably have known, that the solicitation would further the organization's terrorist activity;

"(V) to solicit any individual —

"(aa) to engage in conduct otherwise described in this clause;

"(bb) for membership in a terrorist organization described in clausc (vi)(I) or (vi)(II); or

"(cc) for membership in a terrorist organization described in clause (vi)(III), unless the solicitor can demonstrate that he did not know, and should not reasonably have known, that the solicitation would further the organization's terrorist activity; or

"(VI) to commit an act that the actor knows, or reasonably should know, affords material support, including a safe house, transportation, communications, funds, transfer of funds or other material financial benefit, false documentation or identification, weapons (including chemical, biological, or radiological weapons), explosives, or training —

"(aa) for the commission of a terrorist activity;

"(bb) to any individual who the actor knows, or reasonably should know, has committed or plans to commit a terrorist activity;

"(cc) to a terrorist organization described in clause (vi)(I) or (vi)(II); or

"(dd) to a terrorist organization described in clause (vi)(III), unless the actor can demonstrate that he did not know, and should not reasonably have known, that the act would further the organization's terrorist activity.

This clause shall not apply to any material support the alien afforded to an organization or individual that has committed terrorist activity, if the Secretary of State, after consultation with the Attorney General, or the Attorney General, after consultation with the Secretary of State, concludes in his sole unreviewable discretion, that this clause should not apply."; and

(G) by adding at the end the following new clause :

"(vi) TERRORIST ORGANIZATION DEFINED. — As used in clause (i)(VI) and clause (iv), the term 'terrorist organization' means an organization —

"(I) designated under section 219;

"(II) otherwise designated, upon publication in the Federal Register, by the Secretary of State in consultation with or upon the request of the Attorney General, as a terrorist organization, after finding that the organization engages in the activities described in subclause (I), (II), or (III) of clause (iv), or that the organization provides material support to further terrorist activity; or

"(III) that is a group of two or more individuals, whether organized or not, which engages in the activities described in subclause (I), (II), or (III) of clause (iv)."; and

(2) by adding at the end the following new sub-paragraph :

"(F) ASSOCIATION WITH TERRORIST ORGANIZATIONS. — Any alien who the Secretary of State, after consultation with the Attorney General, or the Attorney General, after consultation with the Secretary of State, determines has been associated with a terrorist organization and intends while in the United States to engage solely, principally, or incidentally in activities that could endanger the welfare, safety, or security of the United States is inadmissible.".

(b) CONFORMING AMENDMENTS. —

(1) Section 237(a)(4)(B) of the Immigration and Nationality Act (8 U.S.C. 1227(a)(4)(B)) is amended by striking "section 212(a)(3)(B)(iii)" and inserting "section 212(a)(3)(B)(iv)".

(2) Section 208(b)(2)(A)(v) of the Immigration and Nationality Act (8 U.S.C. 1158(b)(2)(A)(v)) is amended by striking "or (IV)" and inserting "(IV), or (VI)".

(c) RETROACTIVE APPLICATION OF AMENDMENTS. —

(1) IN GENERAL. — Except as otherwise provided in this subsection, the amendments made by this section shall take effect on the date of the enactment of this Act and shall apply to —

(A) actions taken by an alien before, on, or after such date; and

(B) all aliens, without regard to the date of entry or attempted entry into the United States —

(i) in removal proceedings on or after such date (except for proceedings in which there has been a final administrative decision before such date); or

(ii) seeking admission to the United States on or after such date.

(2) SPECIAL RULE FOR ALIENS IN EXCLUSION OR DEPORTATION PROCEEDINGS. — Notwithstanding any other provision of law, sections 212(a)(3)(B) and 237(a)(4)(B) of the Immigration and Nationality Act, as amended by this Act, shall apply to all aliens in exclusion or deportation proceedings on or after the date of the enactment of this Act (except for proceedings in which there has been a final administrative decision before such date) as if such proceedings were removal proceedings.

(3) SPECIAL RULE FOR SECTION 219 ORGANIZATIONS AND

ORGANIZATIONS DESIGNATED UNDER SECTION 212(a)(3)(B)(vi)(II). —

(A) IN GENERAL. — Notwithstanding paragraphs (1) and (2), no alien shall be considered inadmissible under section 212(a)(3) of the Immigration and Nationality Act (8 U.S.C. 1182(a)(3)), or deportable under section 237(a)(4)(B) of such Act (8 U.S.C. 1227(a)(4)(B)), by reason of the amendments made by subsection (a), on the ground that the alien engaged in a terrorist activity described in subclause (IV)(bb), (V)(bb), or (VI)(cc) of section 212(a)(3)(B)(iv) of such Act (as so amended) with respect to a group at any time when the group was not a terrorist organization designated by the Secretary of State under section 219 of such Act (8 U.S.C. 1189) or otherwise designated under section 212(a)(3)(B)(vi)(II) of such Act (as so amended).

(B) STATUTORY CONSTRUCTION. — Subparagraph (A) shall not be construed to prevent an alien from being considered inadmissible or deportable for having engaged in a terrorist activity —

(i) described in subclause (IV)(bb), (V)(bb), or (VI)(cc) of section 212(a)(3)(B)(iv) of such Act (as so amended) with respect to a terrorist organization at any time when such organization was designated by the Secretary of State under section 219 of such Act or otherwise designated under section 212(a)(3)(B)(vi)(II) of such Act (as so amended); or

(ii) described in subclause (IV)(cc), (V)(cc), or (VI)(dd) of section 212(a)(3)(B)(iv) of such Act (as so amended) with respect to a terrorist organization described in section 212(a)(3)(B)(vi)(III) of such Act (as so amended).

(4) EXCEPTION. — The Secretary of State, in consultation with the Attorney General, may determine that the amendments made by this section shall not apply with

respect to actions by an alien taken outside the United States before the date of the enactment of this Act upon the recommendation of a consular officer who has concluded that there is not reasonable ground to believe that the alien knew or reasonably should have known that the actions would further a terrorist activity.

(c) DESIGNATION OF FOREIGN TERRORIST ORGANIZATIONS. — Section 219(a) of the Immigration and Nationality Act (8 U.S.C. 1189(a)) is amended —

(1) in paragraph (1)(B), by inserting "or terrorism (as defined in section 140(d)(2) of the Foreign Relations Authorization Act, Fiscal Years 1988 and 1989 (22 U.S.C. 2656f(d)(2)), or retains the capability and intent to engage in terrorist activity or terrorism" after "212(a)(3)(B)";

(2) in paragraph (1)(C), by inserting "or terrorism" after "terrorist activity";

(3) by amending paragraph (2)(A) to read as follows :

"(A) NOTICE. —

"(i) TO CONGRESSIONAL LEADERS. — Seven days before making a designation under this subsection, the Secretary shall, by classified communication, notify the Speaker and Minority Leader of the House of Representatives, the President pro tempore, Majority Leader, and Minority Leader of the Senate, and the members of the relevant committees of the House of Representatives and the Senate, in writing, of the intent to designate an organization under this sub-section, together with the findings made under paragraph (1) with respect to that organization, and the factual basis therefor.

"(ii) PUBLICATION IN FEDERAL REGISTER. — The Secretary shall publish the designation in the Federal Register seven days after providing the notification under clause (i).";

(4) in paragraph (2)(B)(i), by striking "subparagraph (A)" and inserting "subparagraph (A)(ii)";

(5) in paragraph (2)(C), by striking "paragraph (2)" and inserting "paragraph (2)(A)(i)";

(6) in paragraph (3)(B), by striking "subsection (c)" and inserting "subsection (b)";

(7) in paragraph (4)(B), by inserting after the first sentence the following : "The Secretary also may redesignate such organization at the end of any 2-year redesignation period (but not sooner than 60 days prior to the termination of such period) for an additional 2-year period upon a finding that the relevant circumstances described in paragraph (1) still exist. Any redesignation shall be effective immediately following the end of the prior 2-year designation or redesignation period unless a different effective date is provided in such redesignation.";

(8) in paragraph (6)(A) —

(A) by inserting "or a redesignation made under paragraph (4)(B)" after "paragraph (1)";

(B) in clause (i) —

(i) by inserting "or redesignation" after "designation" the first place it appears; and

(ii) by striking "of the designation"; and

(C) in clause (ii), by striking "of the designation";

(9) in paragraph (6)(B) —

(A) by striking "through (4)" and inserting "and (3)"; and

(B) by inserting at the end the following new sentence : "Any revocation shall take effect on the date specified in the revocation or upon publication in the Federal Register if no effective date is specified.";

(10) in paragraph (7), by inserting ", or the revocation of a redesignation under paragraph (6)," after "paragraph (5) or (6)"; and

(11) in paragraph (8) —

(A) by striking "paragraph (1)(B)" and inserting "paragraph (2)(B), or if a redesignation under this subsection has become effective under paragraph (4)(B)";

(B) by inserting "or an alien in a removal proceeding" after "criminal action"; and

(C) by inserting "or redesignation" before "as a defense".

SEC. 412. MANDATORY DETENTION OF SUSPECTED TERRORISTS; HABEAS CORPUS; JUDICIAL REVIEW.

(a) IN GENERAL. — The Immigration and Nationality Act (8 U.S.C. 1101 et seq.) is amended by inserting after section 236 the following :

"MANDATORY DETENTION OF SUSPECTED TERRORISTS; HABEAS CORPUS; JUDICIAL REVIEW

"SEC. 236A. (A) DETENTION OF TERRORIST ALIENS. —

"(1) CUSTODY. — The Attorney General shall take into custody any alien who is certified under paragraph (3).

"(2) RELEASE. — Except as provided in paragraphs (5) and (6), the Attorney General shall maintain custody of such an alien until the alien is removed from the United States. Except as provided in paragraph (6), such custody shall be maintained irrespective of any relief from removal for which the alien may be eligible, or any relief from removal granted the alien, until the Attorney General determines that the alien is no longer an alien who may be certified under paragraph (3). If the alien is finally determined not to be removable, detention pursuant to this subsection shall terminate.

"(3) CERTIFICATION. — The Attorney General may certify an alien under this paragraph if the Attorney General has reasonable grounds to believe that the alien —

"(A) is described in section 212(a)(3)(A)(i), 212(a)(3)(A)(iii), 212(a)(3)(B), 237(a)(4)(A)(i), 237(a)(4)(A)(iii), or 237(a)(4)(B); or

"(B) is engaged in any other activity that endangers the national security of the United States.

"(4) NONDELEGATION. — The Attorney General may delegate the authority provided under paragraph (3) only to the

Deputy Attorney General. The Deputy Attorney General may not delegate such authority.

"(5) COMMENCEMENT OF PROCEEDINGS. — The Attorney General shall place an alien detained under paragraph (1) in removal proceedings, or shall charge the alien with a criminal offense, not later than 7 days after the commencement of such detention. If the requirement of the preceding sentence is not satisfied, the Attorney General shall release the alien.

"(6) LIMITATION ON INDEFINITE DETENTION. — An alien detained solely under paragraph (1) who has not been removed under section 241(a)(1)(A), and whose removal is unlikely in the reasonably foreseeable future, may be detained for additional periods of up to six months only if the release of the alien will threaten the national security of the United States or the safety of the community or any person.

"(7) REVIEW OF CERTIFICATION. — The Attorney General shall review the certification made under paragraph (3) every 6 months. If the Attorney General determines, in the Attorney General's discretion, that the certification should be revoked, the alien may be released on such conditions as the Attorney General deems appropriate, unless such release is otherwise prohibited by law. The alien may request each 6 months in writing that the Attorney General reconsider the certification and may submit documents or other evidence in support of that request.

"(b) HABEAS CORPUS AND JUDICIAL REVIEW. —

"(1) IN GENERAL. — Judicial review of any action or decision relating to this section (including judicial review of the merits of a determination made under subsection (a)(3) or (a)(6)) is available exclusively in habeas corpus proceedings consistent with this subsection. Except as provided in the preceding sentence, no court shall have jurisdiction to review, by habeas corpus petition or otherwise, any such action or decision.

"(2) APPLICATION. —

"(A) IN GENERAL. — Notwithstanding any other provision of law, including section 2241(a) of title 28, United States Code, habeas corpus proceedings described in paragraph (1) may be initiated only by an application filed with —

"(i) the Supreme Court;

"(ii) any justice of the Supreme Court;

"(iii) any circuit judge of the United States Court of Appeals for the District of Columbia Circuit; or

"(iv) any district court otherwise having jurisdiction to entertain it.

"(B) APPLICATION TRANSFER. — Section 2241(b) of title 28, United States Code, shall apply to an application for a writ of habeas corpus described in subparagraph (A).

"(3) APPEALS. — Notwithstanding any other provision of law, including section 2253 of title 28, in habeas corpus proceedings described in paragraph (1) before a circuit or district judge, the final order shall be subject to review, on appeal, by the United States Court of Appeals for the District of Columbia Circuit. There shall be no right of appeal in such proceedings to any other circuit court of appeals.

"(4) RULE OF DECISION. — The law applied by the Supreme Court and the United States Court of Appeals for the District of Columbia Circuit shall be regarded as the rule of decision in habeas corpus proceedings described in paragraph (1).

"(c) STATUTORY CONSTRUCTION. — The provisions of this section shall not be applicable to any other provision of this Act.".

(b) CLERICAL AMENDMENT. — The table of contents of the Immigration and Nationality Act is amended by inserting after the item relating to section 236 the following :

"Sec. 236A. Mandatory detention of suspected terrorist; habeas corpus; judicial review.".

(c) REPORTS. — Not later than 6 months after the date of the enactment of this Act, and every 6 months thereafter, the Attorney General shall submit a report to the Committee on the Judiciary of the House of Representatives and the

Committee on the Judiciary of the Senate, with respect to the reporting period, on —

(1) the number of aliens certified under section 236A(a)(3) of the Immigration and Nationality Act, as added by subsection (a);

(2) the grounds for such certifications;

(3) the nationalities of the aliens so certified;

(4) the length of the detention for each alien so certified; and

(5) the number of aliens so certified who —

(A) were granted any form of relief from removal;

(B) were removed;

(C) the Attorney General has determined are no longer aliens who may be so certified; or

(D) were released from detention.

SEC. 413. MULTILATERAL COOPERATION AGAINST TERRORISTS.

Section 222(f) of the Immigration and Nationality Act (8 U.S.C. 1202(f)) is amended —

(1) by striking "except that in the discretion of" and inserting the following : "except that —

"(1) in the discretion of"; and

(2) by adding at the end the following :

"(2) the Secretary of State, in the Secretary's discretion and on the basis of reciprocity, may provide to a foreign government information in the Department of State's computerized visa lookout database and, when necessary and appropriate, other records covered by this section related to information in the database —

"(A) with regard to individual aliens, at any time on a case-by-case basis for the purpose of preventing, investigating, or punishing acts that would constitute a crime in the United States, including, but not limited to, terrorism or trafficking in controlled substances, persons, or illicit weapons; or

"(B) with regard to any or all aliens in the database, pursuant to such conditions as the Secretary of State shall establish in an agreement with the foreign government in which that government agrees to use such information and records for the purposes described in subparagraph (A) or to deny visas to persons who would be inadmissible to the United States.".

SEC. 414. VISA INTEGRITY AND SECURITY.

(a) SENSE OF CONGRESS REGARDING THE NEED TO EXPEDITE IMPLEMENTATION OF INTEGRATED ENTRY AND EXIT DATA SYSTEM. —

(1) SENSE OF CONGRESS. — In light of the terrorist attacks perpetrated against the United States on September 11, 2001, it is the sense of the Congress that —

(A) the Attorney General, in consultation with the Secretary of State, should fully implement the integrated entry and exit data system for airports, seaports, and land border ports of entry, as specified in section 110 of the Illegal Immigration Reform and Immigrant Responsibility Act of 1996 (8 U.S.C. 1365a), with all deliberate speed and as expeditiously as practicable; and

(B) the Attorney General, in consultation with the Secretary of State, the Secretary of Commerce, the Secretary of the Treasury, and the Office of Homeland Security, should immediately begin establishing the Integrated Entry and Exit Data System Task Force, as described in section 3 of the Immigration and Naturalization Service Data Management Improvement Act of 2000 (Public Law 106–215).

(2) AUTHORIZATION OF APPROPRIATIONS. — There is authorized to be appropriated such sums as may be necessary to fully implement the system described in paragraph (1)(A).

(b) DEVELOPMENT OF THE SYSTEM. — In the development of the integrated entry and exit data system under section 110 of the Illegal Immigration Reform and Immigrant Responsibility Act of 1996 (8 U.S.C. 1365a), the Attorney General and the Secretary of State shall particularly focus on —

(1) the utilization of biometric technology; and

(2) the development of tamper-resistant documents readable at ports of entry.

(c) INTERFACE WITH LAW ENFORCEMENT DATABASES. — The entry and exit data system described in this section shall be able to interface with law enforcement databases for use by Federal law enforcement to identify and detain individuals who pose a threat to the national security of the United States.

(d) REPORT ON SCREENING INFORMATION. — Not later than 12 months after the date of enactment of this Act, the Office of Home-land Security shall submit a report to Congress on the information that is needed from any United States agency to effectively screen visa applicants and applicants for admission to the United States to identify those affiliated with terrorist organizations or those that pose any threat to the safety or security of the United States, including the type of information currently received by United States agencies and the regularity with which such information is transmitted to the Secretary of State and the Attorney General.

SEC. 415. PARTICIPATION OF OFFICE OF HOMELAND SECURITY ON ENTRY-EXIT TASK FORCE.

Section 3 of the Immigration and Naturalization Service Data Management Improvement Act of 2000 (Public Law 106–215) is amended by striking "and the Secretary of the Treasury," and inserting "the Secretary of the Treasury, and the Office of Homeland Security".

SEC. 416. FOREIGN STUDENT MONITORING PROGRAM.

(a) FULL IMPLEMENTATION AND EXPANSION OF FOREIGN STUDENT VISA MONITORING PROGRAM REQUIRED. — The Attorney General, in consultation with the Secretary of State, shall fully implement and expand the program established by section 641(a) of the Illegal Immigration Reform and Immigrant Responsibility Act of 1996 (8 U.S.C. 1372(a)).

(b) INTEGRATION WITH PORT OF ENTRY INFORMATION. — For each alien with respect to whom information is collected under section 641 of the Illegal Immigration Reform and Immigrant Responsibility Act of 1996 (8 U.S.C. 1372), the Attorney General, in consultation with the Secretary of State, shall include information on the date of entry and port of entry.

(c) EXPANSION OF SYSTEM TO INCLUDE OTHER APPROVED EDUCATIONAL INSTITUTIONS. — Section 641 of the Illegal Immigration Reform and Immigrant Responsibility Act of 1996 (8 U.S.C.1372) is amended —

(1) in subsection (a)(1), subsection (c)(4)(A), and subsection (d)(1) (in the text above subparagraph (A)), by inserting ", other approved educational institutions," after "higher education" each place it appears;

(2) in subsections (c)(1)(C), (c)(1)(D), and (d)(1)(A), by inserting ", or other approved educational institution," after "higher education" each place it appears;

(3) in subsections (d)(2), (e)(1), and (e)(2), by inserting ", other approved educational institution," after "higher education" each place it appears; and

(4) in subsection (h), by adding at the end the following new paragraph :

"(3) OTHER APPROVED EDUCATIONAL INSTITUTION. — The term 'other approved educational institution' includes any air flight school, language training school, or vocational school, approved by the Attorney General, in consultation with the Secretary of Education and the Secretary of State, under subparagraph (F), (J), or (M) of section 101(a)(15) of the Immigration and Nationality Act.".

(d) AUTHORIZATION OF APPROPRIATIONS. — There is authorized to be appropriated to the Department of Justice $36,800,000 for the period beginning on the date of enactment of this Act and ending on January 1, 2003, to fully implement and expand prior to January 1, 2003, the program established by section 641(a) of the Illegal Immigration Reform and Immigrant Responsibility Act of 1996 (8 U.S.C. 1372(a)).

SEC. 417. MACHINE READABLE PASSPORTS.

(a) AUDITS. — The Secretary of State shall, each fiscal year until September 30, 2007 —

(1) perform annual audits of the implementation of section 217(c)(2)(B) of the Immigration and Nationality Act (8 U.S.C. 1187(c)(2)(B));

(2) check for the implementation of precautionary measures to prevent the counterfeiting and theft of passports; and

(3) ascertain that countries designated under the visa waiver program have established a program to develop tamper-resistant passports.

(b) PERIODIC REPORTS. — Beginning one year after the date of enactment of this Act, and every year thereafter until 2007, the Secretary of State shall submit a report to Congress setting forth the findings of the most recent audit conducted under subsection (a)(1).

(c) ADVANCING DEADLINE FOR SATISFACTION OF REQUIREMENT. — Section 217(a)(3) of the Immigration and Nationality Act (8 U.S.C. 1187(a)(3)) is amended by striking "2007" and inserting "2003".

(d) WAIVER. — Section 217(a)(3) of the Immigration and Nationality Act (8 U.S.C. 1187(a)(3)) is amended —

(1) by striking "On or after" and inserting the following :

"(A) IN GENERAL. — Except as provided in subparagraph (B), on or after"; and

(2) by adding at the end the following :

"(B) LIMITED WAIVER AUTHORITY. — For the period beginning October 1, 2003, and ending September 30, 2007, the Secretary of State may waive the requirement of subparagraph (A) with respect to nationals of a program country (as designated under subsection (c)), if the Secretary of State finds that the program country —

"(i) is making progress toward ensuring that passports meeting the requirement of subparagraph (A) are generally available to its nationals; and

"(ii) has taken appropriate measures to protect against misuse of passports the country has issued that do not meet the requirement of subparagraph (A).".

SEC. 418. PREVENTION OF CONSULATE SHOPPING.

(a) REVIEW. — The Secretary of State shall review how consular officers issue visas to determine if consular shopping is a problem.

(b) ACTIONS TO BE TAKEN. — If the Secretary of State determines under subsection (a) that consular shopping is a problem, the Secretary shall take steps to address the problem and shall submit a report to Congress describing what action was taken.

Subtitle C — Preservation of Immigration Benefits for Victims of Terrorism

SEC. 421. SPECIAL IMMIGRANT STATUS.

(a) IN GENERAL. — For purposes of the Immigration and Nationality Act (8 U.S.C. 1101 et seq.), the Attorney General may provide an alien described in subsection (b) with the status of a special immigrant under section 101(a)(27) of such Act (8 U.S.C. 1101(a(27)), if the alien —

(1) files with the Attorney General a petition under section 204 of such Act (8 U.S.C. 1154) for classification under section 203(b)(4) of such Act (8 U.S.C. 1153(b)(4)); and

(2) is otherwise eligible to receive an immigrant visa and is otherwise admissible to the United States for permanent residence, except in determining such admissibility, the grounds for inadmissibility specified in section 212(a)(4) of such Act (8 U.S.C. 1182(a)(4)) shall not apply.

(b) ALIENS DESCRIBED. —

(1) PRINCIPAL ALIENS. — An alien is described in this sub-section if —

(A) the alien was the beneficiary of —

(i) a petition that was filed with the Attorney General on or before September 11, 2001 —

(I) under section 204 of the Immigration

and Nationality Act (8 U.S.C. 1154) to classify the alien as a family-sponsored immigrant under section 203(a) of such Act (8 U.S.C. 1153(a)) or as an employment-based immigrant under section 203(b) of such Act (8 U.S.C. 1153(b)); or

(II) under section 214(d) (8 U.S.C. 1184(d)) of such Act to authorize the issuance of a non-immigrant visa to the alien under section 101(a)(15)(K) of such Act (8 U.S.C. 1101(a)(15)(K)); or

(ii) an application for labor certification under section 212(a)(5)(A) of such Act (8 U.S.C. 1182(a)(5)(A)) that was filed under regulations of the Secretary of Labor on or before such date; and

(B) such petition or application was revoked or terminated (or otherwise rendered null), either before or after its approval, due to a specified terrorist activity that directly resulted in —

(i) the death or disability of the petitioner, applicant, or alien beneficiary; or

(ii) loss of employment due to physical damage to, or destruction of, the business of the petitioner or applicant.

(2) SPOUSES AND CHILDREN. —

(A) IN GENERAL. — An alien is described in this subsection if —

(i) the alien was, on September 10, 2001, the spouse or child of a principal alien described in paragraph (1); and

(ii) the alien —

(I) is accompanying such principal alien; or

(II) is following to join such principal alien not later than September 11, 2003.

(B) CONSTRUCTION. — For purposes of construing the terms "accompanying" and "following to join" in subparagraph (A)(ii), any death of a principal alien that is described in paragraph (1)(B)(i) shall be disregarded.

(3) GRANDPARENTS OF ORPHANS. — An alien is described in this subsection if the alien is a grandparent of a child, both of whose parents died as a direct result of a specified terrorist activity, if either of such deceased parents was, on September 10, 2001, a citizen or national of the United States or an alien lawfully admitted for permanent residence in the United States.

(c) PRIORITY DATE. — Immigrant visas made available under this section shall be issued to aliens in the order in which a petition on behalf of each such alien is filed with the Attorney General under subsection (a)(1), except that if an alien was assigned a priority date with respect to a petition described in subsection (b)(1)(A)(i), the alien may maintain that priority date.

(d) NUMERICAL LIMITATIONS. — For purposes of the application of sections 201 through 203 of the Immigration and Nationality Act (8 U.S.C. 1151–1153) in any fiscal year, aliens eligible to be provided status under this section shall be treated as special immigrants described in section 101(a)(27) of such Act (8 U.S.C. 1101(a)(27)) who are not described in subparagraph (A), (B), (C), or (K) of such section.

SEC. 422. EXTENSION OF FILING OR REENTRY DEADLINES.

(a) AUTOMATIC EXTENSION OF NONIMMIGRANT STATUS. —

(1) IN GENERAL. — Notwithstanding section 214 of the Immigration and Nationality Act (8 U.S.C. 1184), in the case of an alien described in paragraph (2) who was lawfully present in the United States as a nonimmigrant on September 10, 2001, the alien may remain lawfully in the United States in the same nonimmigrant status until the later of —

(A) the date such lawful nonimmigrant status otherwise would have terminated if this subsection had not been enacted; or

(B) 1 year after the death or onset of disability described in paragraph (2).

(2) ALIENS DESCRIBED. —

(A) PRINCIPAL ALIENS. — An alien is described in this paragraph if the alien was disabled as a direct result of a specified terrorist activity.

(B) SPOUSES AND CHILDREN. — An alien is described in this paragraph if the alien was, on September 10, 2001, the spouse or child of —

(i) a principal alien described in subparagraph (A); or

(ii) an alien who died as a direct result of a specified terrorist activity.

(3) AUTHORIZED EMPLOYMENT. — During the period in which a principal alien or alien spouse is in lawful nonimmigrant status under paragraph (1), the alien shall be provided an "employment authorized" endorsement or other appropriate document signifying authorization of employment not later than 30 days after the alien requests such authorization.

(b) NEW DEADLINES FOR EXTENSION OR CHANGE OF NON-IMMIGRANT STATUS. —

(1) FILING DELAYS. — In the case of an alien who was lawfully present in the United States as a nonimmigrant on September 10, 2001, if the alien was prevented from filing a timely application for an extension or change of nonimmigrant status as a direct result of a specified terrorist activity, the alien's application shall be considered timely filed if it is filed not later than 60 days after it otherwise would have been due.

(2) DEPARTURE DELAYS. — In the case of an alien who was lawfully present in the United States as a nonimmigrant on September 10, 2001, if the alien is unable timely to depart the United States as a direct result of a specified terrorist activity, the alien shall not be considered to have been unlawfully present in the United States during the period beginning on September 11, 2001, and ending on the date of the alien's departure, if such departure occurs on or before November 11, 2001.

(3) SPECIAL RULE FOR ALIENS UNABLE TO RETURN FROM ABROAD. —

(A) PRINCIPAL ALIENS. — In the case of an alien who was in a lawful nonimmigrant status on September 10, 2001, but who was not present in the United States on such date, if the alien was prevented from returning to the United States in order to file a timely application for an extension of nonimmigrant status as a direct result of a specified terrorist activity —

(i) the alien's application shall be considered timely filed if it is filed not later than 60 days after it other-wise would have been due; and

(ii) the alien's lawful nonimmigrant status shall be considered to continue until the later of —

(I) the date such status otherwise would have terminated if this subparagraph had not been enacted; or

(II) the date that is 60 days after the date on which the application described in clause (i) otherwise would have been due.

(B) SPOUSES AND CHILDREN. — In the case of an alien who is the spouse or child of a principal alien described in subparagraph (A), if the spouse or child was in a lawful nonimmigrant status on September 10, 2001, the spouse or child may remain lawfully in the United States in the same nonimmigrant status until the later of —

(i) the date such lawful nonimmigrant status otherwise would have terminated if this subparagraph had not been enacted; or

(ii) the date that is 60 days after the date on which the application described in subparagraph (A) otherwise would have been due.

(4) CIRCUMSTANCES PREVENTING TIMELY ACTION. —

(A) FILING DELAYS. — For purposes of paragraph (1), circumstances preventing an alien from timely acting are —

(i) office closures;

(ii) mail or courier service cessations or delays; and

(iii) other closures, cessations, or delays affecting case processing or travel necessary to satisfy legal requirements.

(B) DEPARTURE AND RETURN DELAYS. — For purposes of paragraphs (2) and (3), circumstances preventing an alien from timely acting are —

(i) office closures;

(ii) airline flight cessations or delays; and

(iii) other closures, cessations, or delays affecting case processing or travel necessary to satisfy legal requirements.

(c) DIVERSITY IMMIGRANTS. —

(1) WAIVER OF FISCAL YEAR LIMITATION. — Notwithstanding section 203(e)(2) of the Immigration and Nationality Act (8 U.S.C. 1153(e)(2)), an immigrant visa number issued to an alien under section 203(c) of such Act for fiscal year 2001 may be used by the alien during the period beginning on October 1, 2001, and ending on April 1, 2002, if the alien establishes that the alien was prevented from using it during fiscal year 2001 as a direct result of a specified terrorist activity.

(2) WORLDWIDE LEVEL. — In the case of an alien entering the United States as a lawful permanent resident, or adjusting to that status, under paragraph (1) or (3), the alien shall be counted as a diversity immigrant for fiscal year 2001 for purposes of section 201(e) of the Immigration and Nationality Act (8 U.S.C. 1151(e)), unless the worldwide level under such section for such year has been exceeded, in which case the alien shall be counted as a diversity immigrant for fiscal year 2002.

(3) TREATMENT OF FAMILY MEMBERS OF CERTAIN ALIENS. — In the case of a principal alien issued an immigrant visa number under section 203(c) of the Immigration and Nationality Act (8 U.S.C. 1153(c))

for fiscal year 2001, if such principal alien died as a direct result of a specified terrorist activity, the aliens who were, on September 10, 2001, the spouse and children of such principal alien shall, until June 30, 2002, if not otherwise entitled to an immigrant status and the immediate issuance of a visa under subsection (a), (b), or (c) of section 203 of such Act, be entitled to the same status, and the same order of consideration, that would have been provided to such alien spouse or child under section 203(d) of such Act as if the principal alien were not deceased and as if the spouse or child's visa application had been adjudicated by September 30, 2001.

(4) CIRCUMSTANCES PREVENTING TIMELY ACTION. — For purposes of paragraph (1), circumstances preventing an alien from using an immigrant visa number during fiscal year 2001 are —

(A) office closures;

(B) mail or courier service cessations or delays;

(C) airline flight cessations or delays; and

(D) other closures, cessations, or delays affecting case processing or travel necessary to satisfy legal requirements.

(d) EXTENSION OF EXPIRATION OF IMMIGRANT VISAS. —

(1) IN GENERAL. — Notwithstanding the limitations under section 221(c) of the Immigration and Nationality Act (8 U.S.C. 1201(c)), in the case of any immigrant visa issued to an alien that expires or expired before December 31, 2001, if the alien was unable to effect entry into the United States as a direct result of a specified terrorist activity, then the period of validity of the visa is extended until December 31, 2001, unless a longer period of validity is otherwise provided under this subtitle.

(2) CIRCUMSTANCES PREVENTING ENTRY. — For purposes of this subsection, circumstances preventing an alien from effecting entry into the United States are —

(A) office closures;

(B) airline flight cessations or delays; and

(C) other closures, cessations, or delays affecting case processing or travel necessary to satisfy legal requirements.

(e) GRANTS OF PAROLE EXTENDED. —

(1) IN GENERAL. — In the case of any parole granted by the Attorney General under section 212(d)(5) of the Immigration and Nationality Act (8 U.S.C. 1182(d)(5)) that expires on a date on or after September 11, 2001, if the alien beneficiary of the parole was unable to return to the United States prior to the expiration date as a direct result of a specified terrorist activity, the parole is deemed extended for an additional 90 days.

(2) CIRCUMSTANCES PREVENTING RETURN. — For purposes of this subsection, circumstances preventing an alien from timely returning to the United States are —

(A) office closures;

(B) airline flight cessations or delays; and

(C) other closures, cessations, or delays affecting case processing or travel necessary to satisfy legal requirements.

(f) VOLUNTARY DEPARTURE. — Notwithstanding section 240B of the Immigration and Nationality Act (8 U.S.C. 1229c), if a period for voluntary departure under such section expired during the period beginning on September 11, 2001, and ending on October 11, 2001, such voluntary departure period is deemed extended for an additional 30 days.

SEC. 423. HUMANITARIAN RELIEF FOR CERTAIN SURVIVING SPOUSES AND CHILDREN.

(a) TREATMENT AS IMMEDIATE RELATIVES. —

(1) SPOUSES. — Notwithstanding the second sentence of section 201(b)(2)(A)(i) of the Immigration and Nationality Act (8 U.S.C. 1151(b)(2)(A)(i)), in the case of an alien who was the spouse of a citizen of the United States at the time of the citizen's death and was not legally separated from the citizen at the time

of the citizen's death, if the citizen died as a direct result of a specified terrorist activity, the alien (and each child of the alien) shall be considered, for purposes of section 201(b) of such Act, to remain an immediate relative after the date of the citizen's death, but only if the alien files a petition under section 204(a)(1)(A)(ii) of such Act within 2 years after such date and only until the date the alien remarries. For purposes of such section 204(a)(1)(A)(ii), an alien granted relief under the preceding sentence shall be considered an alien spouse described in the second sentence of section 201(b)(2)(A)(i) of such Act.

(2) CHILDREN. —

(A) IN GENERAL. — In the case of an alien who was the child of a citizen of the United States at the time of the citizen's death, if the citizen died as a direct result of a specified terrorist activity, the alien shall be considered, for purposes of section 201(b) of the Immigration and Nationality Act (8 U.S.C. 1151(b)), to remain an immediate relative after the date of the citizen's death (regardless of changes in age or marital status thereafter), but only if the alien files a petition under subparagraph (B) within 2 years after such date.

(B) PETITIONS. — An alien described in subparagraph (A) may file a petition with the Attorney General for classification of the alien under section 201(b)(2)(A)(i) of the Immigration and Nationality Act (8 U.S.C. 1151(b)(2)(A)(i)). For purposes of such Act, such a petition shall be considered a petition filed under section 204(a)(1)(A) of such Act (8 U.S.C. 1154(a)(1)(A)).

(b) SPOUSES, CHILDREN, UNMARRIED SONS AND DAUGHTERS OF LAWFUL PERMANENT RESIDENT ALIENS. —

(1) IN GENERAL. — Any spouse, child, or unmarried son or daughter of an alien described in paragraph (3) who is included in a petition for classification as a family-sponsored immigrant under section 203(a)(2) of the Immigration and Nationality Act (8 U.S.C. 1153(a)(2))

that was filed by such alien before September 11, 2001, shall be considered (if the spouse, child, son, or daughter has not been admitted or approved for lawful permanent residence by such date) a valid petitioner for preference status under such section with the same priority date as that assigned prior to the death described in paragraph (3)(A). No new petition shall be required to be filed. Such spouse, child, son, or daughter may be eligible for deferred action and work authorization.

(2) SELF-PETITIONS. — Any spouse, child, or unmarried son or daughter of an alien described in paragraph (3) who is not a beneficiary of a petition for classification as a family-sponsored immigrant under section 203(a)(2) of the Immigration and Nationality Act may file a petition for such classification with the Attorney General, if the spouse, child, son, or daughter was present in the United States on September 11, 2001. Such spouse, child, son, or daughter may be eligible for deferred action and work authorization.

(3) ALIENS DESCRIBED. — An alien is described in this paragraph if the alien —

(A) died as a direct result of a specified terrorist activity; and

(B) on the day of such death, was lawfully admitted for permanent residence in the United States.

(c) APPLICATIONS FOR ADJUSTMENT OF STATUS BY SURVIVING SPOUSES AND CHILDREN OF EMPLOYMENT-BASED IMMIGRANTS. —

(1) IN GENERAL. — Any alien who was, on September 10, 2001, the spouse or child of an alien described in paragraph (2), and who applied for adjustment of status prior to the death described in paragraph (2)(A), may have such application adjudicated as if such death had not occurred.

(2) ALIENS DESCRIBED. — An alien is described in this paragraph if the alien —

(A) died as a direct result of a specified terrorist activity; and

(B) on the day before such death, was —

(i) an alien lawfully admitted for permanent residence in the United States by reason of having been allotted a visa under section 203(b) of the Immigration and Nationality Act (8 U.S.C. 1153(b)); or

(ii) an applicant for adjustment of status to that of an alien described in clause (i), and admissible to the United States for permanent residence.

(d) WAIVER OF PUBLIC CHARGE GROUNDS. — In determining the admissibility of any alien accorded an immigration benefit under this section, the grounds for inadmissibility specified in section 212(a)(4) of the Immigration and Nationality Act (8 U.S.C. 1182(a)(4)) shall not apply.

SEC. 424. "AGE-OUT" PROTECTION FOR CHILDREN.

For purposes of the administration of the Immigration and Nationality Act (8 U.S.C. 1101 et seq.), in the case of an alien —

(1) whose 21st birthday occurs in September 2001, and who is the beneficiary of a petition or application filed under such Act on or before September 11, 2001, the alien shall be considered to be a child for 90 days after the alien's 21st birthday for purposes of adjudicating such petition or application; and

(2) whose 21st birthday occurs after September 2001, and who is the beneficiary of a petition or application filed under such Act on or before September 11, 2001, the alien shall be considered to be a child for 45 days after the alien's 21st birthday for purposes of adjudicating such petition or application.

SEC. 425. TEMPORARY ADMINISTRATIVE RELIEF.

The Attorney General, for humanitarian purposes or to ensure family unity, may provide temporary administrative relief to any alien who —

(1) was lawfully present in the United States on September 10, 2001;

(2) was on such date the spouse, parent, or child of an individual who died or was disabled as a direct result of a specified terrorist activity; and

(3) is not otherwise entitled to relief under any other provision of this subtitle.

SEC. 426. EVIDENCE OF DEATH, DISABILITY, OR LOSS OF EMPLOYMENT.

(a) IN GENERAL. — The Attorney General shall establish appropriate standards for evidence demonstrating, for purposes of this subtitle, that any of the following occurred as a direct result of a specified terrorist activity :

(1) Death.

(2) Disability.

(3) Loss of employment due to physical damage to, or destruction of, a business.

(b) WAIVER OF REGULATIONS. — The Attorney General shall carry out subsection (a) as expeditiously as possible. The Attorney General is not required to promulgate regulations prior to implementing this subtitle.

SEC. 427. NO BENEFITS TO TERRORISTS OR FAMILY MEMBERS OF TERRORISTS.

Notwithstanding any other provision of this subtitle, nothing in this subtitle shall be construed to provide any benefit or relief to —

(1) any individual culpable for a specified terrorist activity; or

(2) any family member of any individual described in paragraph (1).

SEC. 428. DEFINITIONS.

(a) APPLICATION OF IMMIGRATION AND NATIONALITY ACT PROVISIONS. — Except as otherwise specifically provided in this subtitle, the definitions used in the Immigration and Nationality Act (excluding the definitions applicable exclusively to title III of such Act) shall apply in the administration of this subtitle.

(b) SPECIFIED TERRORIST ACTIVITY. — For purposes of this sub-title, the term "specified terrorist activity" means any terrorist activity conducted against the Government or the people of the United States on September 11, 2001.

TITLE V — REMOVING OBSTACLES TO INVESTIGATING TERRORISM

SEC. 501. ATTORNEY GENERAL'S AUTHORITY TO PAY REWARDS TO COMBAT TERRORISM.

(a) PAYMENT OF REWARDS TO COMBAT TERRORISM. — Funds available to the Attorney General may be used for the payment of rewards pursuant to public advertisements for assistance to the Department of Justice to combat terrorism and defend the Nation against terrorist acts, in accordance with procedures and regulations established or issued by the Attorney General.

(b) CONDITIONS. — In making rewards under this section —

(1) no such reward of $250,000 or more may be made or offered without the personal approval of either the Attorney General or the President;

(2) the Attorney General shall give written notice to the Chairmen and ranking minority members of the Committees on Appropriations and the Judiciary of the Senate and of the House of Representatives not later than 30 days after the approval of a reward under paragraph (1);

(3) any executive agency or military department (as defined, respectively, in sections 105 and 102 of title 5, United States Code) may provide the Attorney General with funds for the payment of rewards;

(4) neither the failure of the Attorney General to authorize a payment nor the amount authorized shall be subject to judicial review; and

(5) no such reward shall be subject to any per- or aggregate reward spending limitation established by law, unless that law expressly refers to this section, and no reward paid pursuant to any such offer shall count toward any such aggregate reward spending limitation.

SEC. 502. SECRETARY OF STATE'S AUTHORITY TO PAY REWARDS.

Section 36 of the State Department Basic Authorities Act of 1956 (Public Law 885, August 1, 1956; 22 U.S.C. 2708) is amended —

(1) in subsection (b) —

(A) in paragraph (4), by striking "or" at the end;

(B) in paragraph (5), by striking the period at the end and inserting ", including by dismantling an organization in whole or significant part; or"; and

(C) by adding at the end the following :

"(6) the identification or location of an individual who holds a key leadership position in a terrorist organization.";

(2) in subsection (d), by striking paragraphs (2) and (3) and redesignating paragraph (4) as paragraph (2); and

(3) in subsection (e)(1), by inserting ", except as personally authorized by the Secretary of State if he determines that offer or payment of an award of a larger amount is necessary to combat terrorism or defend the Nation against terrorist acts." after "$5,000,000".

SEC. 503. DNA IDENTIFICATION OF TERRORISTS AND OTHER VIOLENT OFFENDERS.

Section 3(d)(2) of the DNA Analysis Backlog Elimination Act of 2000 (42 U.S.C. 14135a(d)(2)) is amended to read as follows :

"(2) In addition to the offenses described in paragraph (1), the following offenses shall be treated for purposes of this section as qualifying Federal offenses, as determined by the Attorney General :

"(A) Any offense listed in section 2332b(g)(5)(B) of title 18, United States Code.

"(B) Any crime of violence (as defined in section 16 of title 18, United States Code).

"(C) Any attempt or conspiracy to commit any of the above offenses.".

SEC. 504. COORDINATION WITH LAW ENFORCEMENT.

(a) INFORMATION ACQUIRED FROM AN ELECTRONIC SURVEILLANCE. — Section 106 of the Foreign Intelligence Surveillance Act of 1978 (50 U.S.C. 1806), is amended by adding at the end the following :

"(k)(1) Federal officers who conduct electronic surveillance to acquire foreign intelligence information under this title may consult with Federal law enforcement officers to coordinate efforts to investigate or protect against —

"(A) actual or potential attack or other grave hostile acts of a foreign power or an agent of a foreign power;

"(B) sabotage or international terrorism by a foreign power or an agent of a foreign power; or

"(C) clandestine intelligence activities by an intelligence service or network of a foreign power or by an agent of a foreign power.

"(2) Coordination authorized under paragraph (1) shall not preclude the certification required by section 104(a)(7)(B) or the entry of an order under section 105.".

(b) INFORMATION ACQUIRED FROM A PHYSICAL SEARCH. — Section 305 of the Foreign Intelligence Surveillance Act of 1978 (50 U.S.C. 1825) is amended by adding at the end the following :

"(k)(1) Federal officers who conduct physical searches to acquire foreign intelligence information under this title may consult with Federal law enforcement officers to coordinate efforts to investigate or protect against —

"(A) actual or potential attack or other grave hostile acts of a foreign power or an agent of a foreign power;

"(B) sabotage or international terrorism by a foreign power or an agent of a foreign power; or

"(C) clandestine intelligence activities by an intelligence service or network of a foreign power or by an agent of a foreign power.

"(2) Coordination authorized under paragraph (1) shall not preclude the certification required by section 303(a)(7) or the entry of an order under section 304.".

SEC. 505. MISCELLANEOUS NATIONAL SECURITY AUTHORITIES.

(a) TELEPHONE TOLL AND TRANSACTIONAL RECORDS. — Section 2709(b) of title 18, United States Code, is amended —

(1) in the matter preceding paragraph (1), by inserting "at Bureau headquarters or a Special Agent in Charge in a Bureau field office designated by the Director" after "Assistant Director";

(2) in paragraph (1) —

(A) by striking "in a position not lower than Deputy Assistant Director"; and

(B) by striking "made that" and all that follows and inserting the following : "made that the name, address, length of service, and toll billing records sought are relevant to an authorized investigation to protect against international terrorism or clandestine intelligence activities, provided that such an investigation of a United States person is not conducted solely on the basis of activities protected by the first amendment to the Constitution of the United States; and"; and

(3) in paragraph (2) —

(A) by striking "in a position not lower than Deputy Assistant Director"; and

(B) by striking "made that" and all that follows and inserting the following : "made that the information sought is relevant to an authorized investigation to protect against international terrorism or clandestine intelligence activities, provided that such an investigation of a United States person is not conducted solely upon the basis of activities protected by the first amendment to the Constitution of the United States.".

(b) FINANCIAL RECORDS. — Section 1114(a)(5)(A) of the Right to Financial Privacy Act of 1978 (12 U.S.C. 3414(a)(5)(A)) is amended —

(1) by inserting "in a position not lower than Deputy Assistant Director at Bureau headquarters or a Special Agent in Charge in a Bureau field office designated by the Director" after "designee"; and

(2) by striking "sought" and all that follows and inserting "sought for foreign counter intelligence purposes to protect against international terrorism or clandestine intelligence activities, provided that such an investigation of a United States person is not conducted solely upon the basis of activities protected by the first amendment to the Constitution of the United States.".

(c) CONSUMER REPORTS. — Section 624 of the Fair Credit Reporting Act (15 U.S.C. 1681u) is amended —

(1) in subsection (a) —

(A) by inserting "in a position not lower than Deputy Assistant Director at Bureau headquarters or a Special Agent in Charge of a Bureau field office designated by the Director" after "designee" the first place it appears; and

(B) by striking "in writing that" and all that follows through the end and inserting the following : "in writing, that such information is sought for the conduct of an authorized investigation to protect against international terrorism or clandestine intelligence activities, provided that such an investigation of a United States person is not conducted solely upon the basis of activities protected by the first amendment to the Constitution of the United States.";

(2) in subsection (b) —

(A) by inserting "in a position not lower than Deputy Assistant Director at Bureau headquarters or a Special Agent in Charge of a Bureau field office designated by the Director" after "designee" the first place it appears; and

(B) by striking "in writing that" and all that follows through the end and inserting the following : "in writing that such information is sought for the conduct of an authorized investigation to protect against international terrorism or clandestine intelligence activities, provided that such an investigation of a United States person is not conducted solely upon the basis of activities protected by the first amendment to the Constitution of the United States."; and

(3) in subsection (c) —

(A) by inserting "in a position not lower than Deputy Assistant Director at Bureau headquarters or a Special Agent in Charge in a Bureau field office designated by the Director" after "designee of the Director"; and

(B) by striking "in camera that" and all that follows through "States." and inserting the following : "in camera that the consumer report is sought for the conduct of an authorized investigation to protect against international terrorism or clandestine intelligence activities, provided that such an investigation of a United States person is not conducted solely upon the basis of activities protected by the first amendment to the Constitution of the United States.".

SEC. 506. EXTENSION OF SECRET SERVICE JURISDICTION.

(a) CONCURRENT JURISDICTION UNDER 18 U.S.C. 1030. — Section 1030(d) of title 18, United States Code, is amended to read as follows :

"(d)(1) The United States Secret Service shall, in addition to any other agency having such authority, have the authority to investigate offenses under this section.

"(2) The Federal Bureau of Investigation shall have primary authority to investigate offenses under subsection (a)(1) for any cases involving espionage, foreign counterintelligence, information protected against unauthorized disclosure for reasons of national defense or foreign relations, or Restricted Data (as that term is defined in section 11y of the Atomic Energy Act of 1954 (42 U.S.C. 2014(y)), except for offenses affecting the duties of the United States Secret Service pursuant to section 3056(a) of this title.

"(3) Such authority shall be exercised in accordance with an agreement which shall be entered into by the Secretary of the Treasury and the Attorney General.".

(b) REAUTHORIZATION OF JURISDICTION UNDER 18 U.S.C. 1344. — Section 3056(b)(3) of title 18, United States Code, is amended by striking "credit and debit card frauds, and false identification documents or devices" and inserting "access device frauds, false identification documents or devices, and any fraud or other criminal or unlawful activity in or against any federally insured financial institution".

SEC. 507. DISCLOSURE OF EDUCATIONAL RECORDS.

Section 444 of the General Education Provisions Act (20 U.S.C. 1232g), is amended by adding after subsection (i) a new subsection (j) to read as follows :

"(j) INVESTIGATION AND PROSECUTION OF TERRORISM. —

"(1) IN GENERAL. — Notwithstanding subsections (a) through (i) or any provision of State law, the Attorney General (or any Federal officer or employee, in a position not lower than an Assistant Attorney General, designated by the Attorney General) may submit a written application to a court of competent jurisdiction for an ex parte order requiring an educational agency or institution to permit the Attorney General (or his designee) to —

"(A) collect education records in the possession of the educational agency or institution that are relevant to an authorized investigation or prosecution of an offense listed in section 2332b(g)(5)(B) of title 18 United States Code, or an act of domestic or international terrorism as defined in section 2331 of that title; and

"(B) for official purposes related to the investigation or prosecution of an offense described in paragraph (1)(A), retain, disseminate, and use (including as evidence at trial or in other administrative or judicial proceedings) such records, consistent with such guidelines as the Attorney General, after consultation with the Secretary, shall issue to protect confidentiality

"(2) APPLICATION AND APPROVAL. —

"(A) IN GENERAL. — An application under paragraph (1) shall certify that there are specific and articulable facts giving reason to believe that the education records are likely to contain information described in paragraph (1)(A).

"(B) The court shall issue an order described in

paragraph (1) if the court finds that the application for the order includes the certification described in subparagraph (A).

"(3) PROTECTION OF EDUCATIONAL AGENCY OR INSTITUTION. — An educational agency or institution that, in good faith, produces education records in accordance with an order issued under this subsection shall not be liable to any person for that production.

"(4) RECORD-KEEPING. — Subsection (b)(4) does not apply to education records subject to a court order under this sub-section.".

SEC. 508. DISCLOSURE OF INFORMATION FROM NCES SURVEYS.

Section 408 of the National Education Statistics Act of 1994 (20 U.S.C. 9007), is amended by adding after subsection (b) a new subsection (c) to read as follows :

"(c) INVESTIGATION AND PROSECUTION OF TERRORISM. —

"(1) IN GENERAL. — Notwithstanding subsections (a) and (b), the Attorney General (or any Federal officer or employee, in a position not lower than an Assistant Attorney General, designated by the Attorney General) may submit a written application to a court of competent jurisdiction for an ex parte order requiring the Secretary to permit the Attorney General (or his designee) to —

"(A) collect reports, records, and information (including individually identifiable information) in the possession of the center that are relevant to an authorized investigation or prosecution of an offense listed in section 2332b(g)(5)(B) of title 18, United States Code, or an act of domestic or international terrorism as defined in section 2331 of that title; and

"(B) for official purposes related to the investigation or prosecution of an offense described in paragraph (1)(A), retain, disseminate, and use (including as evidence at trial or in other administrative or judicial proceedings) such information, consistent with such guidelines as the Attorney General, after consultation with the Secretary, shall issue to protect confidentiality.

"(2) APPLICATION AND APPROVAL. —

"(A) IN GENERAL. — An application under paragraph (1) shall certify that there are specific and articulable facts giving reason to believe that the information sought is described in paragraph (1)(A).

"(B) The court shall issue an order described in paragraph (1) if the court finds that the application for the order includes the certification described in subparagraph (A).

"(3) PROTECTION. — An officer or employee of the Department who, in good faith, produces information in accordance with an order issued under this subsection does not violate subsection (b)(2) and shall not be liable to any person for that production.".

TITLE VI — PROVIDING FOR VICTIMS OF TERRORISM, PUBLIC SAFETY OFFICERS, AND THEIR FAMILIES

Subtitle A — Aid to Families of Public Safety Officers

SEC. 611. EXPEDITED PAYMENT FOR PUBLIC SAFETY OFFICERS INVOLVED IN THE PREVENTION, INVESTIGATION, RESCUE, OR RECOVERY EFFORTS RELATED TO A TERRORIST ATTACK.

(a) IN GENERAL. — Notwithstanding the limitations of subsection (b) of section 1201 or the provisions of subsections (c), (d), and (e) of such section or section 1202 of title I of the Omnibus Crime Control and Safe Streets Act of 1968 (42 U.S.C. 3796, 3796a), upon certification (containing identification of all eligible payees of benefits pursuant to section 1201 of such Act) by a public agency that a public safety officer employed by such agency was killed or suffered a catastrophic injury producing permanent and total disability as a direct and proximate result of a personal injury sustained in the line of duty as described in section 1201 of such Act in connection with prevention, investigation, rescue, or recovery efforts related to a terrorist attack, the Director of the Bureau of Justice Assistance shall authorize payment to qualified beneficiaries, said payment to be made not later than 30 days after receipt of such certification, benefits described under subpart 1 of part L of such Act (42 U.S.C. 3796 et seq.).

(b) DEFINITIONS. — For purposes of this section, the terms "catastrophic injury", "public agency", and "public safety officer" have the same meanings given such terms in section 1204 of title I of the Omnibus Crime Control and Safe Streets Act of 1968 (42 U.S.C. 3796b).

SEC. 612. TECHNICAL CORRECTION WITH RESPECT TO EXPEDITED PAYMENTS FOR HEROIC PUBLIC SAFETY OFFICERS.

Section 1 of Public Law 107-37 (an Act to provide for the expedited payment of certain benefits for a public safety officer who was killed or suffered a catastrophic injury as a direct and proximate result of a personal injury sustained in the line of duty in connection with the terrorist attacks of September 11, 2001) is amended by —

(1) inserting before "by a" the following : "(containing identification of all eligible payees of benefits pursuant to section 1201)";

(2) inserting "producing permanent and total disability" after "suffered a catastrophic injury"; and

(3) striking "1201(a)" and inserting "1201".

SEC. 613. PUBLIC SAFETY OFFICERS BENEFIT PROGRAM PAYMENT INCREASE.

(a) PAYMENTS. — Section 1201(a) of the Omnibus Crime Control and Safe Streets Act of 1968 (42 U.S.C. 3796) is amended by striking "$100,000" and inserting "$250,000".

(b) APPLICABILITY. — The amendment made by subsection (a) shall apply to any death or disability occurring on or after January 1, 2001.

SEC. 614. OFFICE OF JUSTICE PROGRAMS.

Section 112 of title I of section 101(b) of division A of Public

Law 105–277 and section 108(a) of appendix A of Public Law 106–113 (113 Stat. 1501A–20) are amended —

(1) after "that Office", each place it occurs, by inserting "(including, notwithstanding any contrary provision of law (unless the same should expressly refer to this section), any organization that administers any program established in title 1 of Public Law 90–351)"; and

(2) by inserting "functions, including any" after "all".

Subtitle B — Amendments to the Victims of Crime Act of 1984

SEC. 621. CRIME VICTIMS FUND.

(a) DEPOSIT OF GIFTS IN THE FUND. — Section 1402(b) of the Victims of Crime Act of 1984 (42 U.S.C. 10601(b)) is amended —

(1) in paragraph (3), by striking "and" at the end;

(2) in paragraph (4), by striking the period at the end and inserting "; and"; and

(3) by adding at the end the following :

"(5) any gifts, bequests, or donations to the Fund from private entities or individuals.".

(b) FORMULA FOR FUND DISTRIBUTIONS. — Section 1402(c) of the Victims of Crime Act of 1984 (42 U.S.C. 10601(c)) is amended to read as follows :

"(c) FUND DISTRIBUTION; RETENTION OF SUMS IN FUND; AVAILABILITY FOR EXPENDITURE WITHOUT FISCAL YEAR LIMITATION. —

"(1) Subject to the availability of money in the Fund, in each fiscal year, beginning with fiscal year 2003, the Director shall distribute not less than 90 per cent nor more than 110 per cent of the amount distributed from the Fund in the previous fiscal year, except the Director may distribute up to 120 per cent of the amount distributed in the previous fiscal year in any fiscal year that the total amount available in the Fund is more than 2 times the amount distributed in the previous fiscal year.

"(2) In each fiscal year, the Director shall distribute amounts from the Fund in accordance with subsection (d). All sums not distributed during a fiscal year shall remain in reserve in the Fund to be distributed during a subsequent fiscal year. Notwithstanding any other provision of law, all sums deposited in the Fund that are not distributed shall remain in reserve in the Fund for obligation in future fiscal years, without fiscal year limitation.".

(c) ALLOCATION OF FUNDS FOR COSTS AND GRANTS. — Section 1402(d)(4) of the Victims of Crime Act of 1984 (42 U.S.C. 10601(d)(4)) is amended —

(1) by striking "deposited in" and inserting "to be distributed from";

(2) in subparagraph (A), by striking "48.5" and inserting "47.5";

(3) in subparagraph (B), by striking "48.5" and inserting "47.5"; and

(4) in subparagraph (C), by striking "3" and inserting "5".

(d) ANTITERRORISM EMERGENCY RESERVE. — Section 1402(d)(5) of the Victims of Crime Act of 1984 (42 U.S.C. 10601(d)(5)) is amended to read as follows :

"(5)(A) In addition to the amounts distributed under paragraphs (2), (3), and (4), the Director may set aside up to $50,000,000 from the amounts transferred to the Fund in response to the airplane hijackings and terrorist acts that occurred on September 11, 2001, as an antiterrorism emergency reserve. The Director may replenish any amounts expended from such reserve in subsequent fiscal years by setting aside up to 5 per cent of the amounts remaining in the Fund in any fiscal year after distributing amounts under paragraphs (2), (3) and (4). Such reserve shall not exceed $50,000,000.

"(B) The antiterrorism emergency reserve referred to in subparagraph (A) may be used for supplemental grants under section 1404B and to provide compensation to victims of international terrorism under section 1404C.

"(C) Amounts in the antiterrorism emergency reserve established pursuant to subparagraph (A) may be carried over from fiscal year to fiscal year. Notwithstanding subsection (c) and section 619 of the Departments of Commerce, Justice, and State, the Judiciary, and Related Agencies Appropriations Act, 2001 (and any similar limitation on Fund obligations in any future Act, unless the same should expressly refer to this section), any such amounts carried over shall not be subject to any limitation on obligations from amounts deposited to or available in the Fund.".

(e) VICTIMS OF SEPTEMBER 11, 2001. — Amounts transferred to the Crime Victims Fund for use in responding to the airplane hijackings and terrorist acts (including any related search, rescue, relief, assistance, or other similar activities) that occurred on September 11, 2001, shall not be subject to any limitation on obligations from amounts deposited to or available in the Fund, notwithstanding —

(1) section 619 of the Departments of Commerce, Justice, and State, the Judiciary, and Related Agencies Appropriations Act, 2001, and any similar limitation on Fund obligations in such Act for Fiscal Year 2002; and

(2) subsections (c) and (d) of section 1402 of the Victims of Crime Act of 1984 (42 U.S.C. 10601).

SEC. 622. CRIME VICTIM COMPENSATION.

(a) ALLOCATION OF FUNDS FOR COMPENSATION AND ASSISTANCE. — Paragraphs (1) and (2) of section 1403(a) of the Victims of Crime Act of 1984 (42 U.S.C. 10602(a)) are amended by inserting "in fiscal year 2002 and of 60 percent in subsequent fiscal years" after "40 per cent".

(b) LOCATION OF COMPENSABLE CRIME. — Section 1403(b)(6)(B) of the Victims of Crime Act of 1984 (42 U.S.C. 10602(b)(6)(B)) is amended by striking "are outside the United States (if the compensable crime is terrorism, as defined in section 2331 of title 18), or".

(c) RELATIONSHIP OF CRIME VICTIM COMPENSATION TO MEANSTESTED FEDERAL BENEFIT PROGRAMS. — Section 1403 of the Victims of Crime Act of 1984 (42 U.S.C. 10602) is amended by striking subsection (c) and inserting the following :

"(c) EXCLUSION FROM INCOME, RESOURCES, AND ASSETS FOR PURPOSES OF MEANS TESTS. — Notwithstanding any other law (other than title IV of Public Law 107–42), for the purpose of any maximum allowed income, resource, or asset eligibility requirement in any Federal, State, or local government program using Federal funds that provides medical or other assistance (or payment or reimbursement of the cost of such assistance), any amount of crime victim compensation that the applicant receives through a crime victim compensation program under this section shall not be included in the income, resources, or assets of the applicant, nor shall that amount reduce the amount of the assistance available to the applicant from Federal, State, or local government programs using Federal funds, unless the total amount of assistance that the applicant receives from all such programs is sufficient to fully compensate the applicant for losses suffered as a result of the crime.".

(d) DEFINITIONS OF "COMPENSABLE CRIME" AND "STATE". — Section 1403(d) of the Victims of Crime Act of 1984 (42 U.S.C. 10602(d)) is amended —

(1) in paragraph (3), by striking "crimes involving terrorism,"; and

(2) in paragraph (4), by inserting "the United States Virgin Islands," after "the Commonwealth of Puerto Rico,".

(e) RELATIONSHIP OF ELIGIBLE CRIME VICTIM COMPENSATION PROGRAMS TO THE SEPTEMBER 11TH VICTIM COMPENSATION FUND. —

(1) IN GENERAL. — Section 1403(e) of the Victims of Crime Act of 1984 (42 U.S.C. 10602(e)) is amended by inserting "including the program established under title IV of Public Law 107–42," after "Federal program,".

(2) COMPENSATION. — With respect to any compensation payable under title IV of Public Law 107–42, the failure of a crime victim compensation program, after the effective date of final regulations issued pursuant to section 407 of Public Law 107–42, to provide compensation otherwise required pursuant to section 1403 of the Victims of Crime Act of 1984 (42 U.S.C.

10602) shall not render that program ineligible for future grants under the Victims of Crime Act of 1984.

SEC. 623. CRIME VICTIM ASSISTANCE.

(a) ASSISTANCE FOR VICTIMS IN THE DISTRICT OF COLUMBIA, PUERTO RICO, AND OTHER TERRITORIES AND POSSESSIONS. — Section 1404(a) of the Victims of Crime Act of 1984 (42 U.S.C. 10603(a)) is amended by adding at the end the following :

"(6) An agency of the Federal Government performing local law enforcement functions in and on behalf of the District of Columbia, the Commonwealth of Puerto Rico, the United States Virgin Islands, or any other territory or possession of the United States may qualify as an eligible crime victim assistance program for the purpose of grants under this subsection, or for the purpose of grants under subsection (c)(1).".

(b) PROHIBITION ON DISCRIMINATION AGAINST CERTAIN VICTIMS. — Section 1404(b)(1) of the Victims of Crime Act of 1984 (42 U.S.C. 10603(b)(1)) is amended —

(1) in subparagraph (D), by striking "and" at the end;

(2) in subparagraph (E), by striking the period at the end and inserting "; and"; and

(3) by adding at the end the following :

"(F) does not discriminate against victims because they disagree with the way the State is prosecuting the criminal case.".

(c) GRANTS FOR PROGRAM EVALUATION AND COMPLIANCE EFFORTS. — Section 1404(c)(1)(A) of the Victims of Crime Act of 1984 (42 U.S.C. 10603(c)(1)(A)) is amended by inserting ", program evaluation, compliance efforts," after "demonstration projects".

(d) ALLOCATION OF DISCRETIONARY GRANTS. — Section 1404(c)(2) of the Victims of Crime Act of 1984 (42 U.S.C. 10603(c)(2)) is amended —

(1) in subparagraph (A), by striking "not more than" and inserting "not less than"; and

(2) in subparagraph (B), by striking "not less than" and inserting "not more than".

(e) FELLOWSHIPS AND CLINICAL INTERNSHIPS. — Section 1404(c)(3) of the Victims of Crime Act of 1984 (42 U.S.C. 10603(c)(3)) is amended —

(1) in subparagraph (C), by striking "and" at the end;

(2) in subparagraph (D), by striking the period at the end and inserting "; and"; and

(3) by adding at the end the following :

"(E) use funds made available to the Director under this subsection —

"(i) for fellowships and clinical internships; and

"(ii) to carry out programs of training and special workshops for the presentation and dissemination of information resulting from demonstrations, surveys, and special projects.".

SEC. 624. VICTIMS OF TERRORISM.

(a) COMPENSATION AND ASSISTANCE TO VICTIMS OF DOMESTIC TERRORISM. — Section 1404B(b) of the Victims of Crime Act of 1984 (42 U.S.C. 10603b(b)) is amended to read as follows :

"(b) VICTIMS OF TERRORISM WITHIN THE UNITED STATES. — The Director may make supplemental grants as provided in section 1402(d)(5) to States for eligible crime victim compensation and assistance programs, and to victim service organizations, public agencies (including Federal, State, or local governments) and non-governmental organizations that provide assistance to victims of crime, which shall be used to provide emergency relief, including crisis response efforts, assistance, compensation, training and technical assistance, and ongoing assistance, including during any investigation or prosecution, to victims of terrorist acts or mass violence occurring within the United States.".

(b) ASSISTANCE TO VICTIMS OF INTERNATIONAL TERRORISM. — Section 1404B(a)(1) of the Victims of Crime Act of 1984 (42 U.S.C. 10603b(a)(1)) is amended by striking "who are not persons eligible for compensation under title VIII of the Omnibus Diplomatic Security and Antiterrorism Act of 1986".

(c) COMPENSATION TO VICTIMS OF INTERNATIONAL TERRORISM. — Section 1404C(b) of the Victims of Crime of 1984 (42 U.S.C. 10603c(b)) is amended by adding at the end the following : "The amount of compensation awarded to a victim under this subsection shall be reduced by any amount that the victim received in connection with the same act of international terrorism under title VIII of the Omnibus Diplomatic Security and Antiterrorism Act of 1986.".

TITLE VII — INCREASED INFORMATION SHARING FOR CRITICAL INFRASTRUCTURE PROTECTION

SEC. 701. EXPANSION OF REGIONAL INFORMATION SHARING SYSTEM TO FACILITATE FEDERAL-STATE-LOCAL LAW ENFORCEMENT RESPONSE RELATED TO TERRORIST ATTACKS.

Section 1301 of title I of the Omnibus Crime Control and Safe Streets Act of 1968 (42 U.S.C. 3796h) is amended —

(1) in subsection (a), by inserting "and terrorist conspiracies and activities" after "activities";

(2) in subsection (b) —

(A) in paragraph (3), by striking "and" after the semicolon;

(B) by redesignating paragraph (4) as paragraph (5); and

(C) by inserting after paragraph (3) the following :

"(4) establishing and operating secure information sharing systems to enhance the investigation and prosecution abilities of participating enforcement agencies in addressing multi-juris-dictional terrorist conspiracies and activities; and (5)"; and

(3) by inserting at the end the following :

"(d) AUTHORIZATION OF APPROPRIATION TO THE BUREAU OF JUSTICE ASSISTANCE. — There are authorized to be appropriated to the Bureau of Justice Assistance to carry out this section $50,000,000 for fiscal year 2002 and $100,000,000 for fiscal year 2003.".

TITLE VIII — STRENGTHENING THE CRIMINAL LAWS AGAINST TERRORISM

SEC. 801. TERRORIST ATTACKS AND OTHER ACTS OF VIOLENCE AGAINST MASS TRANSPORTATION SYSTEMS.

Chapter 97 of title 18, United States Code, is amended by adding at the end the following :

"§ 1993. Terrorist attacks and other acts of violence against mass transportation systems

"(a) GENERAL PROHIBITIONS. — Whoever willfully —

"(1) wrecks, derails, sets fire to, or disables a mass transportation vehicle or ferry;

"(2) places or causes to be placed any biological agent or toxin for use as a weapon, destructive substance, or destructive device in, upon, or near a mass transportation vehicle or ferry, without previously obtaining the permission of the mass transportation provider, and with intent to endanger the safety of any passenger or employee of the mass transportation provider, or with a reckless disregard for the safety of human life;

"(3) sets fire to, or places any biological agent or toxin for use as a weapon, destructive substance, or destructive device in, upon, or near any garage, terminal, structure, supply, or facility used in the operation of, or in support of the operation of, a mass transportation vehicle or ferry, without previously obtaining the permission of the mass transportation provider, and knowing or having reason to know such activity would likely derail, disable, or wreck a mass transportation vehicle or ferry used, operated, or employed by the mass transportation provider;

"(4) removes appurtenances from, damages, or otherwise

impairs the operation of a mass transportation signal system, including a train control system, centralized dispatching system, or rail grade crossing warning signal without authorization from the mass transportation provider;

"(5) interferes with, disables, or incapacitates any dispatcher, driver, captain, or person while they are employed in dispatching, operating, or maintaining a mass transportation vehicle or ferry, with intent to endanger the safety of any passenger or employee of the mass transportation provider, or with a reckless disregard for the safety of human life;

"(6) commits an act, including the use of a dangerous weapon, with the intent to cause death or serious bodily injury to an employee or passenger of a mass transportation provider or any other person while any of the foregoing are on the property of a mass transportation provider;

"(7) conveys or causes to be conveyed false information, knowing the information to be false, concerning an attempt or alleged attempt being made or to be made, to do any act which would be a crime prohibited by this subsection; or

"(8) attempts, threatens, or conspires to do any of the aforesaid acts, shall be fined under this title or imprisoned not more than twenty years, or both, if such act is committed, or in the case of a threat or conspiracy such act would be committed, on, against, or affecting a mass transportation provider engaged in or affecting interstate or foreign commerce, or if in the course of committing such act, that person travels or communicates across a State line in order to commit such act, or transports materials across a State line in aid of the commission of such act.

"(b) AGGRAVATED OFFENSE. — Whoever commits an offense under subsection (a) in a circumstance in which —

"(1) the mass transportation vehicle or ferry was carrying a passenger at the time of the offense; or

"(2) the offense has resulted in the death of any person,

shall be guilty of an aggravated form of the offense and shall be fined under this title or imprisoned for a term of years or for life, or both.

"(c) DEFINITIONS. — In this section —

"(1) the term 'biological agent' has the meaning given to that term in section 178(1) of this title;

"(2) the term 'dangerous weapon' has the meaning given to that term in section 930 of this title;

"(3) the term 'destructive device' has the meaning given to that term in section 921(a)(4) of this title;

"(4) the term 'destructive substance' has the meaning given to that term in section 31 of this title;

"(5) the term 'mass transportation' has the meaning given to that term in section 5302(a)(7) of title 49, United States Code, except that the term shall include schoolbus, charter, and sightseeing transportation;

"(6) the term 'serious bodily injury' has the meaning given to that term in section 1365 of this title;

"(7) the term 'State' has the meaning given to that term in section 2266 of this title; and

"(8) the term 'toxin' has the meaning given to that term in section 178(2) of this title.".

(f) CONFORMING AMENDMENT. — The analysis of chapter 97 of title 18, United States Code, is amended by adding at the end :

"1993. Terrorist attacks and other acts of violence against mass transportation systems.".

SEC. 802. DEFINITION OF DOMESTIC TERRORISM.

(a) DOMESTIC TERRORISM DEFINED. — Section 2331 of title 18, United States Code, is amended —

(1) in paragraph (1)(B)(iii), by striking "by assassination or kidnapping" and inserting "by mass destruction, assassination, or kidnapping";

(2) in paragraph (3), by striking "and";

(3) in paragraph (4), by striking the period at the end and inserting "; and"; and

(4) by adding at the end the following :

"(5) the term 'domestic terrorism' means activities that —

"(A) involve acts dangerous to human life that are a violation of the criminal laws of the United States or of any State;

"(B) appear to be intended —

"(i) to intimidate or coerce a civilian population;

"(ii) to influence the policy of a government by intimidation or coercion; or

"(iii) to affect the conduct of a government by mass destruction, assassination, or kidnapping; and

"(C) occur primarily within the territorial jurisdiction of the United States.".

(b) CONFORMING AMENDMENT. — Section 3077(1) of title 18, United States Code, is amended to read as follows :

"(1) 'act of terrorism' means an act of domestic or international terrorism as defined in section 2331;".

SEC. 803. PROHIBITION AGAINST HARBORING TERRORISTS.

(a) IN GENERAL. — Chapter 113B of title 18, United States Code, is amended by adding after section 2338 the following new section :

"§ 2339. Harboring or concealing terrorists

"(a) Whoever harbors or conceals any person who he knows, or has reasonable grounds to believe, has committed, or is about to commit, an offense under section 32 (relating to destruction of aircraft or aircraft facilities), section 175 (relating to biological weapons), section 229 (relating to chemical weapons), section 831 (relating to nuclear materials), paragraph (2) or (3) of section 844(f) (relating to arson and bombing of government property risking or causing injury or death), section 1366(a) (relating to the destruction of an energy facility), section 2280 (relating to violence against maritime navigation), section 2332a (relating to weapons of mass destruction), or section 2332b (relating to acts of terrorism transcending national boundaries) of this title, section 236(a) (relating to sabotage of nuclear facilities or fuel) of the Atomic Energy Act of 1954 (42 U.S.C. 2284(a)), or section 46502 (relating to aircraft piracy) of title 49, shall be fined under this title or imprisoned not more than ten years, or both.".

"(b) A violation of this section may be prosecuted in any Federal judicial district in which the underlying offense was committed, or in any other Federal judicial district as provided by law.".

(b) TECHNICAL AMENDMENT. — The chapter analysis for chapter 113B of title 18, United States Code, is amended by inserting after the item for section 2338 the following :

"2339. Harboring or concealing terrorists.".

SEC. 804. JURISDICTION OVER CRIMES COMMITTED AT U.S. FACILITIES ABROAD.

Section 7 of title 18, United States Code, is amended by adding at the end the following :

"(9) With respect to offenses committed by or against a national of the United States as that term is used in section 101 of the Immigration and Nationality Act —

"(A) the premises of United States diplomatic, consular, military or other United States Government missions or entities in foreign States, including the buildings, parts of buildings, and land appurtenant or ancillary thereto or used for purposes of those missions or entities, irrespective of ownership; and

"(B) residences in foreign States and the land appurtenant or ancillary thereto, irrespective of ownership, used for purposes of those missions or entities or used by United States personnel assigned to those missions or entities.

Nothing in this paragraph shall be deemed to supersede any treaty or international agreement with which this paragraph conflicts. This paragraph does not apply with respect to an offense committed by a person described in section 3261(a) of this title.".

SEC. 805. MATERIAL SUPPORT FOR TERRORISM.

(a) IN GENERAL. — Section 2339A of title 18, United States Code, is amended —

(1) in subsection (a) —

(A) by striking ", within the United States,";

(B) by inserting "229," after "175,";

(C) by inserting "1993," after "1992,";

(D) by inserting ", section 236 of the Atomic Energy Act of 1954 (42 U.S.C. 2284)," after "of this title";

(E) by inserting "or 60123(b)" after "46502"; and

(F) by inserting at the end the following : "A violation of this section may be prosecuted in any Federal judicial district in which the underlying offense was committed, or in any other Federal judicial district as provided by law."; and

(2) in subsection (b) —

(A) by striking "or other financial securities" and inserting "or monetary instruments or financial securities"; and

(B) by inserting "cxpert advice or assistance," after "training,".

(b) TECHNICAL AMENDMENT. — Section 1956(c)(7)(D) of title 18, United States Code, is amended by inserting "or 2339B" after "2339A".

SEC. 806. ASSETS OF TERRORIST ORGANIZATIONS.

Section 981(a)(1) of title 18, United States Code, is amended by inserting at the end the following :

"(G) All assets, foreign or domestic —

"(i) of any individual, entity, or organization engaged in planning or perpetrating any act of domestic or inter-national terrorism (as defined in section 2331) against the United States, citizens or residents of the United States, or their property, and all assets, foreign or domestic, affording any person a source of influence over any such entity or organization;

"(ii) acquired or maintained by any person with the intent and for the purpose of supporting, planning, conducting, or concealing an act of domestic or international terrorism (as defined in section 2331) against the United States, citizens or residents of the United States, or their property; or

"(iii) derived from, involved in, or used or intended to be used to commit any act of domestic or international terrorism (as defined in section 2331) against the United States, citizens or residents of the United States, or their property.".

SEC. 807. TECHNICAL CLARIFICATION RELATING TO PROVISION OF MATERIAL SUPPORT TO TERRORISM.

No provision of the Trade Sanctions Reform and Export Enhancement Act of 2000 (title IX of Public Law 106–387) shall be construed to limit or otherwise affect section 2339A or 2339B of title 18, United States Code.

SEC. 808. DEFINITION OF FEDERAL CRIME OF TERRORISM.

Section 2332b of title 18, United States Code, is amended —

(1) in subsection (f), by inserting "and any violation of section 351(e), 844(e), 844(f)(1), 956(b), 1361, 1366(b), 1366(c), 1751(e), 2152, or 2156 of this title," before "and the Secretary"; and

(2) in subsection (g)(5)(B), by striking clauses (i) through (iii) and inserting the following :

"(i) section 32 (relating to destruction of aircraft or aircraft facilities), 37 (relating to violence at inter-national airports), 81 (relating to arson within special maritime and territorial jurisdiction), 175 or 175b (relating to biological weapons), 229 (relating to chemical weapons), subsection (a), (b), (c), or (d) of section 351 (relating to congressional, cabinet, and Supreme Court assassination and kidnaping), 831 (relating to nuclear materials), 842(m) or (n) (relating to plastic explosives), 844(f)(2) or (3) (relating to arson and bombing of Government property risking or causing death), 844(i) (relating to arson and bombing of property used in interstate commerce), 930(c) (relating to killing or attempted killing during an attack on a Federal facility with a dangerous weapon), 956(a)(1) (relating to conspiracy to murder, kidnap, or maim persons abroad),

1030(a)(1) (relating to protection of computers), 1030(a)(5)(A)(i) resulting in damage as defined in 1030(a)(5)(B)(ii) through (v) (relating to protection of computers), 1114 (relating to killing or attempted killing of officers and employees of the United States), 1116 (relating to murder or man-slaughter of foreign officials, official guests, or internationally protected persons), 1203 (relating to hostage taking), 1362 (relating to destruction of communication lines, stations, or systems), 1363 (relating to injury to buildings or property within special maritime and territorial jurisdiction of the United States), 1366(a) (relating to destruction of an energy facility), 1751(a), (b), (c), or (d) (relating to Presidential and Presidential staff assassination and kidnaping), 1992 (relating to wrecking trains), 1993 (relating to terrorist attacks and other acts of violence against mass transportation systems), 2155 (relating to destruction of national defense materials, premises, or utilities), 2280 (relating to violence against maritime navigation), 2281 (relating to violence against maritime fixed platforms), 2332 (relating to certain homicides and other violence against United States nationals occurring outside of the United States), 2332a (relating to use of weapons of mass destruction), 2332b (relating to acts of terrorism transcending national boundaries), 2339 (relating to harboring terrorists), 2339A (relating to providing material support to terrorists), 2339B (relating to providing material support to terrorist organizations), or 2340A (relating to torture) of this title;

"(ii) section 236 (relating to sabotage of nuclear facilities or fuel) of the Atomic Energy Act of 1954 (42 U.S.C. 2284); or

"(iii) section 46502 (relating to aircraft piracy), the second sentence of section 46504 (relating to assault on a flight crew with a dangerous weapon), section 46505(b)(3) or (c) (relating to explosive or incendiary devices, or endangerment of human life by means of weapons, on aircraft), section 46506 if homicide or attempted homicide is involved (relating to application of certain criminal laws to acts on aircraft), or section 60123(b) (relating to destruction of interstate gas or hazardous liquid pipeline facility) of title 49.".

SEC. 809. NO STATUTE OF LIMITATION FOR CERTAIN TERRORISM OFFENSES.

(a) IN GENERAL. — Section 3286 of title 18, United States Code, is amended to read as follows :

"§ 3286. Extension of statute of limitation for certain terrorism offenses

"(a) EIGHT-YEAR LIMITATION. — Notwithstanding section 3282, no person shall be prosecuted, tried, or punished for any noncapital offense involving a violation of any provision listed in section 2332b(g)(5)(B), or a violation of section 112, 351(e), 1361, or 1751(e) of this title, or section 46504, 46505, or 46506 of title 49, unless the indictment is found or the information is instituted within 8 years after the offense was committed. Notwithstanding the preceding sentence, offenses listed in section 3295 are subject to the statute of limitations set forth in that section.

"(b) NO LIMITATION. — Notwithstanding any other law, an indictment may be found or an information instituted at any time without limitation for any offense listed in section 2332b(g)(5)(B), if the commission of such offense resulted in, or created a forseeable risk of, death or serious bodily injury to another person.".

(b) APPLICATION. — The amendments made by this section shall apply to the prosecution of any offense committed before, on, or after the date of the enactment of this section.

SEC. 810. ALTERNATE MAXIMUM PENALTIES FOR TERRORISM OFFENSES.

(a) ARSON. — Section 81 of title 18, United States Code, is amended in the second undesignated paragraph by striking "not more than twenty years" and inserting "for any term of years or for life".

(b) DESTRUCTION OF AN ENERGY FACILITY. — Section 1366 of title 18, United States Code, is amended —

(1) in subsection (a), by striking "ten" and inserting "20"; and

(2) by adding at the end the following :

"(d) Whoever is convicted of a violation of subsection (a) or (b) that has resulted in the death of any person shall be subject to imprisonment for any term of years or life.".

(c) MATERIAL SUPPORT TO TERRORISTS. — Section 2339A(a) of title 18, United States Code, is amended —

(1) by striking "10" and inserting "15"; and

(2) by striking the period and inserting ", and, if the death of any person results, shall be imprisoned for any term of years or for life.".

(d) MATERIAL SUPPORT TO DESIGNATED FOREIGN TERRORIST ORGANIZATIONS. — Section 2339B(a)(1) of title 18, United States Code, is amended —

(1) by striking "10" and inserting "15"; and

(2) by striking the period after "or both" and inserting ", and, if the death of any person results, shall be imprisoned for any term of years or for life.".

(e) DESTRUCTION OF NATIONALDEFENSE MATERIALS. — Section 2155(a) of title 18, United States Code, is amended —

(1) by striking "ten" and inserting "20"; and

(2) by striking the period at the end and inserting ", and, if death results to any person, shall be imprisoned for any term of years or for life.".

(f) SABOTAGE OF NUCLEAR FACILITIES OR FUEL. — Section 236 of the Atomic Energy Act of 1954 (42 U.S.C. 2284), is amended —

(1) by striking "ten" each place it appears and inserting "20";

(2) in subsection (a), by striking the period at the end and inserting ", and, if death results to any person, shall be imprisoned for any term of years or for life."; and

(3) in subsection (b), by striking the period at the end and inserting ", and, if death results to any person, shall be imprisoned for any term of years or for life.".

(g) SPECIAL AIRCRAFT JURISDICTION OF THE UNITED STATES. — Section 46505(c) of title 49, United States Code, is amended —

(1) by striking "15" and inserting "20"; and

(2) by striking the period at the end and inserting ", and, if death results to any person, shall be imprisoned for any term of years or for life.".

(h) DAMAGING OR DESTROYING AN INTERSTATE GAS OR HAZARDOUS LIQUID PIPELINE FACILITY. — Section 60123(b) of title 49, United States Code, is amended —

(1) by striking "15" and inserting "20"; and

(2) by striking the period at the end and inserting ", and, if death results to any person, shall be imprisoned for any term of years or for life.".

SEC. 811. PENALTIES FOR TERRORIST CONSPIRACIES.

(a) ARSON. — Section 81 of title 18, United States Code, is amended in the first undesignated paragraph —

(1) by striking ", or attempts to set fire to or burn"; and

(2) by inserting "or attempts or conspires to do such an act," before "shall be imprisoned".

(b) KILLINGS IN FEDERAL FACILITIES. — Section 930(c) of title 18, United States Code, is amended —

(1) by striking "or attempts to kill";

(2) by inserting "or attempts or conspires to do such an act," before "shall be punished"; and

(3) by striking "and 1113" and inserting "1113, and 1117".

(c) COMMUNICATIONS LINES, STATIONS, OR SYSTEMS. — Section 1362 of title 18, United States Code, is amended in the first undesignated paragraph —

(1) by striking "or attempts willfully or maliciously to injure or destroy"; and

(2) by inserting "or attempts or conspires to do such an act," before "shall be fined".

(d) BUILDINGS OR PROPERTY WITHIN SPECIAL MARITIME AND TERRITORIAL JURISDICTION. — Section 1363 of title 18, United States Code, is amended —

(1) by striking "or attempts to destroy or injure"; and

(2) by inserting "or attempts or conspires to do such an act," before "shall be fined" the first place it appears.

(e) WRECKING TRAINS. — Section 1992 of title 18, United States Code, is amended by adding at the end the following :

"(c) A person who conspires to commit any offense defined in this section shall be subject to the same penalties (other than the penalty of death) as the penalties prescribed for the offense, the commission of which was the object of the conspiracy.".

(f) MATERIAL SUPPORT TO TERRORISTS. — Section 2339A of title 18, United States Code, is amended by inserting "or attempts or conspires to do such an act," before "shall be fined".

(g) TORTURE. — Section 2340A of title 18, United States Code, is amended by adding at the end the following :

"(c) CONSPIRACY. — A person who conspires to commit an offense under this section shall be subject to the same penalties (other than the penalty of death) as the penalties prescribed for the offense, the commission of which was the object of the conspiracy.".

(h) SABOTAGE OF NUCLEAR FACILITIES OR FUEL. — Section 236 of the Atomic Energy Act of 1954 (42 U.S.C. 2284), is amended —

(1) in subsection (a) —

(A) by striking ", or who intentionally and willfully attempts to destroy or cause physical damage to";

(B) in paragraph (4), by striking the period at the end and inserting a comma; and

(C) by inserting "or attempts or conspires to do such an act," before "shall be fined"; and

(2) in subsection (b) —

(A) by striking "or attempts to cause"; and

(B) by inserting "or attempts or conspires to do such an act," before "shall be fined".

(i) INTERFERENCE WITH FLIGHT CREW MEMBERS AND ATTENDANTS. — Section 46504 of title 49, United States Code, is amended by inserting "or attempts or conspires to do such an act," before "shall be fined".

(j) SPECIAL AIRCRAFT JURISDICTION OF THE UNITED STATES. — Section 46505 of title 49, United States Code, is amended by adding at the end the following :

"(e) CONSPIRACY. — If two or more persons conspire to violate subsection (b) or (c), and one or more of such persons do any act to effect the object of the conspiracy, each of the parties to such conspiracy shall be punished as provided in such subsection.".

(k) DAMAGING OR DESTROYING AN INTERSTATE GAS OR HAZARDOUS LIQUID PIPELINE FACILITY. — Section 60123(b) of title 49, United States Code, is amended —

(1) by striking ", or attempting to damage or destroy,"; and (2) by inserting ", or attempting or conspiring to do such an act," before "shall be fined".

SEC. 812. POST-RELEASE SUPERVISION OF TERRORISTS.

Section 3583 of title 18, United States Code, is amended by adding at the end the following :

"(j) SUPERVISED RELEASE TERMS FOR TERRORISM PREDICATES. — Notwithstanding subsection (b), the authorized term of supervised release for any offense listed in section 2332b(g)(5)(B), the commission of which resulted in, or created a foreseeable risk of, death or serious bodily injury to another person, is any term of years or life.".

SEC. 813. INCLUSION OF ACTS OF TERRORISM AS RACKETEERING ACTIVITY.

Section 1961(1) of title 18, United States Code, is amended —

(1) by striking "or (F)" and inserting "(F)"; and

(2) by inserting before the semicolon at the end the following : ", or (G) any act that is indictable under any provision listed in section 2332b(g)(5)(B)".

SEC. 814. DETERRENCE AND PREVENTION OF CYBERTERRORISM.

(a) CLARIFICATION OF PROTECTION OF PROTECTED

COMPUTERS. — Section 1030(a)(5) of title 18, United States Code, is amended —

(1) by inserting "(i)" after "(A)";

(2) by redesignating subparagraphs (B) and (C) as clauses (ii) and (iii), respectively;

(3) by adding "and" at the end of clause (iii), as so redesignated; and

(4) by adding at the end the following :

"(B) by conduct described in clause (i), (ii), or (iii) of subparagraph (A), caused (or, in the case of an attempted offense, would, if completed, have caused) —

"(i) loss to 1 or more persons during any 1-year period (and, for purposes of an investigation, prosecution, or other proceeding brought by the United States only, loss resulting from a related course of conduct affecting 1 or more other protected computers) aggregating at least $5,000 in value;

"(ii) the modification or impairment, or potential modification or impairment, of the medical examination, diagnosis, treatment, or care of 1 or more individuals;

"(iii) physical injury to any person;

"(iv) a threat to public health or safety; or

"(v) damage affecting a computer system used by or for a government entity in furtherance of the administration of justice, national defense, or national security;".

(b) PROTECTION FROM EXTORTION. — Section 1030(a)(7) of title 18, United States Code, is amended by striking ", firm, association, educational institution, financial institution, government entity, or other legal entity,".

(c) PENALTIES. — Section 1030(c) of title 18, United States Code, is amended —

(1) in paragraph (2) —

(A) in subparagraph (A) —

(i) by inserting "except as provided in subparagraph (B)," before "a fine";

(ii) by striking "(a)(5)(C)" and inserting "(a)(5)(A)(iii)"; and

(iii) by striking "and' at the end;

(B) in subparagraph (B), by inserting "or an attempt to commit an offense punishable under this subparagraph," after "subsection (a)(2)," in the matter preceding clause (i); and

(C) in subparagraph (C), by striking "and" at the end;

(2) in paragraph (3) —

(A) by striking ", (a)(5)(A), (a)(5)(B)," both places it appears; and

(B) by striking "(a)(5)(C)" and inserting "(a)(5)(A)(iii)"; and

(3) by adding at the end the following :

"(4)(A) a fine under this title, imprisonment for not more than 10 years, or both, in the case of an offense under sub-section (a)(5)(A)(i), or an attempt to commit an offense punishable under that subsection;

"(B) a fine under this title, imprisonment for not more than 5 years, or both, in the case of an offense under subsection (a)(5)(A)(ii), or an attempt to commit an offense punishable under that subsection;

"(C) a fine under this title, imprisonment for not more than 20 years, or both, in the case of an offense under sub-section (a)(5)(A)(i) or (a)(5)(A)(ii), or an attempt to commit an offense punishable under either subsection, that occurs after a conviction for another offense under this section.".

(d) DEFINITIONS. — Section 1030(e) of title 18, United States Code is amended —

(1) in paragraph (2)(B), by inserting ", including a computer located outside the United States that is used in a

manner that affects interstate or foreign commerce or communication of the United States" before the semicolon;

(2) in paragraph (7), by striking "and" at the end;

(3) by striking paragraph (8) and inserting the following :

"(8) the term 'damage' means any impairment to the integrity or availability of data, a program, a system, or information;";

(4) in paragraph (9), by striking the period at the end and inserting a semicolon; and

(5) by adding at the end the following :

"(10) the term 'conviction' shall include a conviction under the law of any State for a crime punishable by imprisonment for more than 1 year, an element of which is unauthorized access, or exceeding authorized access, to a computer;

"(11) the term 'loss' means any reasonable cost to any victim, including the cost of responding to an offense, conducting a damage assessment, and restoring the data, program, system, or information to its condition prior to the offense, and any revenue lost, cost incurred, or other consequential damages incurred because of interruption of service; and

"(12) the term 'person' means any individual, firm, corporation, educational institution, financial institution, governmental entity, or legal or other entity.".

(e) DAMAGES IN CIVIL ACTIONS. — Section 1030(g) of title 18, United States Code is amended —

(1) by striking the second sentence and inserting the following : "A civil action for a violation of this section may be brought only if the conduct involves 1 of the factors set forth in clause (i), (ii), (iii), (iv), or (v) of subsection (a)(5)(B). Damages for a violation involving only conduct described in subsection (a)(5)(B)(i) are limited to economic damages."; and

(2) by adding at the end the following : "No action may be brought under this subsection for the negligent

design or manufacture of computer hardware, computer software, or firmware.".

(f) AMENDMENT OF SENTENCING GUIDELINES RELATING TO CERTAIN COMPUTER FRAUD AND ABUSE. — Pursuant to its authority under section 994(p) of title 28, United States Code, the United States Sentencing Commission shall amend the Federal sentencing guidelines to ensure that any individual convicted of a violation of section 1030 of title 18, United States Code, can be subjected to appropriate penalties, without regard to any mandatory minimum term of imprisonment.

SEC. 815. ADDITIONAL DEFENSE TO CIVIL ACTIONS RELATING TO PRE-SERVING RECORDS IN RESPONSE TO GOVERNMENT REQUESTS.

Section 2707(e)(1) of title 18, United States Code, is amended by inserting after "or statutory authorization" the following : "(including a request of a governmental entity under section 2703(f) of this title)".

SEC. 816. DEVELOPMENT AND SUPPORT OF CYBERSECURITY FORENSIC CAPABILITIES.

(a) IN GENERAL. — The Attorney General shall establish such regional computer forensic laboratories as the Attorney General considers appropriate, and provide support to existing computer forensic laboratories, in order that all such computer forensic laboratories have the capability —

(1) to provide forensic examinations with respect to seized or intercepted computer evidence relating to criminal activity (including cyberterrorism);

(2) to provide training and education for Federal, State, and local law enforcement personnel and prosecutors regarding investigations, forensic analyses, and prosecutions of computerrelated crime (including cyberterrorism);

(3) to assist Federal, State, and local law enforcement in enforcing Federal, State, and local criminal laws relating to computer-related crime;

(4) to facilitate and promote the sharing of Federal law enforcement expertise and information about the

investigation, analysis, and prosecution of computer-related crime with State and local law enforcement personnel and prosecutors, including the use of multijurisdictional task forces; and

(5) to carry out such other activities as the Attorney General considers appropriate.

(b) AUTHORIZATION OF APPROPRIATIONS. —

(1) AUTHORIZATION. — There is hereby authorized to be appropriated in each fiscal year $50,000,000 for purposes of carrying out this section.

(2) AVAILABILITY. — Amounts appropriated pursuant to the authorization of appropriations in paragraph (1) shall remain available until expended.

SEC. 817. EXPANSION OF THE BIOLOGICAL WEAPONS STATUTE.

Chapter 10 of title 18, United States Code, is amended —

(1) in section 175 —

(A) in subsection (b) —

(i) by striking "does not include" and inserting "includes";

(ii) by inserting "other than" after "system for"; and

(iii) by inserting "bona fide research" after "protective";

(B) by redesignating subsection (b) as subsection (c); and

(C) by inserting after subsection (a) the following :

"(b) ADDITIONAL OFFENSE. — Whoever knowingly possesses any biological agent, toxin, or delivery system of a type or in a quantity that, under the circumstances, is not reasonably justified by a prophylactic, protective, bona fide research, or other peaceful purpose, shall be fined under this title, imprisoned not more than 10 years, or both. In this subsection, the terms 'biological agent' and 'toxin' do not encompass any biological agent or toxin that is in its naturally occurring environment, if the biological agent or toxin has not been cultivated, collected, or otherwise extracted from its natural source.";

(2) by inserting after section 175a the following :

"SEC. 175b. POSSESSION BY RESTRICTED PERSONS.

"(a) No restricted person described in subsection (b) shall ship or transport interstate or foreign commerce, or possess in or affecting commerce, any biological agent or toxin, or receive any biological agent or toxin that has been shipped or transported in interstate or foreign commerce, if the biological agent or toxin is listed as a select agent in subsection (j) of section 72.6 of title 42, Code of Federal Regulations, pursuant to section 511(d)(l) of the Antiterrorism and Effective Death Penalty Act of 1996 (Public Law 104–132), and is not exempted under subsection (h) of such section 72.6, or appendix A of part 72 of the Code of Regulations.

"(b) In this section :

"(1) The term 'select agent' does not include any such biological agent or toxin that is in its naturally-occurring environment, if the biological agent or toxin has not been cultivated, collected, or otherwise extracted from its natural source.

"(2) The term 'restricted person' means an individual who —

"(A) is under indictment for a crime punishable by imprisonment for a term exceeding 1 year;

"(B) has been convicted in any court of a crime punishable by imprisonment for a term exceeding 1 year;

"(C) is a fugitive from justice;

"(D) is an unlawful user of any controlled substance (as defined in section 102 of the Controlled Substances Act (21 U.S.C. 802));

"(E) is an alien illegally or unlawfully in the United States;

"(F) has been adjudicated as a mental defective or has been committed to any mental institution;

"(G) is an alien (other than an alien lawfully admitted for permanent residence) who is a national of a country as to which the Secretary of State, pursuant to section 6(j) of the Export Administration Act of 1979 (50 U.S.C. App. 2405(j)), section 620A of chapter 1 of part M of the Foreign Assistance Act of 1961 (22 U.S.C. 2371), or section 40(d) of chapter 3 of the Arms Export Control Act (22 U.S.C. 2780(d)), has made a determination (that remains in effect) that such country has repeatedly provided support for acts of international terrorism; or

"(H) has been discharged from the Armed Services of the United States under dishonorable conditions.

"(3) The term 'alien' has the same meaning as in section 1010(a)(3) of the Immigration and Nationality Act (8 U.S.C. 1101(a)(3)).

"(4) The term 'lawfully admitted for permanent residence' has the same meaning as in section 101(a)(20) of the Immigration and Nationality Act (8 U.S.C. 1101(a)(20)).

"(c) Whoever knowingly violates this section shall be fined as provided in this title, imprisoned not more than 10 years, or both, but the prohibition contained in this section shall not apply with respect to any duly authorized United States governmental activity."; and

(3) in the chapter analysis, by inserting after the item relating to section 175a the following :

"175b. Possession by restricted persons.".

TITLE IX — IMPROVED INTELLIGENCE

SEC. 901. RESPONSIBILITIES OF DIRECTOR OF CENTRAL INTELLIGENCE REGARDING FOREIGN INTELLIGENCE COLLECTED UNDER FOREIGN INTELLIGENCE SURVEILLANCE ACT OF 1978.

Section 103(c) of the National Security Act of 1947 (50 U.S.C. 403–3(c)) is amended —

(1) by redesignating paragraphs (6) and (7) as paragraphs (7) and (8), respectively; and

(2) by inserting after paragraph (5) the following new paragraph (6) :

"(6) establish requirements and priorities for foreign intelligence information to be collected under the Foreign Intelligence Surveillance Act of 1978 (50 U.S.C. 1801 et seq.), and provide assistance to the Attorney General to ensure that information derived from electronic surveillance or physical searches under that Act is disseminated so it may be used efficiently and effectively for foreign intelligence purposes, except that the Director shall have no authority to direct, manage, or undertake electronic surveillance or physical search operations pursuant to that Act unless otherwise authorized by statute or Executive order;".

SEC. 902. INCLUSION OF INTERNATIONAL TERRORIST ACTIVITIES WITHIN SCOPE OF FOREIGN INTELLIGENCE UNDER NATIONAL SECURITY ACT OF 1947.

Section 3 of the National Security Act of 1947 (50 U.S.C. 401a) is amended —

(1) in paragraph (2), by inserting before the period the following : ", or international terrorist activities"; and

(2) in paragraph (3), by striking "and activities conducted" and inserting ", and activities conducted,".

SEC. 903. SENSE OF CONGRESS ON THE ESTABLISHMENT AND MAINTENANCE OF INTELLIGENCE RELATIONSHIPS TO ACQUIRE INFORMATION ON TERRORISTS AND TERRORIST ORGANIZATIONS.

It is the sense of Congress that officers and employees of the intelligence community of the Federal Government, acting within the course of their official duties, should be encouraged, and should make every effort, to establish and maintain intelligence relationships with any person, entity, or group for the purpose of engaging in lawful intelligence activities, including the acquisition of information on the identity, location, finances, affiliations, capabilities, plans, or intentions of a terrorist or terrorist organization, or information on any other person, entity, or group (including a foreign government) engaged in harboring, comforting, financing, aiding, or assisting a terrorist or terrorist organization.

SEC. 904. TEMPORARY AUTHORITY TO DEFER SUBMITTAL TO CONGRESS OF REPORTS ON INTELLIGENCE AND INTELLIGENCE-RELATED MATTERS.

(a) AUTHORITY TO DEFER. — The Secretary of Defense, Attorney General, and Director of Central Intelligence each may, during the effective period of this section, defer the date of submittal to Congress of any covered intelligence report under the jurisdiction of such official until February 1, 2002.

(b) COVERED INTELLIGENCE REPORT. — Except as provided in subsection (c), for purposes of subsection (a), a covered intelligence report is as follows :

(1) Any report on intelligence or intelligence-related activities of the United States Government that is required to be submitted to Congress by an element of the intelligence community during the effective period of this section.

(2) Any report or other matter that is required to be submitted to the Select Committee on Intelligence of the Senate and Permanent Select Committee on Intelligence of the House of Representatives by the Department of Defense or the Department of Justice during the effective period of this section.

(c) EXCEPTION FOR CERTAIN REPORTS. — For purposes of subsection (a), any report required by section 502 or 503 of the National Security Act of 1947 (50 U.S.C. 413a, 413b) is not a covered intelligence report.

(d) NOTICE TO CONGRESS. — Upon deferring the date of submittal to Congress of a covered intelligence report under subsection (a), the official deferring the date of submittal of the covered intelligence report shall submit to Congress notice of the deferral. Notice of deferral of a report shall specify the provision of law, if any, under which the report would otherwise be submitted to Congress.

(e) EXTENSION OF DEFERRAL. — (1) Each official specified in sub-section (a) may defer the date of submittal to Congress of a covered intelligence report under the jurisdiction of such official to a date after February 1, 2002, if such official submits to the committees of Congress specified in subsection (b)(2) before February 1, 2002, a certification that preparation and submittal of the covered intelligence report on February 1, 2002, will impede the work of officers or employees who are engaged in counterterrorism activities.

(2) A certification under paragraph (1) with respect to a covered intelligence report shall specify the date on which the covered intelligence report will be submitted to Congress.

(f) EFFECTIVE PERIOD. — The effective period of this section is the period beginning on the date of the enactment of this Act and ending on February 1, 2002.

(g) ELEMENT OF THE INTELLIGENCE COMMUNITY DEFINED. — In this section, the term "element of the intelligence community" means any element of the intelligence community specified or designated under section 3(4) of the National Security Act of 1947 (50 U.S.C. 401a(4)).

SEC. 905. DISCLOSURE TO DIRECTOR OF CENTRAL INTELLIGENCE OF FOREIGN INTELLIGENCE-RELATED INFORMATION WITH RESPECT TO CRIMINAL INVESTIGATIONS.

(a) IN GENERAL. — Title I of the National Security Act of 1947 (50 U.S.C. 402 et seq.) is amended —

(1) by redesignating subsection 105B as section 105C; and

(2) by inserting after section 105A the following new section 105B :

"DISCLOSURE OF FOREIGN INTELLIGENCE ACQUIRED IN CRIMINAL INVESTIGATIONS; NOTICE OF CRIMINAL INVESTIGATIONS OF FOREIGN INTELLIGENCE SOURCES

"SEC. 105B.

(a) DISCLOSURE OF FOREIGN INTELLIGENCE. —

(1) Except as otherwise provided by law and subject to paragraph (2), the Attorney General, or the head of any other department or agency of the Federal Government with law enforcement responsibilities, shall expeditiously disclose to the Director of Central Intelligence, pursuant to guidelines developed by the Attorney General in consultation with the Director, foreign intelligence acquired by an element of the

Department of Justice or an element of such department or agency, as the case may be, in the course of a criminal investigation.

"(2) The Attorney General by regulation and in consultation with the Director of Central Intelligence may provide for exceptions to the applicability of paragraph (1) for one or more classes of foreign intelligence, or foreign intelligence with respect to one or more targets or matters, if the Attorney General determines that disclosure of such foreign intelligence under that paragraph would jeopardize an ongoing law enforcement investigation or impair other significant law enforcement interests.

"(b) PROCEDURES FOR NOTICE OF CRIMINAL INVESTIGATIONS. — Not later than 180 days after the date of enactment of this section, the Attorney General, in consultation with the Director of Central Intelligence, shall develop guidelines to ensure that after receipt of a report from an element of the intelligence community of activity of a foreign intelligence source or potential foreign intelligence source that may warrant investigation as criminal activity, the Attorney General provides notice to the Director of Central Intelligence, within a reasonable period of time, of his intention to commence, or decline to commence, a criminal investigation of such activity.

"(c) PROCEDURES. — The Attorney General shall develop procedures for the administration of this section, including the disclosure of foreign intelligence by elements of the Department of Justice, and elements of other departments and agencies of the Federal Government, under subsection (a) and the provision of notice with respect to criminal investigations under subsection (b).".

(b) CLERICAL AMENDMENT. — The table of contents in the first section of that Act is amended by striking the item relating to section 105B and inserting the following new items :

"Sec. 105B. Disclosure of foreign intelligence acquired in criminal investigations; notice of criminal investigations of foreign intelligence sources.

"Sec. 105C. Protection of the operational files of the National Imagery and Mapping Agency.".

SEC. 906. FOREIGN TERRORIST ASSET TRACKING CENTER.

(a) REPORT ON RECONFIGURATION. — Not later than February 1, 2002, the Attorney General, the Director of Central Intelligence, and the Secretary of the Treasury shall jointly submit to Congress a report on the feasibility and desirability of reconfiguring the Foreign Terrorist Asset Tracking Center and the Office of Foreign Assets Control of the Department of the Treasury in order to establish a capability to provide for the effective and efficient analysis and dissemination of foreign intelligence relating to the financial capabilities and resources of international terrorist organizations.

(b) REPORT REQUIREMENTS. — (1) In preparing the report under subsection (a), the Attorney General, the Secretary, and the Director shall consider whether, and to what extent, the capacities and resources of the Financial Crimes Enforcement Center of the Department of the Treasury may be integrated into the capability contemplated by the report.

(2) If the Attorney General, Secretary, and the Director determine that it is feasible and desirable to undertake the reconfiguration described in subsection (a) in order to establish the capability described in that subsection, the Attorney General, the Secretary, and the Director shall include with the report under that subsection a detailed proposal for legislation to achieve the reconfiguration.

SEC. 907. NATIONAL VIRTUAL TRANSLATION CENTER.

(a) REPORT ON ESTABLISHMENT. — (1) Not later than February 1, 2002, the Director of Central Intelligence shall, in consultation with the Director of the Federal Bureau of Investigation, submit to the appropriate committees of Congress a report on the establishment and maintenance within the intelligence community of an element for purposes of providing timely and accurate translations of foreign intelligence for all other elements of the intelligence community. In the report, the element shall be referred to as the "National Virtual Translation Center".

(2) The report on the element described in paragraph (1) shall discuss the use of state-of-the-art communications technology, the integration of existing translation capabilities in the intelligence community, and the utilization of remote-connection capacities so as to minimize the need for a central physical facility for the element.

(b) RESOURCES. — The report on the element required by subsection (a) shall address the following :

(1) The assignment to the element of a staff of individuals possessing a broad range of linguistic and translation skills appropriate for the purposes of the element.

(2) The provision to the element of communications capabilities and systems that are commensurate with the most current and sophisticated communications capabilities and systems available to other elements of intelligence community.

(3) The assurance, to the maximum extent practicable, that the communications capabilities and systems provided to the element will be compatible with communications capabilities and systems utilized by the Federal Bureau of Investigation in securing timely and accurate translations of foreign language materials for law enforcement investigations.

(4) The development of a communications infrastructure to ensure the efficient and secure use of the translation capabilities of the element.

(c) SECURE COMMUNICATIONS. — The report shall include a discussion of the creation of secure electronic communications between the element described by subsection (a) and the other elements of the intelligence community.

(d) DEFINITIONS. — In this section :

(1) FOREIGN INTELLIGENCE. — The term "foreign intelligence" has the meaning given that term in section 3(2) of the National Security Act of 1947 (50 U.S.C. 401a(2)).

(2) ELEMENT OF THE INTELLIGENCE COMMUNITY. — The term "element of the intelligence community" means any element of the intelligence community specified

or designated under section 3(4) of the National Security Act of 1947 (50 U.S.C. 401a(4)).

SEC. 908. TRAINING OF GOVERNMENT OFFICIALS REGARDING IDENTIFICATION AND USE OF FOREIGN INTELLIGENCE.

(a) PROGRAM REQUIRED. — The Attorney General shall, in consultation with the Director of Central Intelligence, carry out a program to provide appropriate training to officials described in subsection (b) in order to assist such officials in —

(1) identifying foreign intelligence information in the course of their duties; and

(2) utilizing foreign intelligence information in the course of their duties, to the extent that the utilization of such information is appropriate for such duties.

(b) OFFICIALS. — The officials provided training under subsection (a) are, at the discretion of the Attorney General and the Director, the following :

(1) Officials of the Federal Government who are not ordinarily engaged in the collection, dissemination, and use of foreign intelligence in the performance of their duties.

(2) Officials of State and local governments who encounter, or may encounter in the course of a terrorist event, foreign intelligence in the performance of their duties.

(c) AUTHORIZATION OF APPROPRIATIONS. — There is hereby authorized to be appropriated for the Department of Justice such sums as may be necessary for purposes of carrying out the program required by subsection (a).

TITLE X — MISCELLANEOUS

SEC. 1001. REVIEW OF THE DEPARTMENT OF JUSTICE.

The Inspector General of the Department of Justice shall designate one official who shall —

(1) review information and receive complaints alleging

abuses of civil rights and civil liberties by employees and officials of the Department of Justice;

(2) make public through the Internet, radio, television, and newspaper advertisements information on the responsibilities and functions of, and how to contact, the official; and

(3) submit to the Committee on the Judiciary of the House of Representatives and the Committee on the Judiciary of the Senate on a semi-annual basis a report on the implementation of this subsection and detailing any abuses described in paragraph (1), including a description of the use of funds appropriations used to carry out this subsection.

SEC. 1002. SENSE OF CONGRESS.

(a) FINDINGS. — Congress finds that —

(1) all Americans are united in condemning, in the strongest possible terms, the terrorists who planned and carried out the attacks against the United States on September 11, 2001, and in pursuing all those responsible for those attacks and their sponsors until they are brought to justice;

(2) Sikh-Americans form a vibrant, peaceful, and law-abiding part of America's people;

(3) approximately 500,000 Sikhs reside in the United States and are a vital part of the Nation;

(4) Sikh-Americans stand resolutely in support of the commitment of our Government to bring the terrorists and those that harbor them to justice;

(5) the Sikh faith is a distinct religion with a distinct religious and ethnic identity that has its own places of worship and a distinct holy text and religious tenets;

(6) many Sikh-Americans, who are easily recognizable by their turbans and beards, which are required articles of their faith, have suffered both verbal and physical assaults as a result of misguided anger toward Arab-Americans and Muslim-Americans in the wake of the September 11, 2001 terrorist attack;

(7) Sikh-Americans, as do all Americans, condemn acts of prejudice against any American; and

(8) Congress is seriously concerned by the number of crimes against Sikh-Americans and other Americans all across the Nation that have been reported in the wake of the tragic events that unfolded on September 11, 2001.

(b) SENSE OF CONGRESS. — Congress —

(1) declares that, in the quest to identify, locate, and bring to justice the perpetrators and sponsors of the terrorist attacks on the United States on September 11, 2001, the civil rights and civil liberties of all Americans, including Sikh-Americans, should be protected;

(2) condemns bigotry and any acts of violence or discrimination against any Americans, including Sikh-Americans;

(3) calls upon local and Federal law enforcement authorities to work to prevent crimes against all Americans, including Sikh-Americans; and

(4) calls upon local and Federal law enforcement authorities to prosecute to the fullest extent of the law all those who commit crimes.

SEC. 1003. DEFINITION OF "ELECTRONIC SURVEILLANCE".

Section 101(f)(2) of the Foreign Intelligence Surveillance Act (50 U.S.C. 1801(f)(2)) is amended by adding at the end before the semicolon the following : ", but does not include the acquisition of those communications of computer trespassers that would be permissible under section 2511(2)(i) of title 18, United States Code".

SEC. 1004. VENUE IN MONEY LAUNDERING CASES.

Section 1956 of title 18, United States Code, is amended by adding at the end the following :

"(i) VENUE. — (1) Except as provided in paragraph (2), a prosecution for an offense under this section or section 1957 may be brought in —

"(A) any district in which the financial or monetary transaction is conducted; or

"(B) any district where a prosecution for the underlying specified unlawful activity could be brought, if the defendant participated in the transfer of the proceeds of the specified unlawful activity from that district to the district where the financial or monetary transaction is conducted.

"(2) A prosecution for an attempt or conspiracy offense under this section or section 1957 may be brought in the district where venue would lie for the completed offense under paragraph (1), or in any other district where an act in furtherance of the attempt or conspiracy took place.

"(3) For purposes of this section, a transfer of funds from 1 place to another, by wire or any other means, shall constitute a single, continuing transaction. Any person who conducts (as that term is defined in subsection (c)(2)) any portion of the transaction may be charged in any district in which the transaction takes place.".

SEC. 1005. FIRST RESPONDERS ASSISTANCE ACT.

(a) GRANT AUTHORIZATION. — The Attorney General shall make grants described in subsections (b) and (c) to States and units of local government to improve the ability of State and local law enforcement, fire department and first responders to respond to and prevent acts of terrorism.

(b) TERRORISM PREVENTION GRANTS. — Terrorism prevention grants under this subsection may be used for programs, projects, and other activities to —

(1) hire additional law enforcement personnel dedicated to intelligence gathering and analysis functions, including the formation of full-time intelligence and analysis units;

(2) purchase technology and equipment for intelligence gathering and analysis functions, including wire-tap, pen links, cameras, and computer hardware and software;

(3) purchase equipment for responding to a critical incident, including protective equipment for patrol officers such as quick masks;

(4) purchase equipment for managing a critical incident, such as communications equipment for improved

interoperability among surrounding jurisdictions and mobile command posts for overall scene management; and

(5) fund technical assistance programs that emphasize coordination among neighboring law enforcement agencies for sharing resources, and resources coordination among law enforcement agencies for combining intelligence gathering and analysis functions, and the development of policy, procedures, memorandums of understanding, and other best practices.

(c) ANTITERRORISM TRAINING GRANTS. — Antiterrorism training grants under this subsection may be used for programs, projects, and other activities to address —

(1) intelligence gathering and analysis techniques;

(2) community engagement and outreach;

(3) critical incident management for all forms of terrorist attack;

(4) threat assessment capabilities;

(5) conducting followup investigations; and

(6) stabilizing a community after a terrorist incident.

(d) APPLICATION. —

(1) IN GENERAL. — Each eligible entity that desires to receive a grant under this section shall submit an application to the Attorney General, at such time, in such manner, and accompanied by such additional information as the Attorney General may reasonably require.

(2) CONTENTS. — Each application submitted pursuant to paragraph (1) shall —

(A) describe the activities for which assistance under this section is sought; and

(B) provide such additional assurances as the Attorney General determines to be essential to ensure compliance with the requirements of this section.

(e) MINIMUM AMOUNT. — If all applications submitted by a State or units of local government within that State have not been funded under this section in any fiscal year, that

State, if it qualifies, and the units of local government within that State, shall receive in that fiscal year not less than 0.5 per cent of the total amount appropriated in that fiscal year for grants under this section.

(f) AUTHORIZATION OF APPROPRIATIONS. — There are authorized to be appropriated $25,000,000 for each of the fiscal years 2003 through 2007.

SEC. 1006. INADMISSIBILITY OF ALIENS ENGAGED IN MONEY LAUNDERING.

(a) AMENDMENT TO IMMIGRATION AND NATIONALITY ACT. — Section 212(a)(2) of the Immigration and Nationality Act (8 U.S.C. 1182(a)(2)) is amended by adding at the end the following :

"(I) MONEY LAUNDERING. — Any alien —

"(i) who a consular officer or the Attorney General knows, or has reason to believe, has engaged, is engaging, or seeks to enter the United States to engage, in an offense which is described in section 1956 or 1957 of title 18, United States Code (relating to laundering of monetary instruments); or

"(ii) who a consular officer or the Attorney General knows is, or has been, a knowing aider, abettor, assister, conspirator, or colluder with others in an offense which is described in such section; is inadmissible.".

(b) MONEY LAUNDERING WATCHLIST. — Not later than 90 days after the date of the enactment of this Act, the Secretary of State shall develop, implement, and certify to the Congress that there has been established a money laundering watchlist, which identifies individuals worldwide who are known or suspected of money laundering, which is readily accessible to, and shall be checked by, a consular or other Federal official prior to the issuance of a visa or admission to the United States. The Secretary of State shall develop and continually update the watchlist in cooperation with the Attorney General, the Secretary of the Treasury, and the Director of Central Intelligence.

SEC. 1007. AUTHORIZATION OF FUNDS FOR DEA POLICE TRAINING IN SOUTH AND CENTRAL ASIA.

In addition to amounts otherwise available to carry out section 481 of the Foreign Assistance Act of 1961 (22 U.S.C. 2291), there is authorized to be appropriated to the President not less than $5,000,000 for fiscal year 2002 for regional antidrug training in the Republic of Turkey by the Drug Enforcement Administration for police, as well as increased precursor chemical control efforts in the South and Central Asia region.

SEC. 1008. FEASIBILITY STUDY ON USE OF BIOMETRIC IDENTIFIER SCANNING SYSTEM WITH ACCESS TO THE FBI INTEGRATED AUTOMATED FINGERPRINT IDENTIFICATION SYSTEM AT OVERSEAS CONSULAR POSTS AND POINTS OF ENTRY TO THE UNITED STATES.

(a) IN GENERAL. — The Attorney General, in consultation with the Secretary of State and the Secretary of Transportation, shall conduct a study on the feasibility of utilizing a biometric identifier (fingerprint) scanning system, with access to the database of the Federal Bureau of Investigation Integrated Automated Fingerprint Identification System, at consular offices abroad and at points of entry into the United States to enhance the ability of State Department and immigration officials to identify aliens who may be wanted in connection with criminal or terrorist investigations in the United States or abroad prior to the issuance of visas or entry into the United States.

(b) REPORT TO CONGRESS. — Not later than 90 days after the date of the enactment of this Act, the Attorney General shall submit a report summarizing the findings of the study authorized under subsection (a) to the Committee on International Relations and the Committee on the Judiciary of the House of Representatives and the Committee on Foreign Relations and the Committee on the Judiciary of the Senate.

SEC. 1009. STUDY OF ACCESS.

(a) IN GENERAL. — Not later than 120 days after enactment of this Act, the Federal Bureau of Investigation shall study and report to Congress on the feasibility of providing to airlines access via computer to the names of passengers who are suspected of terrorist activity by Federal officials.

(b) AUTHORIZATION. — There are authorized to be appropriated not more than $250,000 to carry out subsection (a).

SEC. 1010. TEMPORARY AUTHORITY TO CONTRACT WITH LOCAL AND STATE GOVERNMENTS FOR PERFORMANCE OF SECURITY FUNCTIONS AT UNITED STATES MILITARY INSTALLATIONS.

(a) IN GENERAL. — Notwithstanding section 2465 of title 10, United States Code, during the period of time that United States armed forces are engaged in Operation Enduring Freedom, and for the period of 180 days thereafter, funds appropriated to the Department of Defense may be obligated and expended for the purpose of entering into contracts or other agreements for the performance of security functions at any military installation or facility in the United States with a proximately located local or State government, or combination of such governments, whether or not any such government is obligated to provide such services to the general public without compensation.

(b) TRAINING. — Any contract or agreement entered into under this section shall prescribe standards for the training and other qualifications of local government law enforcement personnel who perform security functions under this section in accordance with criteria established by the Secretary of the service concerned.

(c) REPORT. — One year after the date of enactment of this section, the Secretary of Defense shall submit a report to the Committees on Armed Services of the Senate and the House of Representatives describing the use of the authority granted under this section and the use by the Department of Defense of other means to improve the performance of security functions on military installations and facilities located within the United States.

SEC. 1011. CRIMES AGAINST CHARITABLE AMERICANS.

(a) SHORT TITLE. — This section may be cited as the "Crimes Against Charitable Americans Act of 2001".

(b) TELEMARKETING AND CONSUMER FRAUD ABUSE. — The

Tele-marketing and Consumer Fraud and Abuse Prevention Act (15 U.S.C. 6101 et seq.) is amended —

(1) in section 3(a)(2), by inserting after "practices" the second place it appears the following : "which shall include fraudulent charitable solicitations, and";

(2) in section 3(a)(3) —

(A) in subparagraph (B), by striking "and" at the end;

(B) in subparagraph (C), by striking the period at the end and inserting "; and"; and

(C) by adding at the end the following :

"(D) a requirement that any person engaged in telemarketing for the solicitation of charitable contributions, donations, or gifts of money or any other thing of value, shall promptly and clearly disclose to the person receiving the call that the purpose of the call is to solicit charitable contributions, donations, or gifts, and make such other disclosures as the Commission considers appropriate, including the name and mailing address of the charitable organization on behalf of which the solicitation is made."; and

(3) in section 7(4), by inserting ", or a charitable contribution, donation, or gift of money or any other thing of value," after "services".

(c) RED CROSS MEMBERS OR AGENTS. — Section 917 of title 18, United States Code, is amended by striking "one year" and inserting "5 years".

(d) TELEMARKETING FRAUD. — Section 2325(1) of title 18, United States Code, is amended —

(1) in subparagraph (A), by striking "or" at the end;

(2) in subparagraph (B), by striking the comma at the end and inserting "; or";

(3) by inserting after subparagraph (B) the following :

"(C) a charitable contribution, donation, or gift of money or any other thing of value,"; and

(4) in the flush language, by inserting "or charitable contributor, or donor" after "participant".

SEC. 1012. LIMITATION ON ISSUANCE OF HAZMAT LICENSES.

(a) LIMITATION. —

(1) IN GENERAL. — Chapter 51 of title 49, United States Code, is amended by inserting after section 5103 the following new section :

"§ 5103a. Limitation on issuance of hazmat licenses

"(a) LIMITATION. —

"(1) ISSUANCE OF LICENSES. — A State may not issue to any individual a license to operate a motor vehicle transporting in commerce a hazardous material unless the Secretary of Transportation has first determined, upon receipt of a notification under subsection (c)(1)(B), that the individual does not pose a security risk warranting denial of the license.

"(2) RENEWALS INCLUDED. — For the purposes of this section, the term 'issue', with respect to a license, includes renewal of the license.

"(b) HAZARDOUS MATERIALS DESCRIBED. — The limitation in sub-section (a) shall apply with respect to —

"(1) any material defined as a hazardous material by the Secretary of Transportation; and

"(2) any chemical or biological material or agent determined by the Secretary of Health and Human Services or the Attorney General as being a threat to the national security of the United States.

"(c) BACKGROUND RECORDS CHECK. —

"(1) IN GENERAL. — Upon the request of a State regarding issuance of a license described in subsection (a)(1) to an individual, the Attorney General —

"(A) shall carry out a background records check regarding the individual; and

"(B) upon completing the background records check, shall notify the Secretary of Transportation of the completion and results of the background records check.

"(2) SCOPE. — A background records check regarding an individual under this subsection shall consist of the following :

"(A) A check of the relevant criminal history data bases.

"(B) In the case of an alien, a check of the relevant data bases to determine the status of the alien under the immigration laws of the United States.

"(C) As appropriate, a check of the relevant international data bases through Interpol–U.S. National Central Bureau or other appropriate means.

"(d) REPORTING REQUIREMENT. — Each State shall submit to the Secretary of Transportation, at such time and in such manner as the Secretary may prescribe, the name, address, and such other information as the Secretary may require, concerning —

"(1) each alien to whom the State issues a license described in subsection (a); and

"(2) each other individual to whom such a license is issued, as the Secretary may require.

"(e) ALIEN DEFINED. — In this section, the term 'alien' has the meaning given the term in section 101(a)(3) of the Immigration and Nationality Act.".

(2) CLERICAL AMENDMENT. — The table of sections at the beginning of such chapter is amended by inserting after the item relating to section 5103 the following new item :

"5103a. Limitation on issuance of hazmat licenses.".

(b) REGULATION OF DRIVER FITNESS. — Section 31305(a)(5) of title 49, United States Code, is amended —

(1) by striking "and" at the end of subparagraph (A);

(2) by inserting "and" at the end of subparagraph (B); and

(3) by adding at the end the following new subparagraph :

"(C) is licensed by a State to operate the vehicle after having first been determined under section 5103a of this title as not posing a security risk warranting denial of the license.".

(c) AUTHORIZATION OF APPROPRIATIONS. — There is authorized to be appropriated for the Department of Transportation and the Department of Justice such amounts as may be necessary to carry out section 5103a of title 49, United States Code, as added by subsection (a).

SEC. 1013. EXPRESSING THE SENSE OF THE SENATE CONCERNING THE PROVISION OF FUNDING FOR BIOTERRORISM PREPAREDNESS AND RESPONSE.

(a) FINDINGS. — The Senate finds the following :

(1) Additional steps must be taken to better prepare the United States to respond to potential bioterrorism attacks.

(2) The threat of a bioterrorist attack is still remote, but is increasing for a variety of reasons, including —

(A) public pronouncements by Osama bin Laden that it is his religious duty to acquire weapons of mass destruction, including chemical and biological weapons;

(B) the callous disregard for innocent human life as demonstrated by the terrorists' attacks of September 11, 2001;

(C) the resources and motivation of known terrorists and their sponsors and supporters to use biological warfare;

(D) recent scientific and technological advances in agent delivery technology such as aerosolization that have made weaponization of certain germs much easier; and

(E) the increasing access to the technologies and expertise necessary to construct and deploy chemical and biological weapons of mass destruction.

(3) Coordination of Federal, State, and local terrorism research, preparedness, and response programs must be improved.

(4) States, local areas, and public health officials must have enhanced resources and expertise in order to respond to a potential bioterrorist attack.

(5) National, State, and local communication capacities must be enhanced to combat the spread of chemical and biological illness.

(6) Greater resources must be provided to increase the capacity of hospitals and local health care workers to respond to public health threats.

(7) Health care professionals must be better trained to recognize, diagnose, and treat illnesses arising from biochemical attacks.

(8) Additional supplies may be essential to increase the readiness of the United States to respond to a bio-attack.

(9) Improvements must be made in assuring the safety of the food supply.

(10) New vaccines and treatments are needed to assure that we have an adequate response to a biochemical attack.

(11) Government research, preparedness, and response programs need to utilize private sector expertise and resources.

(12) Now is the time to strengthen our public health system and ensure that the United States is adequately prepared to respond to potential bioterrorist attacks, natural infectious disease outbreaks, and other challenges and potential threats to the public health.

(b) SENSE OF THE SENATE. — It is the sense of the Senate that the United States should make a substantial new investment this year toward the following :

(1) Improving State and local preparedness capabilities by upgrading State and local surveillance epidemiology, assisting in the development of response plans, assuring adequate staffing and training of health professionals to diagnose and care for victims of bioterrorism, extending the electronics communications networks and training personnel, and improving public health laboratories.

(2) Improving hospital response capabilities by assisting hospitals in developing plans for a bioterrorist attack and improving the surge capacity of hospitals.

(3) Upgrading the bioterrorism capabilities of the Centers for Disease Control and Prevention through improving rapid identification and health early warning systems.

(4) Improving disaster response medical systems, such as the National Disaster Medical System and the Metropolitan Medical Response System and Epidemic Intelligence Service.

(5) Targeting research to assist with the development of appropriate therapeutics and vaccines for likely bioterrorist agents and assisting with expedited drug and device review through the Food and Drug Administration.

(6) Improving the National Pharmaceutical Stockpile program by increasing the amount of necessary therapies (including smallpox vaccines and other post-exposure vaccines) and ensuring the appropriate deployment of stockpiles.

(7) Targeting activities to increase food safety at the Food and Drug Administration.

(8) Increasing international cooperation to secure dangerous biological agents, increase surveillance, and retrain biological warfare specialists.

SEC. 1014. GRANT PROGRAM FOR STATE AND LOCAL DOMESTIC PREPAREDNESS SUPPORT.

(a) IN GENERAL. — The Office for State and Local Domestic Preparedness Support of the Office of Justice Programs shall make a grant to each State, which shall be used by the State, in conjunction with units of local government, to enhance the capability of State and local jurisdictions to prepare for and respond to terrorist acts including events of terrorism involving weapons of mass destruction and biological, nuclear, radiological, incendiary, chemical, and explosive devices.

(b) USE OF GRANT AMOUNTS. — Grants under this section may be used to purchase needed equipment and to provide training and technical assistance to State and local first responders.

(c) AUTHORIZATION OF APPROPRIATIONS. —

(1) IN GENERAL. — There is authorized to be appropriated to carry out this section such sums as necessary for each of fiscal years 2002 through 2007.

(2) LIMITATIONS. — Of the amount made available to carry out this section in any fiscal year not more than 3 per cent may be used by the Attorney General for salaries and administrative expenses.

(3) MINIMUM AMOUNT. — Each State shall be allocated in each fiscal year under this section not less than 0.75 per cent of the total amount appropriated in the fiscal year for grants pursuant to this section, except that the United States Virgin Islands, America Samoa, Guam, and the Northern Mariana Islands each shall be allocated 0.25 per cent.

SEC. 1015. EXPANSION AND REAUTHORIZATION OF THE CRIME IDENTIFICATION TECHNOLOGY ACT FOR ANTITERRORISM GRANTS TO STATES AND LOCALITIES.

Section 102 of the Crime Identification Technology Act of 1998 (42 U.S.C. 14601) is amended —

(1) in subsection (b) —

(A) in paragraph (16), by striking "and" at the end;

(B) in paragraph (17), by striking the period and inserting "; and"; and

(C) by adding at the end the following :

"(18) notwithstanding subsection (c), antiterrorism purposes as they relate to any other uses under this section or for other antiterrorism programs."; and

(2) in subsection (e)(1), by striking "this section" and all that follows and inserting "this section $250,000,000 for each of fiscal years 2002 through 2007.".

SEC. 1016. CRITICAL INFRASTRUCTURES PROTECTION.

(a) SHORT TITLE. — This section may be cited as the "Critical Infrastructures Protection Act of 2001".

(b) FINDINGS. — Congress makes the following findings :

(1) The information revolution has transformed the conduct of business and the operations of government as well as the infrastructure relied upon for the defense and national security of the United States.

(2) Private business, government, and the national security apparatus increasingly depend on an interdependent network of critical physical and information infrastructures, including telecommunications, energy, financial services, water, and transportation sectors.

(3) A continuous national effort is required to ensure the reliable provision of cyber and physical infrastructure services critical to maintaining the national defense, continuity of government, economic prosperity, and quality of life in the United States.

(4) This national effort requires extensive modeling and analytic capabilities for purposes of evaluating appropriate mechanisms to ensure the stability of these complex and inter-dependent systems, and to underpin policy recommendations, so as to achieve the continuous viability and adequate protection of the critical infrastructure of the Nation.

(c) POLICY OF THE UNITED STATES. — It is the policy of the United States —

(1) that any physical or virtual disruption of the operation of the critical infrastructures of the United States be rare, brief, geographically limited in effect, manageable, and minimally detrimental to the economy, human and government services, and national security of the United States;

(2) that actions necessary to achieve the policy stated in paragraph (1) be carried out in a public-private partnership involving corporate and non-governmental organizations; and

(3) to have in place a comprehensive and effective program to ensure the continuity of essential Federal Government functions under all circumstances.

(d) ESTABLISHMENT OF NATIONAL COMPETENCE FOR CRITICAL INFRASTRUCTURE PROTECTION. —

(1) SUPPORT OF CRITICAL INFRASTRUCTURE PROTECTION AND CONTINUITY BY NATIONAL INFRASTRUCTURE SIMULATION AND ANALYSIS CENTER. — There shall be established the National Infrastructure Simulation and Analysis Center (NISAC) to serve as a source of national competence to address critical infrastructure protection and continuity through support for activities related to counterterrorism, threat assessment, and risk mitigation.

(2) PARTICULAR SUPPORT. — The support provided under paragraph (1) shall include the following :

(A) Modeling, simulation, and analysis of the systems comprising critical infrastructures, including cyber infrastructure, telecommunications infrastructure, and physical infrastructure, in order to enhance understanding of the large-scale complexity of such systems and to facilitate modification of such systems to mitigate the threats to such systems and to critical infrastructures generally.

(B) Acquisition from State and local governments and the private sector of data necessary to create and maintain models of such systems and of critical infrastructures generally.

(C) Utilization of modeling, simulation, and analysis under subparagraph (A) to provide education and training to policymakers on matters relating to —

(i) the analysis conducted under that subparagraph;

(ii) the implications of unintended or unintentional disturbances to critical infrastructures; and

(iii) responses to incidents or crises involving critical infrastructures, including the continuity of government and private sector activities through and after such incidents or crises.

(D) Utilization of modeling, simulation, and analysis under subparagraph (A) to provide recommendations to policymakers, and to departments and agencies of the Federal Government and private sector persons and entities upon request, regarding means of enhancing the stability of, and preserving, critical infrastructures.

(3) RECIPIENT OF CERTAIN SUPPORT. — Modeling, simulation, and analysis provided under this subsection shall be provided, in particular, to relevant Federal, State, and local entities responsible for critical infrastructure protection and policy.

(e) CRITICAL INFRASTRUCTURE DEFINED. — In this section, the term "critical infrastructure" means systems and assets, whether physical or virtual, so vital to the United States that the incapacity or destruction of such systems and assets would have a debilitating impact on security, national economic security, national public health or safety, or any combination of those matters.

(f) AUTHORIZATION OF APPROPRIATIONS. — There is hereby authorized for the Department of Defense for fiscal year 2002, $20,000,000 for the Defense Threat Reduction Agency for activities of the National Infrastructure Simulation and Analysis Center under this section in that fiscal year.

Speaker of the House of Representatives.

Vice President of the United States and President of the Senate.

